'O ke kanaka ke kuleana o ka moe
   The privilege of man is to dream
— *Hawaiian proverb*

CLAUS SPRECKELS
The Sugar King in Hawaii

CLAUS SPRECKELS

1828–1908

CLAUS SPRECKELS

The Sugar King in Hawaii

By JACOB ADLER

*Illustrated
by Joseph Feher*

UNIVERSITY OF HAWAII PRESS, HONOLULU
1966

Copyright 1966 by the University of Hawaii Press
Manufactured in the United States of America by the
Kingsport Press, Inc.
Designed by Joseph Feher
Library of Congress Catalog Card Number 65–28712

For M.R. *and* T.C.A.

Preface

Claus Spreckels, who built a sugar empire in California and in the Hawaiian Kingdom, died over half a century ago. Much of what has been written about his Hawaiian career makes him out to be a scoundrel. Beyond question he was a man of consequence in the islands. How much consequence? And for good or evil? That is what I have tried to find out.

Spreckels became a card-playing crony and financial backer of Hawaii's last king, the merry David Kalakaua, who reigned from 1874 to 1891. He formed an alliance with that monarch's "evil angel," Premier Walter Murray Gibson. For a time, the unlikely Kalakaua-Gibson-Spreckels triumvirate controlled the kingdom. Later, after the overthrow of King Kalakaua's sister, Queen Liliuokalani, who reigned from 1891 to 1893, Spreckels attempted to put her back on the throne.

In Hawaii his reputation for rascality lives on. In many ways, as the following pages will show, the reputation was well earned. But his contributions to the development of the island kingdom remain largely unsung. This book tries to throw some light on these.

The story deals with Spreckels' rise and fall in Hawaii. It tells of the clash of a mainland entrepreneur with an island community. It records his initial warm reception, his gradually tightening grip on the Hawaiian Kingdom, his spreading monopoly of the sugar industry, his conflicts with the conservative businessmen, his sudden fall from political power, and the consequent decline of his economic power.

In the islands Claus Spreckels was the outlander in the Veblenian sense, the invader, the interloper. He was unfettered by the Hawaiian culture or by that culture as modified by the missionaries from Boston. His own cultural heritage was rather akin to that of the lusty whalers who were constantly at odds with the Hawaiian missionaries, or to that of contemporary robber barons, whose rapaciously acquisitive age nevertheless brought startling material progress to the common man.

Historians may argue whether economic development in the United States would have taken place rapidly without the moguls. As to Hawaii, there is less room for argument. Spreckels towered over the Hawaiian sugar industry; there was no one else of comparable stature. Without him the island sugar industry could hardly have gone forward as fast as it did.

In the minds of many islanders Spreckels strides through the pages of Hawaiian history as an opportunist who drained the island kingdom and gave nothing in return. It is easy to remember his ruthlessness, his arrogance, his corruption of king, cabinet, and legislature; and easy to forget his contributions to the development of the kingdom.

Economic development is a complicated affair which includes thousands of things—not all strictly economic—and thousands of persons, from industrial giants to menial laborers. Within a given period of such development it may be a fruitless task to choose "the most important person." Yet, if for late nineteenth-century Hawaii a choice were to be made, the title might well go to Claus Spreckels. In the islands, sugar was a dominant fact of economic life, and in sugar Spreckels was king.

JACOB ADLER

Honolulu, Hawaii, 1965

viii

Acknowledgments

T*he* story of Claus Spreckels in Hawaii has been a fascinating quest, in the pursuit of which I have had much help. My chief intellectual debt is to the late Professor Ralph S. Kuykendall, the foremost historian of Hawaii. He generously permitted me to read parts of the manuscript for the third volume (on the Kalakaua dynasty) of his definitive *Hawaiian Kingdom*.

Charles H. Hunter, Professor of History at the University of Hawaii, has given me vigorous and helpful criticism. For comment on major parts of the manuscript I am indebted to Shelley M. Mark, Director of Planning and Economic Development, State of Hawaii; Daniel M. Slate, Professor of Economics, University of Illinois; James H. Shoemaker, Vice-President for Research, Bank of Hawaii; and Henry David and Carter Goodrich, former professors of economics, Columbia University.

Parts of the work have been read by Professors Harold S. Roberts, Charles A. Moore, Arthur J. Marder, A. Grove Day, W. W. Cordray, William E. Huntsberry, and Russell Taussig; and also by Miss Albertine Loomis of the Hawaiian Historical Society, and Meiric K. Dutton, former President of the Society.

For perceptive criticism of the manuscript from the viewpoint of the average reader, I am indebted to Mrs. Margaret Solomon.

Any errors remaining are chargeable, of course, solely to my account.

For help in gathering material I am greatly obliged to Miss Agnes

Acknowledgments

Conrad, Archivist of the State of Hawaii, and her staff, especially Henry C. K. Choy, Mrs. Aurora Domingo, Jack Mathews, Mrs. Philomena A. Morrison, and Mrs. Doris Takeshita; Miss Janet E. Bell, Curator of the Hawaiian and Pacific Collection, Gregg M. Sinclair Library, University of Hawaii, and her staff; Mrs. Clara C. Ching, Assistant Librarian for Documents and Maps, Sinclair Library; Mrs. Willowdean C. Handy, former Librarian of the Hawaiian Historical Society; and Miss Bernice Judd, former Librarian of the Hawaii Mission Children's Society.

I am also indebted to:

The University of Hawaii Press Committee, and especially to Thomas Nickerson, Director of the Press, and Mrs. Aldyth V. Morris, former Managing Editor, for encouraging publication of this work.

Robert W. Sparks, Managing Editor of the University of Hawaii Press, for educating me on the many details of getting a book into print.

Joseph Feher, Artist-Historian of the Bishop Museum and the Honolulu Academy of Arts, not only for designing and illustrating this book but also for many hours of conversation about things Hawaiian.

The time from conception to birth for this book has been over-long. But I am glad to acknowledge that parts of it, in different form, have appeared in *Hawaiian Historical Society Annual Reports, Paradise of the Pacific, Honolulu Advertiser, Honolulu Star-Bulletin, Numismatist, Berliner Numismatische Zeitschrift, Explorations in Entrepreneurial History, California Historical Society Quarterly, Business History Review, Pacific Historical Review,* and *Agricultural History.*

Let me add a bit of harmless information which nevertheless acknowledges a very real debt. This book was written mainly in Waikiki coffee shops and hotel lobbies. No phones rang. The passers-by did not interrupt or disturb me.

Finally, my greatest debt of all—to my wife, for reasons that anyone who has ever tried to write can easily guess.

J. A.

CONTENTS

Contents

CHAPTER I

Spreckels and Reciprocity

In the afternoon of August 24, 1876, the steamer "City of San Francisco" appeared off the island of Oahu in the Hawaiian kingdom. The lookout at Diamond Head point reported that the ship was "decked with bunting from bowsprit to spanker boom" —an assurance of good news aboard. Honolulans deserted the streets of the town and hurried to the wharves. By the first boat from the steamer came a message that the Reciprocity Treaty between Hawaii and the United States had passed the Senate on August 14 and had been signed by President Grant the next day.

As the word spread, faces in the crowd lighted up. "The sudden joy did not break out in cheers—it was too deep for that—but men shook hands heartily with their neighbors in silence." [1]

The ship carrying news of the Reciprocity Treaty also brought Claus Spreckels, a rich San Francisco sugar refiner, to Hawaii for the first time. [2] This was no mere coincidence. Although he had originally opposed the treaty, Spreckels now moved swiftly to take advantage of it. During a three-week stay in the islands he bought up over half the anticipated 14,000-ton sugar crop for 1877, [3] before the full price rise caused by the treaty could take effect.

Spreckels' move caused a sensation in California and Hawaii. Particularly loud outcries came from other San Francisco sugar brokers and refiners less alert than Spreckels.[4] Besides advancing his own refining interests, he also made plans to become a sugar producer himself in the islands. He would thus gain the two-cent a pound increase which the duty-free entry of sugar to the United States gave Hawaiian planters.

An understanding of the treaty that formed the backdrop for Spreckels' dramatic arrival in the islands requires some discussion of the Hawaiian economy, especially of sugar. When the first shot of the American Revolution was fired in 1775, Hawaii was still a subsistence economy untouched by Western influence. Soon after Captain Cook discovered the islands in 1778, they became a stopping point for ships in the Pacific. Hawaii was a link in the China trade, although in the beginning hardly more than a provisioning station. The first natural resource to be exported in any great quantity was sandalwood, prized by the Chinese as incense for their temples. By 1830 the sandalwood forests had been stripped, but the kingdom was able to fall back on the growing Pacific whaling trade. After reaching a peak in 1859, this trade declined rapidly. By 1876 whaling was of little importance. Sugar had become the main prop of the Hawaiian economy.[5]

During the century after its discovery Hawaii had changed from a subsistence economy to one largely oriented toward trade. Sugar was the chief export. "The haole ["white foreigner"] merchants and planters and missionaries had reformed the Island economic structure essentially after their own image. Their plantations, stores, steamships, churches, and weekly brass band were drowning the traditions of the past. Hawaii was bound tightly in the expanding commercial network of the world; and Hawaii's future was the future of its plantation economy." [6]

From 1778—when Captain Cook found cane growing wild in the islands—to 1825, only a few persons tried to grow sugar commercially and to process it: a Chinese, Wong Tze Chun (1802); a Spaniard, Don Francisco de Paula Marín (1819); and an Italian, Lavinia (1823). John Wilkinson, an Englishman, set out 100 acres of cane in 1825 in Manoa Valley, Oahu, under the

4

patronage of Governor Boki. Some sugar, molasses, and rum were made; but in a few years the plantation was abandoned. One reason was that Queen Regent Kaahumanu, because of missionary influence, frowned on the making of rum.[7]

The American firm of Ladd and Company founded the first more or less permanent, stable plantation in 1835, at Koloa on the island of Kauai. The company leased about one thousand acres from Kamehameha III at $300 a year. Three hundred acres of this tract were good cane land. At first the sugar was of poor quality, and up to 1842 it was hardly merchantable. The plantation began to prosper, however, when a Dr. R. W. Wood took control in 1848. Because of the example it set, the establishment of Koloa was especially significant. The Hawaiian system of cultivating plots on shares for the chiefs produced less sugar per acre than the wage system at Koloa. The plantation also demonstrated the advantages of large-scale sugar culture as compared with haphazard growing on small tracts.[8]

Exports of sugar amounted to only 4 tons in 1836; by 1876 they totaled around 13,000 tons a year.[9] In this 40-year period before reciprocity the Hawaiian sugar industry made much progress with respect to problems of land, labor, technology, financing, and marketing. The Reciprocity Treaty was to contribute mightily to the further solution of all these problems.

LAND. One of the obstacles faced by pioneers of the sugar industry was the native land system. Foreigners generally could not own land; they had difficulty even in getting leases. The land system also impeded the development of sugar mill technology, because there was little incentive to experiment and make costly improvements as long as large, fee simple tracts were not to be had.[10]

The first mills were necessarily temporary affairs for grinding sugar from small, scattered tracts. Co-ordination of mill and field practices had to await the development of large-scale growing. Another technological problem related to land was that of irrigation. Much land otherwise suitable for sugar did not have enough rainfall.

5

The *Mahele* ("division") of 1848 practically overturned the old Hawaiian land system, and is generally acknowledged as one of the most important events in the history of the kingdom. Lands were divided among the king, the government, and the people. By 1850, foreigners could own land in fee.[11] The Reciprocity Treaty of 1876 also influenced the land problem, for the resulting price increase of sugar encouraged growers to put marginal land into cane. The treaty thus extended the area devoted to cane, and also encouraged irrigation and heavy use of fertilizer.[12]

LABOR. Hawaii never suffered a warlike conquest by an outsider. Yet the introduction of Western civilization brought about a "benevolent" destruction of the native economy which was quite as complete as though Hawaii had been overrun by invading armies. Disease, liquor, and the ways of the white man took a heavy toll. Between 1778 and 1876, the native population fell from about 300,000 to 50,000.[13] This fall markedly increased the labor problems faced by the sugar planters.

In the early days, Hawaiian labor, though of questionable efficiency, was still plentiful. But planters had trouble with the chiefs, who distrusted the foreigners' wage system. The chiefs also resented the planters' efforts to attract laborers away from their small plots. These Hawaiians cultivated for themselves and for the chiefs. John Wilkinson had trouble in getting labor for the Manoa plantation he started in 1825, and the operators of Koloa plantation ran into the same problem.[14]

The gold rush attracted Hawaiian laborers to California, thus accentuating the planters' labor problem. Moreover the demand in California for Hawaiian potatoes and other vegetables caused sugar workers to turn to growing these crops. Many of the laws passed in the 1840's and 1850's reflected the growing concern with labor problems. Vagrants could be seized and indentured for not over one year. Hawaiians had to get special permission to join whaling fleets, and whalers had to deposit a bond of $100 a man. Hawaiians could not emigrate to the California gold fields without permission from the king.

In 1850 the Hawaiian legislature passed a contract labor law providing that anyone over twenty could bind himself for not more than five years.[15] The contract labor law, together with immigration, provided an important though controversial solution to the planters' labor problem. In the year the law was passed the Royal Hawaiian Agricultural Society was formed. One of its purposes was to give attention to ways of obtaining labor. Under impetus of the society, about three hundred Chinese were brought in during 1852, inaugurating the policy of bringing contract laborers to Hawaii. Their contracts provided for a term of five years, passage from China, and payment of three dollars a month plus room, board, and clothing.[16]

About two thousand Chinese were brought in between 1852 and 1874.[17] After reciprocity the tide of immigration became a flood; 55,000 immigrant laborers came to Hawaii between 1887 and 1890, including Chinese, Japanese, and Portuguese.[18] Some of the immigrants later returned to their homelands. Many of the abler ones tended to leave the plantations to farm for themselves, or to become merchants, mechanics, and artisans in Honolulu. Honolulans complained of the competition, and planters complained of the loss of labor.[19]

TECHNOLOGY. The pioneers of the Hawaiian sugar industry had little technical knowledge. One must wonder at—and admire—their brashness in daring to hope they could produce sugar commercially. They learned from experience, often at heavy cost. Gradually the mills and methods of cultivation improved. The planters soon realized that profitable cane-growing required large-scale operation; but their lack of capital and inability to obtain land presented obstacles not easy to overcome. From 1850 on, however, when the land problem had been partially solved (by the land reform of 1848), there was a continuing trend toward increasing the scale of operation. Larger and more permanent mills were built. There was also more dovetailing of mill and field practices.

The earliest mills used wooden rollers driven by animal or water power. In 1838 there were 22 mills, 20 run by animal power

7

and 2 by water. Of 22 mills in 1861, 9 were run by steam, 12 by water, and only 1 by animal power.[20] By this time, iron rollers had replaced those made of wood.

At first the cane juice was merely boiled in whalers' try-pots. The vacuum pan, introduced in the early 1860's, permitted quicker boiling of sugar without scorching. In 1851 D. M. Weston prepared a centrifugal from descriptions he had seen. This machine permitted quicker separation of sugar from molasses, and thus made possible sugar of higher quality. Weston founded the Honolulu Iron Works in 1853, and the company made excellent mill machinery, although much British and American equipment continued to be imported.[21]

Improvements were also applied in the fields. About 1850 Samuel Burbank of Koloa devised a heavy, deep plow. Manuring of cane fields began at Lihue, Kauai, in the 1860's but the use of fertilizer was not common in Hawaii.[22] An improved variety of cane (called Lahaina cane, after the port of entry on Maui) was introduced in 1854 from Tahiti.[23] Irrigation was practiced from the beginning on a small scale. W. H. Rice, in 1856, built the first fairly large project, a ditch several miles long at Lihue, Kauai.[24]

FINANCING. In the early days the planters relied mostly on their own meager savings for financing. Gradually, funds from commerce in Honolulu were channeled into the sugar industry. Both individual merchants and mercantile houses invested in sugar. The decline of whaling in the 1860's hastened this trend, because it left the merchants looking for investment outlets. Mainly through financing, either by loans or direct investment, the mercantile houses, or agencies as they came to be called, gained a large measure of control over the sugar industry. Ladd and Company, the first of these agencies, had a central office in Honolulu for managing the affairs of Koloa plantation on Kauai.[25]

Before 1858 there was little financial capital, and the means for mobilizing existing capital were poor. Judge William L. Lee, president of the Royal Hawaiian Agricultural Society, said in

8

1852 that lack of capital was the greatest obstacle to agricultural progress in the islands.[26] Honolulans had no locally owned bank until that of Bishop and Company was started in 1858, although in 1854 a California bank had operated a branch in Honolulu for about a year.[27] In the 1840's the government made loans directly to planters and traders, but it discontinued this practice about 1850 because money was needed for public improvements.[28] In 1880, when the planters were experiencing temporary financial stress, the government made a loan of $250,000 to the Bishop bank. The bank, in turn, made loans to the planters.[29]

From the gold rush days, the chief source of foreign capital had been San Francisco, the natural market for Hawaiian sugar. San Francisco sugar brokers gave credit on island crops. With reciprocity, San Francisco became even more important as a capital market for Hawaii. The treaty also brought about some direct investment by Californians in Hawaiian plantations. By far the most important of these foreign "interlopers" was Claus Spreckels.[30]

Another significant source of capital, especially as sugar became more profitable under the treaty, was plantation earnings in excess of dividends paid. While no detailed study is available, there can be little doubt that over the years the plantations have received a large share of their financing from retained earnings.

MARKETING. Solutions to the problems of the Hawaiian sugar industry were of little value without a solution to the final problem of markets. Soon after the founding of Koloa plantation in 1835 it became clear that the local market, including provisioning of ships, could not absorb the potential output of sugar. As we have already seen, the first recorded export, 4 tons, took place in 1836; [31] by 1840 exports had climbed to 180 tons.

Some sugar was shipped to Sydney, Valparaiso, and the eastern United States.[32] In a few years the settlement of California and Oregon was to furnish an expanding market for island sugar. Under the stimulus of the gold rush, exports increased to 327 tons in 1849 and to 375 tons in 1850. Prices were high, but Philippine, Chinese, and Batavian sugars also poured into the Cali-

9

fornia market, so that it was soon glutted. Hawaiian planters, moreover, had shipped much sugar of inferior quality, and this caused a price decline in the West Coast market. For these reasons, and also because of a drought that hurt production, exports in 1851 amounted to only 10 tons.[33]

The high United States tariff and competition from low-cost sugars of the Philippines, China, and Batavia also impeded the marketing of island sugar on the West Coast. Between 1848 and 1852 Hawaii made the first of many efforts to solve these problems. What was wanted was a reciprocity treaty to gain duty-free entry of Hawaiian sugar into the United States.[34] But these first efforts were fruitless and no such treaty was then obtained.

During the Civil War the next notable advance in Hawaiian sugar exports took place. Sugar-growing in the southern United States was, of course, disrupted. Exports from Hawaii increased over tenfold, from 722 tons in 1860 to 7,659 tons in 1865. To some extent, high American tariffs offset high prices.[35] Then too, overexpansion in the island sugar industry caused postwar difficulties. These were aggravated by the failure of Brooks and Company, a San Francisco sugar broker. In Honolulu, Walker, Allen and Company, which had connections with Brooks, also failed, and several plantations in which Walker, Allen and Company were interested had to be liquidated.[36]

Strangely enough, the improving quality of Hawaiian sugar caused marketing problems in the 1860's. The higher grades of Hawaiian-milled sugar competed with second-grade sugar refined in San Francisco. The San Francisco refiners therefore tried to persuade the island planters to turn out more low grades in return for a reduction of San Francisco imports from the Philippines, China, and Batavia. For a few years an agreement along these lines was in effect, but it soon lapsed.[37]

With the opening of a steamer line between the British colonies and Hawaii in the 1870's, the planters looked to Australia and New Zealand for expansion of markets, but most of the sugar still went to the United States. Many planters felt—and they were quite right as later events proved—that there was almost no problem within the Hawaiian sugar industry, including marketing, that a reciprocity treaty with the United States could not solve. The treaty was finally achieved, and went into effect on September 9, 1876.

The reaction of Honolulu to reciprocity was well put by the editor of the *Pacific Commercial Advertiser*. Noting that four new plantations were already being planned, he wrote: "Now is the time for capital to invest for the seven years of plenty." [38] The editor of the *Hawaiian Gazette* called for establishment of plantations as joint stock companies for ease in securing capital. "Let us be wide awake," he also said, "and meet Fortune half-way, for we may rest assured that Fortune will not come more than halfway to meet us. The grand prize for which we have prayed and labored for the last twenty years has become ours." [39]

The treaty provided for duty-free admission of about fifteen Hawaiian products to the United States. Of these, sugar and rice were the principal ones, and sugar soon became by far the more important. The Hawaiian sugar planters got almost the entire benefit of the tariff remission, about two cents a pound.[40] The benefit to producers represented the normal effect of removing the duty on a product whose price was chiefly determined by the world market.

The treaty was to remain in force for seven years, to 1883. After that it could be terminated by either country on one year's notice. Neither country gave notice. After some delay, the treaty was renewed in 1887, with a controversial amendment giving the United States the right to use Pearl Harbor.[41] Joy over renewal gave way to gloom a few years later when the McKinley Tariff of 1890 brought near disaster to Hawaii. This tariff nullified the advantage of reciprocity to the island kingdom. All foreign sugar was admitted duty-free to the United States, and growers in that country were given a bounty of two cents a pound. The price of Hawaiian sugar fell from $100 to $60 a ton. A few years later, however, the Wilson-Gorman tariff of 1894 (replacing the McKinley Tariff) restored the benefits of reciprocity to Hawaii.

The Reciprocity Treaty continued in force until annexation of Hawaii by the United States in 1898.[42]

No Hawaiian historian would question that the Reciprocity Treaty was one of the most significant events in the economic history of the kingdom. The treaty also had vast political, social, and cultural consequences. For good or ill, it completed the conversion of Hawaii to virtually a one-crop economy in which sugar was king. "The sole support of the country is sugar," stated the *Bulletin* (Honolulu) in 1884. "It was once the whaling fleet, but whalers having deserted us, we had to discover a new industry, and we found sugar. What other industries have we to fall back upon should sugar fail us? Nothing." [43] Between 1876 and 1898, sugar exports increased from 13,000 to 229,000 tons a year.[44]

The treaty stimulated immigration, mainly from Asia, and thus made Hawaii a blend of many cultures. By making sugar more profitable, the treaty accelerated investment, including that from British and American sources. Increased profits and investments made advances possible in sugar technology, both in field and mill. The treaty was responsible, however, for some wasteful practices. Large profits encouraged the entry of marginal producers and also the use of marginal lands.[45] Since profitable sugar-growing requires large-scale operation, reciprocity brought about concentrations of economic power, especially in the hands of the Honolulu sugar agencies.

By assuring a duty-free market on the West Coast, the treaty also led to closer political and commercial ties between Hawaii and the United States. Reciprocity was therefore a factor in eventual annexation in 1898. In 1875 Hawaiian sugar accounted for only 1 per cent of United States consumption; by 1898 it accounted for 10 per cent.[46] Greater need for transport, because of enlarged sugar production and the resulting economic boom, caused expansion of steamship lines between Hawaii and the West Coast. Spreckels' Oceanic Steamship Company dominated this route in the last two decades of the nineteenth century.

SUGAR AGENCY SYSTEM. Another feature of Spreckels' rise to power after reciprocity was his partnership in 1880 in William

G. Irwin and Company. During the last quarter of the nineteenth century this firm became one of the leading sugar agencies in the kingdom. The agency system as it was practiced in the islands has no close parallel elsewhere. The sugar factors or agencies grew out of the merchandising houses established in the early years of the nineteenth century to provision the whaling fleets. The merchant predecessors of the agencies were exporters, importers, financiers—experienced businessmen in a kingdom where "business" in the Western sense was almost unknown until after 1800.

The transition from merchant to sugar agent was a natural one. With the decline of whaling after 1850, those merchandising houses which had prospered now looked more and more to the rising sugar industry. The struggling planters had enough trouble merely growing cane. For financing (in addition to sources already discussed), warehousing, marketing, purchase of supplies and equipment, the planters turned to the Honolulu merchants. Here they could get help—for a price. The agency system grew out of the need for specialization and division of labor which had to be developed if both agent and planter were to prosper.[47]

Many of the plantation owners and managers looked upon the agent as a necessary evil. They regarded him as "nonproductive" in the sense that he had little to do with the growing of cane and furnished only "services." This was the age-old complaint of the grower against the middleman who stood between him and the consumer. Since one of the chief functions of the agent was the lending of money against crops until they could be sold, planters felt the resentment that a debtor often feels toward a creditor, no matter how necessary the creditor's services may be. As the *Gazette* said: "Few of the planters have had the necessary funds of their own, and have had to depend on the commission houses for most of their funds. For this, of course, they had to pay liberally. . . . Still the interest and commissions which the planter had to pay looked enormously large to the planter and absorbed nearly all his profits until the [reciprocity] treaty came to his relief." [48]

13

The way Spreckels took advantage of the Reciprocity Treaty by hastening to Hawaii was typical of his ability to adapt himself to what he could not change. The United States favored the treaty on primarily political rather than commercial grounds. Political expansionists, hearkening to the cry of "Manifest Destiny!," saw in the treaty an instrument for maintaining the paramount influence which the United States had acquired in Hawaii. Certain West Coast commercial interests, particularly the merchants of San Francisco, favored reciprocity because the West Coast was the main outlet for Hawaii's external trade. Other commercial interests in the United States were either indifferent to the treaty or actively. hostile. The New York refiners and southern planters opposed the treaty because they did not want competition from foreign duty-free sugar. The San Francisco refiners, in contrast to the merchants, fought reciprocity for the same reason. Claus Spreckels led the attack.

Spreckels said later, in 1885, "When they began to agitate this treaty I was opposed to it . . . I was afraid they would drive me out of business, as they had the color [of the sugar] too high." [49] The higher-grade Hawaiian-milled sugars, known as grocery grades, went to market without further refining. They competed with the San Francisco refiners' second-grade refined product known as coffee sugars. Naturally, the refiners made no profit on the Hawaiian grocery grades.

The San Francisco refiners in February, 1875, sent a protest against the proposed reciprocity treaty to the entire California delegation in the United States Congress. The refiners argued (1) that transfer of refining from the West Coast to the Hawaiian Islands would spell disaster to "home industry"; (2) that West Coast consumers would have to pay more for sugar because Hawaii would get control of the market; (3) that the treaty would violate "favored nation" clauses in agreements with other countries, and would thus damage the foreign trade of the United States; (4) that the American planters in Hawaii were "self-expatriated" citizens. It was scarcely possible that the government would kill the fatted calf for them and "refuse a kid to those who have zealously endeavored to cultivate and improve the paternal farm." [50] This protest was signed by the major refiners in the San Francisco area, led by Claus Spreckels who was then head of the California Sugar Refinery.

These refiners sent another protest in March, 1875, to California Representative John K. Luttrell. In it they claimed (1) that the Hawaiian Islands could produce 75,000 tons [51] of sugar a year, or 40,000 tons more than the annual consumption of all states and territories west of the Rockies, and that the excess would go east to compete with sugar production of the southern planters and eastern refiners; (2) that duty-free admission of sugar would cost the United States almost $4,000,000 a year; (3) that "should . . . overshadowing national requirements render it politic to sanction reciprocity," grades higher than thirteen Dutch Standard should not come in duty-free, and that lack of such a restriction "would destroy the most important [refining] interests of this coast, and at the East, which represent millions of capital and give employment to thousands of skilled workmen." [52] In summary, the chief arguments against the treaty were that it would cause damage to home industry and consumers, violate the favored nation clauses, create a monopoly, and bring loss of revenue.

These were Spreckels' views in the early part of 1875. Later in that year J. C. Pflueger of Hackfeld and Company (a Honolulu sugar agency) talked with Spreckels and tried to get the refiners to reverse their stand against reciprocity or at least to remain neutral. Otherwise, said Pflueger, the Hawaiian sugar planters would withhold a large part of the 1876 crop from the San Francisco refiners. He won Spreckels over, and got him to wire the California delegation in Washington that the refiners were dropping their opposition. In the United States Congress some members then charged that the Hawaiian planters and the California refiners had combined to defraud the government.[53] Despite this and other charges, laws to put the reciprocity treaty in effect were passed. By September, 1876, the treaty was in force and Spreckels was in Hawaii to turn it to his profit.

CHAPTER II

King Kalakaua and King Claus

S*preckels* arrived in Hawaii in the third year of King Kalakaua's reign (1874–1891).[1] Born in 1836, Kalakaua came from a family of high chiefs, though he was not of the Kamehameha line. After the death of Lunalilo in 1874, the last of that line, Kalakaua came to power by election over Queen Emma, widow of Kamehameha IV. Queen Emma had been supported by the British in Honolulu, Kalakaua by the Americans. Native Hawaiian support was divided. Some of the Americans feared that if Queen Emma should gain the throne it would be difficult to secure a reciprocity treaty with the United States. After Kalakaua's election by the legislature, in a vote of 39 to 6, Queen Emma's followers rioted and sacked the courthouse. It was the beginning of a turbulent reign.

Kalakaua wanted to restore power to the crown, as did his sister Liliuokalani, who succeeded him in 1891. Attempts by Hawaiian nationalists to strengthen the monarchy were no doubt partly responsible for its overthrow in the Revolution of 1893. Largely under American missionary influence, the Hawaiian kingdom had been converted in the 1840's to a constitutional monarchy. From the Western point of view this change was one of the necessary political conditions for the economic development of Hawaii. Europeans and Americans were not likely to make large investments there until Western ideas about law and property rights had found favor.

A year before his election over Queen Emma, Kalakaua had been defeated by Lunalilo in the campaign for the throne. In this campaign Kalakaua made it clear that he favored revision of the constitution to restore the king to his earlier position of absolute power. Kalakaua's attempts to carry out this idea and to revive Hawaiian nationalism were later to alienate British and American residents of Honolulu. His political ambitions conflicted with their economic interests.[2]

At first Kalakaua did little to antagonize the foreign community. His early cabinet appointments were well received and gave some promise of political stability. Cabinet changes later took place so often that many persons in the community were disturbed. Kalakaua made a visit to the United States in 1874, which helped to create a favorable atmosphere for passage of the reciprocity treaty. As the first king of any country to visit the United States, he was warmly received wherever he went. His tour became a triumph. He called on President Grant and was presented to both houses of Congress.

All the good will created by Kalakaua among the foreign residents of Honolulu soon vanished. He aligned himself with Walter Murray Gibson, an adventurer and many-sided controversial genius who had come to Hawaii in 1861 as a Mormon missionary.[3] After carving out, by highly questionable methods, something of an empire for himself on the island of Lanai, Gibson was excommunicated by the Mormon Church. He then looked toward politics in Honolulu to further his ambitions. With the cry of "Hawaii for the Hawaiians!" he was elected to the legislature in 1878 by a large majority, and became the leader of the Hawaiian faction. He spoke Hawaiian fluently. Beyond any doubt he was a brilliant student of Hawaiian customs and traditions.

Together, Kalakaua and Gibson (later joined by Spreckels) instituted a regime of political corruption unlike anything known in the previous 40 years of constitutional government in Hawaii.

17

Appropriations were made without reference to probable tax receipts. Members of the legislature favorable to the regime were rewarded with other offices, since there was no law against holding two offices. The royal franking privilege was abused, especially with respect to imports of liquor (often used to influence elections), so that customs revenues were lost. Lands were leased illegally without public auction. Exemptions were sold to lepers so they could avoid segregation at the leper settlement. Roads were neglected and road money misappropriated. Cabinet members were arbitrarily and frequently dismissed, which made it difficult to get competent persons to serve. Once Gibson himself was at the same time premier, minister of foreign affairs, minister of interior, attorney general, president of the board of health, and member of the boards of education and immigration. He became known as "minister of everything."

Members of the Kalakaua-Gibson-Spreckels triumvirate had diverse ambitions. Kalakaua was interested in strengthening the monarchy and reviving Hawaiian nationalism. Gibson appears to have been an opportunist who wanted power for its own sake. Kalakaua felt he needed Gibson because Gibson understood both the Hawaiian ways and those of the foreigners and was an astute politician. Spreckels lent financial support to the government. In return, he sought political favors that would further his economic ambitions. However, as a property owner, planter, and businessman, he wanted political stability and he therefore opposed the wilder schemes of Kalakaua and Gibson.

Whatever the faults of the Kalakaua regime, the kingdom was prospering under the influence of reciprocity. Kalakaua decided to learn more about the ways of foreigners by making a tour of the world. One excuse for the trip was to seek foreign labor for the sugar plantations. Among those who accompanied the king were his chamberlain, C. H. Judd, and Attorney General W. N. Armstrong. Armstrong was also named commissioner of immigration, in keeping with the ostensible aim of the trip. The party was received with royal honors at many of the principal capitals in Europe and Asia. Kalakaua took a special interest in military displays and in court pomp and etiquette. At the courts of Oriental potentates he got some new ideas about how to be a king and about what it meant to be an absolute monarch. His return to Honolulu on October 29, 1881, was welcomed with "a magnificent reception, triumphal arches, torches blazing at noonday, and extravagant adulation of every description." [4]

Kalakaua prepared for a formal coronation on February 12, 1883, the ninth anniversary of his accession. What he had seen on his trip influenced preparations for the event. Two crowns and other regalia were ordered from London. The ceremony was to be a combination of Hawaiian and Western rites. All the major powers sent representatives to the coronation. It thus became an international event directing world attention to Hawaii. In a Napoleonic gesture, Kalakaua placed the crown on his head with his own hands, and then he also crowned his queen, Kapiolani.

A few years later, on November 16, 1886, the kingdom celebrated Kalakaua's fiftieth birthday. Among other events there was an elaborate *ho'okupu* ("gift-giving"), in keeping with ancient Hawaiian custom. In a gesture worthy of him, Gibson presented Kalakaua with a pair of elephant tusks mounted on a *koa* wood stand, inscribed: "The horns of the righteous shall be exalted." The police department gave a check for $570. The value of the gifts came to about $10,000. A torchlight parade, a historical procession, a *luau* ("feast") for 1,500 persons, and an elaborate jubilee ball, all helped to make the birthday a festive occasion.

This surface gaiety could not, however, hide the drift of the Kalakaua regime toward trouble. In successive legislatures of 1882, 1884, and 1886, the opposition to the regime remained strong, particularly on the part of the white foreigners who were members of the Honolulu business community. In 1884 the finance committee of the legislature presented a sensational report on the mishandling of funds. The Kalakaua-Gibson-Spreckels triumvirate fell apart in October, 1886, with the departure of Spreckels for San Francisco.

After Spreckels' departure, Gibson and Kalakaua were busy

with schemes (hatched earlier, mainly by Gibson) to establish the primacy of Hawaii among the Pacific islands. A parody of the Monroe Doctrine had been sent to the powers, intended to discourage them from further annexations in the Pacific. Many of the powers did not even bother to reply. Kalakaua commissioned J. E. Bush as envoy to Samoa, Tonga, and other islands of Polynesia. In February, 1887, Hawaii and Samoa entered into a political confederation.

Kalakaua felt he needed a navy to maintain his "Primacy of the Pacific." The kingdom bought an English 170-ton steamer, the "Explorer," for $20,000, refitted her at a cost of $50,000, and renamed her the "Kaimiloa" ("explorer"). Captained by G. E. G. Jackson, a retired British naval officer, and manned in part by a crew from the Honolulu reform school, the ship set sail in May, 1887, for Samoa. It was an unfortunate voyage. Robert Louis Stevenson later wrote: "The Kaimiloa was from the first a scene of disaster and dilapidation; the stores were sold; the crew revolted: for a great part of the night she was in the hands of mutineers." [5] Germany became concerned about Hawaii's ambitions in the Pacific, and as a gentle hint sent a few warships to Samoa. Bush was recalled on July 7, 1887. The "Kaimiloa" arrived in Honolulu in September and was later sold at auction for $2,800 as junk.

The corruption of the Kalakaua regime, the efforts of the king to establish a strong monarchy, and fears of the foreign propertied classes in Honolulu at the revival of Hawaiian nationalism resulted in a bloodless revolution in 1887 which deprived Kalakaua of much of his power. An opium-bribe affair in which the king was involved set off the revolution. Gibson was toppled as premier and charged with embezzlement. Although the charges were dropped, some hotheads talked of lynching Gibson. He was permitted to leave the kingdom, nevertheless, and he died in 1888 in California. Kalakaua, while on a trip to the United States, died in 1891 in San Francisco. One of the few persons present at the deathbed was Claus Spreckels. He was the last survivor of the once powerful triumvirate.

Spreckels was born in the village of Lamstedt, Germany, on July 9, 1828, the eldest of six children of Diedrich and Gesche Baack Spreckels.[6] Herr Diedrich was a *Köthner,* a person who supplemented his livelihood as a villager by farming a small plot of ground. After meager education, young Claus went to work for neighboring farmers, receiving bed and board and little more. Farming out children was a custom of the poor villagers of Lamstedt, especially during the harvest season, because it meant at least one less mouth to feed at home.[7] In the poverty of Spreckels' youth an Adlerian psychologist might well find the key to his later drive for wealth and power.

During the revolutionary ferment of the 1840's Claus Spreckels decided to leave Germany. He became a part of that process by which some of the most energetic and resourceful persons in Europe reached the United States. Of emigration between 1845 and 1856 from the region around Lamstedt to America, W. Klenck has said: "On the question, 'Who were the emigrants?' we should note that they were probably among the most venture-some persons in their native district. Timid persons who thought about the matter too much preferred to remain at home. Since those who emigrated were used to hard work, and knew how to 'pitch in,' almost all of them prospered in America."[8] Klenck goes on to say that of the emigrants from Lamstedt, Spreckels became the richest and most famous.

Spreckels borrowed steerage-passage money from a friend and sailed from Bremen in 1846. He landed at Charleston, South Carolina, with one German thaler in his pocket. Soon he found work in a grocery store; in a few weeks he paid back his passage money.[9] When his employers decided to retire, Spreckels bought the store. Within a year he paid off the purchase price. By 1852 he was well enough established to marry his childhood sweetheart, Anna Christina Mangels, who was then working as a housemaid in New York City. Restless to search out new opportunities, Spreckels sold his Charleston grocery in 1855 and moved to New York. There he bought out the Samson Moore grocery at West Broadway and Anthony streets. The business prospered;

within a year he was able to make a trip back to Germany with his family.

On his return to New York he made a decision that was to place him in the area where he gained his greatest fame. His brother Bernard, who had been operating a grocery in San Francisco, gave him a firsthand account of the opportunities in California, still burning with the gold-rush fever. Claus bought his brother's store and sold his own New York store to his brother-in-law, Claus Mangels.

Spreckels sailed from New York for Panama, made the trek overland, and then boarded the steamer "John L. Stephens," reaching San Francisco in July, 1856. The grocery business turned out to be profitable but did not occupy all his time and energy, so he looked about for other ventures. He started a brewery in 1857. Soon he sold the grocery for $50,000, and in 1863 he also sold the brewery for $75,000. He was thirty-five years old and already a fairly rich man. He next turned his attention to a field that was to occupy him for much of his life—sugar refining.

Together with his brother Peter, his brother-in-law Claus Mangels, and others, Spreckels organized the Bay Sugar Refinery in 1863 in San Francisco. The business was incorporated the following year. There is no evidence that Spreckels knew much about refining at this time, but he saw opportunities for profit and he was willing to learn. He returned to New York, where he studied the operations of sugar refineries by going to work in one of them. He then bought the machinery of the bankrupt United States Refinery and shipped it to San Francisco.

Chiefly because of Spreckels' direction, the Bay Sugar Refinery was successful from the start, and he soon became impatient to expand. When the directors demurred, he sold out his interest. From this time on he seldom got involved in any venture that he could not control. He was essentially a lone operator who prized his independence of action.

He went back to Germany in 1865 to increase his knowledge of refining. For eight months he worked as a common laborer in a Magdeburg beet sugar refinery. Upon return to California, he considered going into beet sugar but decided the time was not yet ripe because labor and other costs were too high. He organized the California Sugar Refinery, however, obtaining cane sugar from the Hawaiian Islands, the Philippines, China, and Java. The capital behind the new refinery was $300,000. Claus Spreckels had the controlling interest and was the first president. His brother Peter and his brother-in-law Claus Mangels were also associated with him in this venture.

Plant capacity at the start was 25,000 to 30,000 pounds a day. This was expanded to 125,000 pounds a day in 1869, and 250,000 pounds in 1871. With the stimulus of the Reciprocity Treaty in 1876, Hawaiian sugar production expanded, and practically all of it was refined in San Francisco. The California Sugar Refinery built an entirely new plant at a cost of $1,000,000. When completed in 1881 it was the most modern refinery in America. In one way or another, by purchase, merger, or price war, Spreckels had eliminated most competing West Coast refiners. He had become the acknowledged sugar king of California.

There can be little doubt that the success of the refinery resulted from Spreckels' personal leadership. He drove himself relentlessly to improve the product and lower the cost. His labors in New York and Magdeburg had been only the beginning. He was ever on the alert for new machinery and new methods. In 1868 he patented a process for speeding the refining of sugar. He also invented a process for making cube sugar direct from the centrifugals. By 1869 he was sick from overwork and went to Germany for eighteen months for his health. He came back fully restored.

By the 1880's, Spreckels' achievements in refining on the West Coast attracted the attention of the sugar trust, operating mainly on the East Coast, with some control also in the Midwest. The principal holding company for the trust's extensive operations was the American Sugar Refining Company. The trust in 1887 made overtures to Spreckels for a share of the West Coast market. These overtures Spreckels rebuffed. "No, thank you," he said in effect; "I'll continue to run things on the West Coast by myself."

23

The trust then began a war against Spreckels by getting control of the American Sugar Refinery in San Francisco (not to be confused with the American Sugar Refining Company, the trust's parent company). A few years before the trust got control of American Sugar Refinery, Honolulu sugar agencies unfriendly to Spreckels had vainly tried to break his monopoly by making contracts with this West Coast refinery. Spreckels himself had no financial interest in the American refinery at this time, but he had an arrangement to give it a minor share of the West Coast market. Ironically, the American Sugar Refinery's plant was that of the old Bay Sugar Company through which Spreckels had got his start in sugar.

The state of California in 1888 brought suit against American Sugar Refinery on the ground it had violated California law by selling out to the trust. There is no proof that Spreckels instigated the lawsuit, but he may well have supported it behind the scenes. Legal harassment of American Sugar Refinery was obviously to his advantage in his battle with the trust. The refinery was forced to close. After a long court fight, it was permitted to reopen in 1890. During the two years it was closed, Spreckels solidified his West Coast position by taking additional business for his own California Sugar Refinery, business that otherwise might have gone to American.

A more dramatic battle in Spreckels' war with the sugar trust was set off by his invasion of the East Coast. No incident better illustrates his character as a no-holds-barred, bare-knuckle fighter. Spreckels scraped together about $5,000,000, hardly enough to match the resources of the trust, which were around $50,000,000. He set out to build a refinery in Philadelphia and indicated "it was his intention to fight the trust on its own ground and demonstrate it was not omnipotent." [10] He bought a Philadelphia site in 1888 and the next year completed a refinery at a cost of $3,000,000. With the latest in machinery and equipment, Spreckels felt confident he could process sugar at a lower cost than could the trust.

He engaged in a bitter price war with the trust refiners from

1889 to 1891, in retaliation against the trust's efforts to sell sugar below cost on the West Coast. By 1891 the combatants were ready to come to terms in the thus far profitless war. In that year the trust obtained a 45 per cent interest in Spreckels' Philadelphia Refinery, and the next year a controlling interest. Spreckels made a profit of about $3,000,000 on the sale of his stock. In 1891 the trust also obtained a 50 per cent interest in Spreckels' California Sugar Refinery. It then became the Western Sugar Refinery. Though the results of the battle were something of a stalemate, Spreckels must be judged the victor when one considers the relative size of the opponents.

For raw material for his refinery Spreckels had come to depend almost entirely on Hawaiian cane sugar, including that grown by his own company. His political power in Hawaii had waned and he faced possible government hostility to his economic interests in the islands by the autumn of 1886. The Hawaiian planters, moreover, were growing restive under Spreckels' control. Spreckels now turned to beet sugar as a possible solution to these problems and as a fulfillment of his dream of more than twenty years before, when he had worked in a Magdeburg beet sugar refinery.

The record of beet sugar in California was largely one of failure before Spreckels got into it. He had a ranch at Aptos, California, where he experimented with beet growing. In 1887 he again went to Germany for his health, but he also made a further study of the processing of beets. He bought machinery having a capacity of fifty tons a day and shipped it to California. In November, 1887, he met with the farmers of Pajaro Valley, California, to discuss a possible beet sugar refinery at Watsonville. At this meeting he said: "I am now in my sixtieth year, and it would kill me to fail in what I undertake to do. It is not money that is an object to me, but I want the people of California to be able to show that Claus Spreckels has done something for this state when his bones are at rest." [11]

He put up $440,000 for the project, and six associates put up $10,000 each. The Watsonville beet sugar refinery, known as the Western Beet Sugar Company, began grinding in 1888. In the first year 2,920,000 pounds of beets were processed. Spreckels educated the farmers in beet sugar production by talking with them and by having articles on the subject published in farm journals. He also offered prizes to growers and guaranteed a market for their crops by making firm contracts. The capacity of the Watsonville refinery was increased in 1892 from 350 to 700 tons a day, and later to 1,000 tons.

Encouraged by the progress at Watsonville, Spreckels decided to build another plant. He went to Germany in 1896 and spent eight weeks at Maschinenfabrik Grevenbroich developing plans for new machinery. On his return he spoke at a meeting of some two thousand farmers from the vicinity of Salinas and explained that the new factory would spend over $1,000,000 a year for beets, labor, fuel, etc. When one of the farmers addressed him as "Sir Claus" (he had been "knighted" by King Kalakaua), he said: "If you want to give me a title, I have two. I was a colonel on the Governor's staff and I am the 'sugar king.' When I shall have built this big refinery, however, I will no longer be the 'sugar king'; but the 'emperor' of the sugar industry." [12] The refinery was built about five miles south of Salinas at a place later called Spreckels. Completed in 1899, the plant had a capacity of 3,000 tons of beets a day, more than that of all other California beet sugar plants combined.

Besides cane and beet sugar refining, Claus Spreckels had many other commercial interests, including railroads, steamships, real estate, public utilities, and banking. Some of these ventures were related to sugar, some grew out of his search for investment outlets for his wealth, and some merely resulted from the fact that he saw things that needed doing and went ahead and did them. Certainly from the age of about forty Spreckels could have relaxed, sat back, and lived from the income of his wealth. But this was not the character of the man. To the end of his life he was a doer, a maker, a builder. It would be a great mistake to view his life as merely a constant search for money and power. Work was one of his greatest pleasures, and he had a tremendous pride of workmanship in the Veblenian sense. Again, using

Veblen's terms, Spreckels was both a financial capitalist and an industrial capitalist, but more the latter than the former. His continuing drive and energy, even in his sixties and seventies, far surpassed that of many a younger man.

In railroading, Spreckels helped to break the monopoly of the Southern Pacific Railroad on the route into San Francisco. Merchants of the city often complained of high railroad freight rates. They made numerous vain attempts in the eighties and nineties to restore competition, including efforts to ship by boat from New York by way of Cape Horn. The merchants formed the Traffic Association of California in 1891 to wrestle with the problem. A few years later the association appointed a committee to meet with citizens of San Joaquin Valley about starting a railroad to compete with Southern Pacific on the last leg of the San Francisco route. The necessary funds could not be raised.

At another meeting held at the San Francisco Chamber of Commerce in January, 1895, Spreckels was present. He pledged $50,000 for a San Joaquin Valley railroad. This spark caught fire. Spreckels headed a committee of 12 which decided upon a capital of $6,000,000. He subscribed $500,000 and "persuaded" two of his sons, John and Adolph, to subscribe $100,000 each. Under Spreckels' leadership the committee soon raised the rest of the money and incorporated the San Francisco and San Joaquin Valley Railroad on February 25, 1895. Spreckels was chosen president. The company broke ground at Stockton in July, 1895, and by October 1896, the road had been completed to Fresno. At a huge celebration there the participants lauded Spreckels' role in the building of the road. By July, 1898, the road was complete from Stockton to Bakersfield, with a loop into Visalia, and 279 miles of track were in use. Having fully accomplished its chief purpose, which was to force the Southern Pacific to reduce freight rates, the Valley line was sold to the Santa Fe Railroad around 1900.[13]

Spreckels bought heavily in San Francisco real estate between 1890 and 1900, and this was his chief financial interest near the time of his death. In 1895 he bought a corner lot at Market and

Third streets as a site for the Spreckels Building, the tallest of its time in San Francisco. The building withstood the earthquake of 1906, though it was damaged. Spreckels took great pride in this structure. On some floors ornate bronze doorknobs with the initials "C.S." can still be seen. The building is now known as the Central Tower.

Indirectly, the building caused Spreckels to enter the public utility business. Not far away stood two plants of the San Francisco Gas and Electric Company. The smoke from these plants smudged the sides of the Spreckels Building and annoyed the tenants. After protests by Spreckels, the utility company made vain efforts in 1897 and 1898 to abate the nuisance by using anthracite coal and automatic stokers. In August, 1898, Spreckels ran into Joseph B. Crockett, president of San Francisco Gas and Electric, at the Pacific Union Club, and again complained of the smoke. Crockett said, in effect, "I never talk business at the club." The few words of this rebuff were doubtless the most costly that Crockett ever spoke. Spreckels went back to his office and made plans to produce electricity.

He started the Independent Electric Light and Power Company in March, 1899. Two years later he also founded the Independent Gas and Power Company. At seventy-three years of age, Spreckels was still a determined fighter. He engaged in an unremitting rate war with San Francisco Gas and Electric which drove the stock of that company from $100 to $30. The company moved in 1903 to merge with its rivals and completed arrangements with all companies except those of Spreckels. He refused to merge but offered to sell. "The records show . . . that he . . . made a clear profit of $1,214,000 as recompense for the coal smoke that had smudged the walls and windows of his office building." [14] The Pacific Gas and Electric Company of California is a successor to all the merged companies and those of Spreckels.

Spreckels was a director of the First National Bank of San Francisco and also of the First Federal Trust Company. Among the assets of his estate at his death were 1,000 shares of Mercantile Trust Company stock, appraised at $215,000, and 1,083 shares of

First National Bank stock, appraised at $271,000. The total estate was about $11,000,000, but before his death in 1908 Spreckels had disposed of about $40,000,000, mostly by gift to his sons John and Adolph.

Between 1846, when he landed at Charleston as a penniless immigrant youth, and 1908, Claus Spreckels had come far. What in his career stands out? First, his enormous appetite for purposeful work. Second, his ability to see opportunities and make the most of them. Third, his character as a relentless, determined, and resourceful fighter. His methods were ruthless but to some extent a product of the social climate of the times. This, it will be recalled, was the era of the robber barons. Of these, Spreckels was not the most important but he was by no means the least.

The following chapters deal with Claus Spreckels' Hawaiian period—more narrowly, with his years of greatest power in the islands, 1876 to 1886, and also with his attempted political comeback after the Hawaiian Revolution of 1893. With a combination of stubborn drive, vast wealth, a thorough knowledge of sugar, and the ability to promote favorable political alignments for economic purposes, Spreckels gained control of the Hawaiian sugar industry to an extent not since attained. Politically, he made and unmade cabinets, and no cabinet opposing him could stay in power for long. He became variously known as "the sugar king of Hawaii," "the power behind the throne," "the second king," "the uncrowned king of Hawaii," or "the maker and breaker of cabinets." In some satirical pamphlets of the time he was called "His Royal Saccharinity," "Sir Silvergilt," or "Herr Von Boss."

There is a considerable oral tradition with respect to the Spreckels era in Hawaii, particularly about his card-playing relationship with King Kalakaua. Much of this folklore has no doubt been distorted and embellished in the retelling. It may nevertheless throw light on some parts of the truth. One example of this lore concerns the break between Spreckels and Kalakaua over the London loan.[15]

One day in 1886 Kalakaua, Spreckels, and two visiting admirals, one American and the other British, were playing a game of euchre at Kalakaua's boathouse. Outside, the Royal Hawaiian Band played. Relations between the king and Spreckels were somewhat strained because of Spreckels' demands regarding conditions under which he would renew his loans to the kingdom. Reportedly, these conditions included control by Spreckels of Honolulu's wharves, waterworks, and electric light plant (as security). Still friendly, nevertheless, Spreckels and Kalakaua were partners against the admirals in the card game.

Spreckels held three kings, an ace, and one low card. He turned to one of the admirals and said: "If this were poker I would have the winning hand here."

In jest, the admiral offered to bet. He then showed his hand containing three aces.

"My four kings would still win over your aces," said Spreckels.

"Where is the fourth king?" asked Kalakaua.

"I am the fourth king," said Spreckels.

Kalakaua rose in anger. As he strode off, the band played "God Save the King." Spreckels bowed in the direction of the band leader. It is said that Kalakaua consulted that same night with his adviser George Macfarlane about a loan in London to break Spreckels' grip on the kingdom.[16]

CHAPTER III

Water Rights and
Cabinet Shuffles

S*preckels* knew that one of his main problems in starting a sugar plantation on the dry plains of Maui would be how to get water for irrigation. As he tried to solve this problem his influence reached into the throne room and into the Hawaiian cabinet. The pulling and hauling over certain water rights on Maui marks Spreckels' first interference in Hawaiian politics to gain economic goals, and the start of his rise to power in the kingdom.

The importance of water in sugar culture can best be understood from the fact that about two thousands pounds of water are needed to produce one pound of sugar.[1] In the Hawaiian Islands the heaviest rainfall occurs in the mountains. In many lowland areas otherwise suited to sugar growing, the rainfall is not enough to assure a profitable yield. The Hawaiian sugar industry has therefore had to pioneer large-scale irrigation. Ditches, flumes, aqueducts, mountain tunnels, and artesian wells have all played a role.[2]

During the few years before Spreckels first came to the islands, many newspaper articles emphasized the importance of irrigation and called upon the government to undertake it. This would increase land available for agriculture, according to the *Pacific Commercial Advertiser*, and would therefore increase sugar production and exports. Irrigation would enhance the value of government lands and they could then be sold at a price that would amply repay the cost of getting water.[3] The editor thought that private enterprise could not do the job: "Neither the capital for speculation, the public spirit and enterprise, nor the energy exist among us to undertake [irrigation] works. . . . Consequently if the Government refuses to move . . . it is clear that nobody else will move." [4]

The editor also said that government control of irrigation would avoid the "danger of a tyrannizing monopoly." He called attention to the plains of Maui: "With water the change that would come over this now barren and worthless 'kula' ["district"] would be almost magical. It would convert the desert waste into productive lands, the seat of thriving industries, and add immensely to the wealth of the country." [5]

Some residents of Maui had petitioned the legislature in 1872 for a public irrigation project on the central part of the island; but the petition had been rejected. The government said the engineering difficulties were great, and the cost would be at least $200,000. The *Advertiser* thought the cost would not be over $100,000, and the investment would "prove better than a gold mine." [6]

Despite the pessimism of the newspapers about the ability of private enterprise to get the irrigation job done, H. P. Baldwin and S. T. Alexander, Maui planters, obtained a government lease dated September 30, 1876, and began construction of the so-called Hamakua ditch. This was the first large irrigation project on Maui. When Spreckels arrived in Honolulu on August 24, 1876, his imagination may well have been stirred by the following newspaper account of this work:

The energetic manager of Haiku plantation, East Maui, will soon commence operation for digging a ditch to bring the waters of Haleakala down on to the cane fields. The route of the proposed ditch has been carefully surveyed and demonstrated to be perfectly feasible, and the amount of water is surprisingly large, equal, as Mr. Alexander assures us, to the combined volume of Waihee, Wailuku and Waikapu [rivers]! The right of way and water will be granted by the government, which is all the aid he requires to complete the enterprise. Without the treaty, the bringing down of this water would be a "bonanza" to East Maui, but with the treaty—it simply assures a magnificent near future for the planters of that region.[7]

Just two days after this article appeared, Spreckels left Honolulu to spend several days on Maui. He explored the undeveloped land and water resources of the island. Alexander pointed out to him that the central plains needed only water to produce abundant sugar crops.[8] Spreckels later claimed it was at this time that he got the idea for his own ditch, and that immediately on return to San Francisco in September, 1876, he consulted Hermann Schussler, a well-known irrigation engineer, about the project.[9] More than a year went by, however, before Spreckels returned to Maui.

There was much talk of another ditch in the same area even before the Hamakua ditch was finished. The *Advertiser* reported: "[It is said] that the Royal Commissioners will approve of another water-way, *makai* ["seaward"] of the present ditch by which they hope to lay many acres on the plain under water." [10] Reports of drought early in 1878 gave dramatic emphasis to the need for more irrigation, though such need was already well understood. The dry spell was a common topic of conversation, with generally depressing effect. "Should we not have copious showers of rain, and that shortly, too," lamented the *Hawaiian Gazette*, "the result will doubtless be disastrous." [11] The drought ended in late April, 1878, but not before widespread damage had been done to the crops.[12]

Only a few weeks before Spreckels returned to Maui in May, 1878, a writer in the *Advertiser* noted that sugar is a soil-exhausting crop and that before long the planters would have to seek new land. The writer called attention to the dry Wailuku Commons of central Maui: "By proper engineering works the surplus waters of the valleys which now run to waste in the sea could be made to irrigate the entire 'commons' and raise thereon enormous crops of cane. And it will surely be done some day." [13]

As this statement appeared, Spreckels and his engineer, Hermann Schussler, were preparing to leave San Francisco to make the prophecy come true. After arrival in Honolulu in late May, 1878, they went to Maui to study a plan for bringing water from the northern slopes of Mount Haleakala ("House of the Sun") to the plains of the Wailuku and Waikapu commons. They examined the site of the proposed ditch and the streams to be tapped, and determined how to carry out the work.

Schussler organized a survey party which included an engineering assistant, eight Hawaiians, a Japanese cook, and a mule driver. The Hawaiians carried the chains and stakes and other surveying equipment; the cook and the driver looked after the tent and other camping supplies. Plodding along mountain trails overhung with tropical shrubbery, the party first surveyed the area near the headwaters of the proposed ditch. Schussler determined the probable course of the waterway, sizes and strength of piping to be used, and the character of the soil at various points, especially its capacity for carrying water without too much seepage. He also estimated the cost of the work which would extend some thirty miles, intersecting many ravines and gulches. Much of the survey was over rugged terrain, but Schussler finished it in about two weeks. He also made a topographical map of the area to be watered. The ditch was planned so it would run along the upper edge of the land and in this way maximum use could be made of gravity so that there would be little need for pumps.[14]

Spreckels now had a plan for his project. Two chief obstacles still stood in the way: he owned no sugar land on Maui and he owned no water rights. The first of these problems he solved by buying from Henry Cornwell an undivided half-interest in 16,000 acres of the Waikapu Commons. Also, Spreckels leased 24,000 acres of crown lands on the adjoining Wailuku Commons from the government, at $1,000 a year.[15] The problem of the water rights proved somewhat more difficult.

Spreckels presented a petition to the king and ministry on June 24, 1878. He requested the desired water rights at $500 a year.

36

According to the petition, many advantages would accrue to the Hawaiian kingdom from an extensive irrigation system on Maui. "A large district now lying waste [would] be brought to a high state of cultivation." [16] The ministry did not immediately grant the rights, but accepted the petition for consideration. On the same day, Walter Murray Gibson, then a member of the legislature, brought in a motion of no confidence in the ministry. This was defeated, 26 to 19.[17]

Spreckels was not a man to put up with delay. On the night of July 1 he, King Kalakaua, and several other persons met at a hotel. About two o'clock in the morning the king sent a messenger to rout the ministers from their beds and notify them they were dismissed. According to the historian W. D. Alexander, "Such an arbitrary and despotic act was without precedent in Hawaiian history." [18] The editor of the *Gazette* expressed the general mystification over the dismissal of the cabinet:

We do not for a moment question the right or the prerogative of His Majesty to change the Ministry as and when he pleases, and no doubt the reasons which moved the King to act with decision and promptness were sufficiently strong and controlling in their character to justify his action. What those reasons were, we are not only ignorant of, but under and in view of the circumstances, at a loss to conjecture.[19]

The new cabinet was made up as follows: S. G. Wilder, Minister of the Interior, vice J. Mott Smith; J. M. Kapena, Minister of Foreign Relations, vice H. A. Peirce; S. K. Kaai, Minister of Finance, vice J. M. Kapena; Edward Preston, Attorney General, vice A. S. Hartwell.[20] This cabinet, on July 8, granted Spreckels the desired water rights.

Of the change in the cabinet James H. Wodehouse, British commissioner in Hawaii, wrote to the Foreign Office: "The Ministers declare that their overthrow was caused by a great Californian [*sic*] capitalist, but I cannot say how much truth there is in this statement." [21] James M. Comly, United States minister-resident, reported as follows to the secretary of state:

Meantime, the various assaults upon the Ministry culminated in a sudden decision by the King to rudely and unceremoniously dismiss the whole of them. According [sic] messengers were sent ... with peremptory orders to the Ministry to hand in all their resignations the next morning early. I have been told by the Ministers themselves that the order was couched in most insulting terms. ... The action of the King was totally unexpected by all parties. Various explanations are offered for the extraordinary haste requiring the use of messengers at the dead of night. ... One thing is known, however: The King spent the evening up to about 11 or 12 o'clock with Claus Spreckels and Wm. H. Dimond. ... Dimond [a San Francisco sugar broker and commission agent] is a confidential agent of the Pacific Mail S. S. Co., and is here to secure an enlargement ... of the subsidy now paid to that Company. ... What influences were brought to bear on His Majesty by Spreckels and Dimond is not known; but after spending the time in their company until about midnight, His Majesty reached such an elevation that he dismissed his Ministers.[22]

On the same day that the lease granting the water rights was signed, S. K. Kaai, newly appointed minister of finance, spoke to a meeting of native Hawaiians at Kaumakapili Church. The theme of the meeting turned out to be: *E mahalo i ka ona miliona* ("Let us give thanks to the multimillionaire"). The meeting passed resolutions thanking Spreckels for his investments in Hawaii, and thanking the king for appointing two Hawaiians to the ministry. A letter to the editor of the *Gazette* commented:

It was thought by the promoters of the meeting that it was best to publicly thank Mr. C. Spreckels for his noble and magnanimous conduct during his late visit to Honolulu. Possibly it appeared to the native mind that a speculation—which has in it somewhat of a savor of monopoly— was a disinterested investment of money in these Islands for the benefit of the nation; that it exhibited a benevolence which should call forth the admiration of all classes—from the highest to the lowest. Perhaps it was wise to praise the power of money, and to inculcate its worship as a worthy public sentiment; but its introduction into politics as an element of discussion is certainly not wise. Hitherto the Hawaiians have been free from its influence, and happy will it be for them if they never have to contend with its subversive power.[23]

This meeting was probably designed to promote public acceptance of Spreckels. Kaai may also have felt the need to justify the cabinet's grant of water rights to Spreckels for what must have seemed to the public a small annual payment. Water rights have always been important in Hawaii—the native word for wealth is *waiwai*, literally "water-water"—and even before the coming of the *haole* ("white foreigner") these rights were subject to a complex system of regulation, remnants of which still survive.

Rumors of a pay-off by Spreckels soon began to spread. In October, 1878, the *Advertiser* cited parts of an article that had appeared in the *Alta California* on September 5. Because of the Reciprocity Treaty, said the article, many new investments were being made in sugar. The Hawaiians were delighted with the boldness of American capitalists, and Californians could readily adapt themselves to circumstances. A "certain high personage" in Hawaii had become involved in debts which it was not convenient to pay. "This knot was dexterously cut by a California capitalist who begged . . . to take the loan at a less [*sic*] rate of interest. . . . The interests of the capitalist have not suffered by his adroit stroke of finesse." [24]

As one might suspect from the above account, much had been going on behind the scenes. Kalakaua's cashbook and letters from C. C. Harris, chief justice of the Hawaiian supreme court, to E. H. Allen, Hawaiian minister at Washington, throw additional light on what took place. The king's cashbook, kept by his chamberlain, contains the following entry:

Bills payable
    Amount 4 notes dated July 8, 1878, given by His Majesty favor of Claus Spreckels for $10,000 each at 2, 3, 4 & 5 years with int. at 7 per cent per annum payable semiannually and secured by net receipts of Crown Lands. ....$40,000.[25]

The date of these notes is the same as that of Spreckels' lease of the Maui water rights.

If any further mystery exists about what happened, it is cleared up by Harris's account to Allen:

On Spreckels' arrival he had been "greatly entertained" by the king. As far as the request for water rights was concerned, the cabinet dismissed on July 1, 1878, was not averse to granting whatever it could legally grant. A. S. Hartwell, the subsequently deposed attorney general, was, however, of a cautious turn of mind. He drafted the lease, went over it with Spreckels and Schussler, and then redrafted it several times. Chief Justice Harris was also consulted and seemed to understand what was wanted. Spreckels then heard rumors that certain sugar interests on Maui would oppose his lease. Harris told Hartwell he would go to see Spreckels and Schussler, and draw up the paper himself. While Harris was talking to Hartwell, the latter received a note by messenger from Kalakaua saying that "he hoped the matter would be attended to as his [the king's] interest was suffering." [26]

Harris, the account continues, went to Schussler's room at the hotel and found Kalakaua, Sam Parker,[27] W. H. Dimond, Spreckels, and Schussler, all drinking champagne. They invited Harris to take a drink, but he declined because the room was crowded and warm. He told Schussler that he would help him draft the lease and then returned to his own room. Since Schussler did not come to his room, Harris went back at nine o'clock and again at eleven but did not go into the room because the king was still there. Next morning Mott Smith showed Harris the note requesting his (Mott Smith's) resignation, which he had been roused from his bed to receive. Then, according to Harris:

I immediately sent for Schutzler [sic] & Spreckles [sic] to their several rooms & taxed them with it. They said they had not done it & I answered, you have done it by finding unnecessary fault & reporting to the King statements which enemys [sic] have made & have not told him what I told you Mr. Schutzler last night. Besides you have offered the King pecuniary considerations, & then alarmed him by telling him you would withdraw from the enterprise. They asked me how I knew that? I answered, I guessed at it; because that is the way you talked to me yesterday, & you talked to the King the same way, and I know that because the King's action has followed directly upon his leaving your room. The fact was that the King went immediately to Preston's and got him out of bed, & told him he was going to appoint him Attorney General, & sent a note to Green.

Schutzler & Spreckles replied to me, we are only defending our own interests, I said & it is the first time money has been used in this country to procure official favors, and now with the King. You have injured our pride & done damage to those who are doing good to you, & who have spent an immensity of time & trouble in bringing your plan into shape, & who didn't want, & couldn't be induced to take a dollar of your money. They denied that they had used pecuniary considerations.

I replied to them, gentlemen, will you undertake to deny me that you have promised the King a gift of $10,000 & a loan of $40,000 at 7%—

holding out in my hand a Note of the King's in which he said that Mr. S had offered him to lend him $40,000 at 7% to pay some Notes which were then running at 12%. Of course there was nothing that could be said. The $10,000 has since arrived and been received by the King, by Draft on the California Bank on Bishop & Co.[28]

The next morning C. R. Bishop (a banker, and husband of Bernice Pauahi Paki, a high chiefess) went to the king and tried to reason with him about the cabinet dismissal. Bishop urged Kalakaua to confer again with Harris, but the king had made up his mind and would not listen.[29] Increasingly thereafter, Kalakaua and the "palace party" were to be at odds with the more conservative element in the Honolulu community.

Thus, using political influence to serve his economic ambitions, Spreckels began his rise to power in the kingdom. His money, which had begun to play a role in Hawaiian politics was to be an important factor for some eight years. Not only were there loans to the king and later to the kingdom, but also, according to the Harris account quoted above, "gifts" of money to the king.

Presumably the first of the four notes for $10,000 each given to Spreckels by Kalakaua was paid when it fell due in July, 1880. The 1880 legislature, in discussing the assumption of the balance of the loan by the government, mentioned a figure of $30,000. L. Aholo, a Hawaiian member of the legislature, introduced a resolution on August 5 that:

The Minister of Finance be authorized to pay to the Commissioners of Crown Lands the sum of Thirty Thousand Dollars for the purpose of cancelling certain notes of His Majesty now held by Capitalists, the money to be returned by said Commissioners into the Treasury with interest thereon at a rate not to exceed five per cent per annum, by payments from time to time of one fourth of the income of said lands.[30]

Just who was behind this resolution by Aholo is not clear, but it is doubtful that he would have dared to introduce it without Kalakaua's consent. Aholo said only that he thought "this was a thing that ought to be done," and therefore he had brought it in.[31]

Godfrey Rhodes said this was "a very extraordinary bill . . . to be brought before the Assembly. . . . It appears to be part of the

$40,000 for which the last Ministry went out of office." [32] He also said the king could not be sued and that those who had made loans to him should just wait until he was able to repay them. Attorney General Preston said that the crown lands could not be legally encumbered in any way.

All other cabinet members pleaded ignorance of the background of Aholo's resolution. Gibson said that, as the matter concerned the person of the sovereign, it should have originated with the "constitutional advisers of the King" (the ministers). It should not, therefore, have been brought in by other members of the legislature. After some further debate, the assembly referred the resolution to a special committee.[33] "It is bad enough," commented the *Gazette,* "that the formation and existence of such debts are known unofficially, without parading the matter before the world." [34]

While the resolution was still in committee the *Gazette* also said about the proposed takeover of the debt by the government: "It may as well be said at once and to the point, that there is only one opinion among the public, and that is stern condemnation." [35] The majority report of the committee nevertheless recommended adoption of a resolution which differed only slightly from that brought in earlier by Aholo:

Resolved, That the Minister of Finance be and he is hereby authorized and empowered to advance by way of Loan to the Commissioners of Crown Lands the sum of Thirty Thousand Dollars to be used by them in taking up outstanding Notes of His Majesty to that amount, and to be repaid to the Minister of Finance in yearly installments of not less than Six Thousand Dollars each with interest at the rate of five per cent per annum.[36]

A. S. Cleghorn, a noble of the kingdom, favored adoption of the majority report. He was "opposed to His Majesty being under any obligation to anyone out of the country." It was advisable that all such matters be in the hands of the government. He also said he had "no objection to Mr. Spreckels, he is a gentleman who is doing a great deal of good for the country, but it would be better if he were paid off and the notes thereby redeemed." [37]

As precedent for paying the king's debts, Gibson cited a case in which the government of Great Britain had assumed $2,000,000 in debts of King George IV. By a vote of 30 to 6 the legislature rejected a motion to postpone acceptance of the majority report. Both the report and the resolution were then adopted.[38]

Spreckels' loan to the king had been the subject of many rumors. Now it had become a matter of public record. Even though repayment was to be made by Kalakaua out of income from the crown lands, the kingdom's assumption of the debt disturbed those in the community who wanted economy in government. "So the country is to be saddled with the payment of that $30,000 after all," wrote the editor of the *Gazette*. "Dear country, won't you pay our private debts too?" [39]

CHAPTER IV

The Spreckels Ditch

The lease of July 8, 1878, which Spreckels obtained at the same time that he made the loan of $40,000 to Kalakaua, set forth that the water rights granted to him were deemed by the king and ministry "to be for the benefit of the agricultural interests and the general welfare of the Hawaiian Kingdom." After commenting on the expense and labor for the necessary ditches and aqueducts, the lease continued: "The Hawaiian Government is not now ready or willing to undertake such works, and incur such expenses." [1]

The term of the lease was for 30 years at $500 a year. Spreckels had authority to "take, draw off, conduct away, and use the waters not heretofore utilized of the hereinafter named creeks, streams, watersources and flowing in and through the same from and on the northerly and northeasterly slopes of Mount Haleakala on the Island of Maui, Kingdom of Hawaii, into the Pacific Ocean." A detailed description of the creeks, streams, and water sources then followed. Spreckels had the right to build such ditches, aqueducts, and pipelines as he thought proper to conduct away the designated waters, not including waters already in use at the date of his lease. He could enter upon government lands to build and maintain the ditch system. The lease set a three-year limit for completing a specified portion of the ditch, and six years for over-all completion.

The Hawaiian government had the right to purchase the ditch system at cost at any time after its completion. If the right of purchase was exercised by the government, Spreckels had the option to buy all the water the ditch could furnish, at $1.25 per 100,000 cubic feet. This price was to remain in effect to the end of the 30-year term. Thereafter, for another 30-year term he could buy all the water the ditch could furnish, the rate to be adjusted every 10 years by agreement or arbitration. If the kingdom did not exercise the right of purchase during the first period of the lease, Spreckels could renew it for another term, the rent to be set by agreement or arbitration.

It is clear from the lease that Spreckels had the right to use all the water the ditch could deliver at maximum capacity for a 60-year period from July 1, 1878, provided he exercised his right of renewal at the end of the first term. This does not appear to be consistent with the statement referred to above that the lease was "for the benefit of the agricultural interests and the general welfare." In the short run it was mainly in the interest and for the welfare of Spreckels; however, in the long run, there were undoubtedly certain advantages to the kingdom. Irrigation on the scale contemplated was of such general benefit in increasing the sugar crop that it could well have been done by the government. As set forth in the lease, the kingdom did not have the means to carry out the work. Spreckels did—and in carrying it out he contributed to the economic development of the country. He made central Maui a region of tall cane.

With water rights and land for cane-growing secured, Spreckels was ready to build the ditch. He lost no time. Both Spreckels and Schussler left the islands on July 9, 1878 (only one day after the lease of water rights was signed) to buy needed equipment. Schussler went to Pittsburgh to obtain a large quantity of boiler plate which was to be made into water pipe by the Risdon Iron Works of San Francisco.[2] In mid-October the *Hawaiian Gazette* reported that a large amount of material for construction, including pipes and machinery, was on its way from the East. A large number of mechanics and laborers would be needed. "With the energy, enterprise and push of Colonel Spreckels [said the editor] ... it may be confidently expected that he will infuse new life into the business of these Islands, and ... the results will tell upon the commerce and industries of the Kingdom." [3] The *Pacific Commercial Advertiser* thought that, besides stimulating all branches of trade and commerce, Spreckels' project would attract more capital to the islands.[4]

The Hawaiian Commercial Company was formed about this time in San Francisco, with Claus Spreckels, F. F. Low, F. W. Babcock, Hermann Schussler, and Hermann Bendell as directors. One object of the company was to build irrigation works to increase the area devoted to sugar and the total output of sugar in the Hawaiian Islands.[5] At least two of the directors were well qualified on problems of water supply. Babcock was president of the Spring Valley Water Works of San Francisco, and Schussler was chief engineer of the same company.

Schussler returned to the islands on November 5, 1878, with a corps of assistants and mechanics. In Honolulu and on Maui he recruited an additional work force of 250 white and Chinese laborers (later increased to 350).[6] The bark "Fremont" soon left San Francisco for Kahului, Maui, with water pipes, building equipment, horses, and mules. From Kahului the pipes, varying in diameter from 35 to 41 inches, were shipped by coastal schooners to Maliko Landing near the line of the proposed ditch.[7]

The following notice appeared in early December, 1878, in both the *Gazette* and the *Advertiser:*

Mr. Claus Spreckels of California intends to construct a large ditch on the Island of Maui for irrigating purposes. Any person or persons willing to excavate or dig 500 feet or more of this ditch by contract, and be paid for such work either by the number of cubic feet or by the number of running feet of the ditch excavated, are requested to apply to H. Schussler, Haiku, Maui, or to Wm. G. Irwin & Co., Honolulu, who will give them necessary information.

November 23, 1878

Claus Spreckels
by H. Schussler[8]

Both papers commented favorably on the notice. The *Advertiser* thought this was a novel plan, but a good one. It would give employment to small groups of Hawaiians and also enable them to go into business for themselves. The editor added: "In this work of bringing down water on the rich but heretofore barren plains ... whereby our products of sugar will be vastly increased, Mr. Spreckels (while of course benefiting himself) will be doing a grand work toward the development of Hawaii." [9]

Under Schussler's able supervision the construction of the ditch went forward. He set up work camps, and a depot where the pipes were boiled in an asphalt bath. Horses, mules, and bullocks carried the pipes to the various gulches, and bridges were built to carry the pipes across. Mile after mile of clay soil was scooped out. As streams were crossed, side ditches connected them with the main fall. One of these side ditches, costing $25,000, was four miles long, with three tunnels through solid rock.[10]

Schussler reported in late March, 1879, on a test of the partly finished ditch. The water was let in and the test was completely satisfactory. The engineer expressed himself "enthusiastically as to the ultimate success of the enterprise." [11] Since the Spreckels interests were not yet ready to use the water, it was run off into the fields of the Haiku plantation in northeast Maui.

It was now being said that the title "Big Ditch," by which the Hamakua ditch of Baldwin and Alexander had been known, would hereafter belong to the Spreckels ditch. The work was going ahead "systematically and rapidly." [12] Late May, 1879, saw the crossing of the most formidable obstacle—pipes were put across the vast gulch of Maliko. Soon the water would be run into the "great Maui desert" on the central plains.[13]

In June, 1878, the *Gazette* hailed the anticipated completion of the work. It would boost "the sugar yield of these islands [by] not less than 12,000 tons ... per annum" for the Spreckelsville plantation alone. It would "give employment to several thousand workmen of all grades and scatter a large sum of money among our people." It would "swell the revenues of the Kingdom." Also, Spreckels' work would be a stimulus to other investors.[14]

47

Schussler left for San Francisco in September, 1879. The work of the water engineer was done; that of the planter and mill builder was still ahead.[15] In the same month 30 teams began plowing on the commons. Two thousand acres were to be planted to cane. "With the rich soil in that locality [said the *Advertiser*] ... combined with the irrigation of the Spreckels ditch, a yield may be expected of from 4 to 5 tons per acre, say 9,000 tons." [16]

The *Gazette* noted in March, 1880, that a reservoir almost half a mile wide was being built to store the surplus waters of the ditch. Remarked the editor: "[This reservoir] will make a marvelous change in the landscape of the hitherto barren plains. Already the houses and canefields have produced a change so great that one coming back after a year's absence would hardly know the locality." [17] The reservoir was nearly finished by mid-April and water was being stored; the ditch itself was now carrying water at full capacity.[18]

Because of a dry spell a few months later, the water in the ditch was quite low. Said the editor of the *Gazette*: "The 'Ona Miliona' ["multimillionaire"] Mr. Spreckels and Mr. Schussler have been out looking at the gulches ... so of course it [the water supply] will boom again soon." [19]

Some ten years later H. M. Whitney, a keen observer of and commentator on the Hawaiian sugar industry, wrote:

> On the sandy isthmus connecting East and West Maui, and on a plain which was formerly an arid desert, where neither a tree and scarcely a blade of grass could formerly be found, can now be seen green pastures, beautiful flower gardens, avenues of trees and twelve thousand acres of growing sugar cane, and a sugar mill capable of manufacturing 100 to 110 tons of sugar per day.
>
> This great change has been brought about by storing the rain gifts of the clouds which have fallen on barren rocks forty miles distant, which for numberless ages have run to waste in the sea below. The work of transferring this water from the mountains to these fertile plains was an immense undertaking, and is by far the grandest piece of engineering that these islands can boast.[20]

This "grand piece of engineering" involved some thirty miles of ditch, tunnels, pipes, flumes, and trestles. It crossed thirty gulches, some over 2,000 feet wide and 400 feet deep. Twenty-eight tunnels, 3 by 8 feet, some of them 500 feet long, had been cut through solid rock. Twenty-one thousand feet of pipe had been used. The ditch itself was 8 feet wide by 5 feet deep, with a fall of about 3 feet to the mile. It delivered up to 60 cubic feet of water a second. All this involved an outlay of about $500,000, the largest amount spent on any irrigation project in the Hawaiian Islands up to 1880.[21]

The Spreckels ditch ran from the northern slopes of Mount Haleakala in east Maui to the central part of the island. A few years later, in 1882, Spreckels built the Waihee ditch that tapped the streams on the mountainous slopes of west Maui.[22] With this second ditch he became the first to bring water to the plains from both ends of the island.

The Spreckels ditch invites comparison with the earlier Hamakua ditch of Baldwin and Alexander. The Hamakua ditch was 17 miles long, delivered about 40,000,000 gallons of water a day, and cost $80,000. The Spreckels ditch was 30 miles long, delivered about 60,000,000 gallons a day, and, as already noted, cost about half a million dollars. This ditch was built *makai* ("seaward") of the Hamakua ditch.[23] Both were pioneering works, but the Hamakua ditch was the first large irrigation project on the island of Maui. It is to Spreckels' credit as an entrepreneur that he promptly evaluated and grasped the importance of the Baldwin and Alexander work. He imitated its good features, profited from their experience, and avoided their mistakes.

Considering the limited resources at their command, the work of Baldwin and Alexander must be judged the greater achievement. It was harder for them to raise $80,000 than it was for Spreckels to raise $500,000.[24] They could not afford the competent engineering talent represented by Hermann Schussler.

One of the hazards that Baldwin and Alexander overcame was a September 30, 1878, completion date which was of more than passing concern to Spreckels. Their lease was so worded that if the Hamakua ditch was not completed by this date, all rights in

49

the water and in the construction so far done would revert to the government. This meant in effect that such rights would revert to Spreckels, because his lease covered the same general area as the Hamakua lease, subject to "prior or vested rights" of other persons. It is little wonder that Spreckels followed the progress of the Hamakua ditch with much interest. Baldwin and Alexander finished their project with great difficulty, just a few days before the deadline.[25]

In the campaign for election to the 1886 legislature, Lorrin A. Thurston, one of Spreckels' most consistent detractors, charged that he had acquired water rights unlawfully at Waihee and other places. The editor of the *Advertiser* called Thurston a "young and immature politician" and added:

This [Thurston's speech] is doing a gross injustice to a man who introduced more capital, employs more labor, puts more money in circulation, and stimulates trade and commerce more largely ... than any other man ... in the Kingdom outside his business associates.

Furthermore the social condition of the natives along the line of the ditch ... is greatly improved from what it was before that important work was commenced. The natives do not now live in abject poverty. They have frame houses, are well fed and clothed, and land formerly unproductive along the line of the ditch is now cultivated, water being furnished by seepage.... Neither have the taxpayers ... any cause of complaint, because the utilization of that water has turned an arid plain, which contributed nothing in taxes, into the most extensive and productive sugar plantation in the Kingdom, one year's taxes upon which amount to double the selling value of the property when Colonel Spreckels took it in hand.[26]

In spite of frequent controversy with Thurston and other persons, Spreckels' search for water did not end with the Spreckels and Waihee ditches. He was often busy with plans to extend them, to get more water through artesian wells, and to use the water more efficiently. The search went on even after the reversal of his political fortunes in the islands.[27] The year 1893 was a depression year in Honolulu and a year of political setbacks for Spreckels. Nevertheless, while he was on one of his inspection trips to the Spreckelsville plantation, his mind was full of new ways to get water. He found additional springs and had wells dug at various points between Kahului and Spreckelsville, with good results.[28] He also made plans in that same year to build an electric plant in the Iao Valley of west Maui. The electricity was to run pumping stations to increase the water supply.[29]

And so, Spreckels transformed the vast dry plains of central Maui into a region of green fields. The Spreckels ditch provided the best demonstration at the time that large-scale irrigation in the Hawaiian sugar industry was both feasible and profitable. The ditch made possible the largest sugar plantation in the Hawaiian Islands. Maui owed much of its wealth to Spreckels' enterprise and example. Moreover, in the sugar-based Hawaiian economy, the ditch furthered the progress of the entire kingdom. Trade with San Francisco was stimulated because sugar was the chief export and most of it went to that city for refining. The ditch resulted in more employment in the islands and more government revenues. It set an example for others, inspired confidence, and lured potential investors.

CHAPTER V

Princess Ruth and
the Crown Lands

T_{he} crown lands Claus Spreckels had leased on Maui were at first little more than cow pastures. By 1880, the once dust-dry plains were watered by the Spreckels ditch and began to give promise of the great plantation they would one day become. Since he had already plunged $500,000 into irrigation alone, the cost-conscious sugar king saw that his venture would soon represent an outlay of many millions. The 30-year term of his lease would probably not give enough time to develop a multimillion dollar sugar estate properly. Spreckels realized that he might lose expensive improvements at the end of the lease. How, then, could he get a title in fee? He turned to what would seem at first a somewhat unlikely solution to his problem: Princess Ruth Keelikolani's doubtful claim to half the crown lands of the kingdom.

By ancient custom, land in the islands belonged to conquering chiefs. They in turn made assignments to lesser chiefs, and so on down to commoners who had uncertain tenure on small tracts of land. The commoners owed military and other services to the chiefs, as well as part of the products of the soil. Rights in land were revocable. They depended on the whims of the chiefs and the fortunes of war; but in practice the tenant-commoners enjoyed a fair measure of stability.

After Kamehameha I conquered the islands around the end of the eighteenth century (the island of Kauai did not yield until 1810) he became the virtual owner of almost all land in the kingdom. By the time of his death in 1819 problems were beginning to arise because newcomers wanted ownership in fee. Little was done about land questions during the reign of Kamehameha II (1819–1824), but during that of Kamehameha III (1825–1854) a revolution occurred in the system. The *Mahele* ("division") of 1848 with its related events divided lands among the king, the government, and the people. By 1850, foreigners could own land outright.

Kamehameha III dealt with the king's lands (consisting of about one million acres and later known as crown lands) as his private property: he sold, mortgaged, and leased them at will. Kamehameha IV (1854–1863) and V (1863–1872) continued to deal with the crown lands as prviate property, with resulting shrinkage. Early in the reign of Kamehameha V, however, a supreme court decision of May 27, 1864, and an act of the legislature on January 3, 1865, made the lands inalienable. The decision and the act set forth the view that the crown lands were meant to descend only to successors to the throne. This view was based on an instrument of Kamehameha III and a confirmatory statute of 1848 setting up the crown lands.[1]

Princess Ruth Keelikolani,[2] a high chiefess, claimed that as a descendant of the Kamehamehas she had a half interest in the crown lands. Her claim was valid only if the lands were considered to be private property. However, according to the supreme court decision of May 27, 1864, and the act of January 3, 1865, they were not private property. There is no question that Princess Ruth was of high birth; but a genealogical study by Stokes casts much doubt on her claim that she was of the Kamehameha line.[3] At best, then, her interest in the crown lands was somewhat shadowy.

At the going rate of about $1.50 an acre in 1880, the crown lands were worth perhaps $1,500,000. Princess Ruth's claim to a half interest, if valid, was thus worth $750,000. Because of the clouded title, it is hard to imagine that a shrewd businessman would buy the claim. Claus Spreckels had engaged in some minor business dealings with the princess who was rich and owned a large amount of land in her own name. On September 13, 1880, Spreckels bought her claim to the crown lands for $10,000. He also made a loan to her of $60,000 at 6 per cent which enabled her to pay off 12 per cent notes of the same amount held by other persons.[4] The deed reads in part:

> I, Ruth Keelikolani of Honolulu ... in consideration of the sum of ten thousand dollars ... paid to me by Claus Spreckels ... do hereby bargain, sell, remise, release and forever quitclaim ... the several lands reserved by His late Majesty, Kamehameha the Third, to himself as his own private property and mentioned ... in and by a certain act ... passed on the seventh day of June, in the year of our Lord one thousand eight hundred and forty eight, entitled "An Act relating to the lands of His Majesty the King and of the Government to be the private lands of His Majesty Kamehameha the Third, and commonly called and known as the Crown Lands." ... And all my estate, right, title and interest ... of and to the said land and of all other lands commonly called ... Crown Lands, ... and whether belonging to me or to which I may now be entitled as heir to his said Majesty Kamehameha the Third, or to their late Majesties Kamehameha the Fourth, Kamehameha the Fifth, my father His Highness the late M. Kekuanaoa, or in any other manner or right whatsoever.[5]

The editor of the *Pacific Commercial Advertiser* chuckled at the stupidity of the sugar king: "H. R. H. K—made a good thing in getting a cool $10,000 for a quitclaim to a nominal interest." [6] The editor also said: "The purchase by Col. Spreckels of certain alleged claims has occasioned many inquiries as to the nature of these claims, and, being looked upon as a move rather political than speculative, has excited much public interest." [7] As it turned out, Spreckels looked at the purchase as *both* "political and speculative."

What caused Princess Ruth to sell her claim is not clear. Some hypotheses may be suggested: (1) She knew her claim was worthless and, feeling that Spreckels was buying "a pig in a poke," she quickly took the $10,000.[8] (2) She knew what Spreckels was up to; payments to her were for her influence as a high chiefess to help him get title to the crown lands of the Spreckelsville plantation. (3) She relied on advice from the manager of her estate, S. K. Kaai, who was unduly influenced by Spreckels to persuade her to sell.[9]

Soon after the sale, rumors of a law suit by Spreckels were rife in Honolulu. Said the *Saturday Press:* "Ostensibly the case will be to decide ... the validity of the sale of certain real estate by ... Ruth Keelikolani; the real issue however will be, who is the lawful heir of the Kamehamehas." [10] The editor thought the question was of great importance.

It is doubtful that Spreckels had any intent of pressing his claim to a half interest in all the crown lands. He wanted, rather, to protect the now valuable property of his Spreckelsville plantation. Purchase of Princess Ruth's claim gave him the lever he needed.[11] He sought legal advice in both Honolulu and California. Among those in Honolulu who gave him opinions that he had good title to half the crown lands were: W. R. Castle, a former attorney general; A. S. Hartwell, who had been deposed as attorney general in 1878 just before the grant of Maui water rights to Spreckels; Edward Preston, who had been attorney general when the water rights were granted.[12]

The "highest legal talent in California" also agreed with the opinions of these Honolulans.[13] Although as private attorneys, Castle and Hartwell gave Spreckels favorable opinions, they were not "Spreckels men." Both were vigorous opponents of the "palace party" headed by King Kalakaua, Gibson, and Spreckels. Preston, however, was at this time pretty much in the Spreckels camp. His opinion given on May 17, 1882, was as follows:

I have for some time given the question of the title to the "Crown Lands" my serious consideration.

I feel quite certain that these lands were intended to be the private lands of Kamehameha the 3rd and that they descended to his heirs and devisees.

The King was not the sole owner of the lands in the Kingdom as a person, but as head of the State, and had to provide for the Government of the Country out of the revenue of the lands.

When the lands were divided (not by himself of his own will, but by the consent of the Council of Chiefs) he retained for his own private use and of his heirs the lands called Crown Lands and disposed of some of them accordingly, devising the residue by Will to his adopted child and heir Kamehameha the 4th, on whose death they descended, as I am of the opinion, to his Queen (Emma) and his father.

The queen has conveyed her rights to the Government and it appears to me that the other moiety descended to Kamehameha the 5th and his Sister Luka [Princess Ruth] who succeeded as heir to her brother on his death intestate in 1872.

Under these circumstances of course, in my opinion the decision of the Supreme Court and the law declaring these lands inalienable are inoperative and void as against Mr. Spreckels' grantor, and I therefore do not hesitate to say that under his conveyance he is entitled to one half of the so called "Crown Lands."

[signed] Edward Preston
May 17, 1882[14]

Three days later, on May 20, Kalakaua appointed Preston attorney general. Two months later Preston introduced in the legislature a bill to give Spreckels title to the crown lands of the Spreckelsville plantation. It seems a fair question whether Preston, having given a private opinion to Spreckels, was a proper person to advise the legislature on the bill.

One fact overshadows all the legal ammunition gathered by Spreckels: Princess Ruth had sold for $10,000 a claim to land worth $750,000. Would she have sold her claim at such a huge discount if she thought it was really worth much? The legal merit of the Spreckels interest, moreover, is beside the point when one considers his relationship to Gibson, Preston, and Kaai. As cabinet members, they later supported the land bill in the legislature.

The Gibson cabinet came to power after one headed by W. L. Green had resigned. Green's cabinet had been fighting Kalakaua's policies. The change, effective May 20, 1882, was as follows: Walter Murray Gibson, Premier and Minister of Foreign Relations, vice W. L. Green; Simon K. Kaai, Minister of Interior, vice W. N. Armstrong; Edward Preston, Attorney General, vice W. N. Armstrong; J. E. Bush, Minister of Finance, vice J. S. Walker.[15]

One writer indicates that a reason for the fall of the Green ministry was its unwillingness to alienate the crown lands of

Wailuku in favor of Spreckels.[16] This may be, but there were other reasons of more general importance. That cabinet was somewhat disorganized and no longer had the support of the legislature and the king. Besides, the cabinet showed no enthusiasm for Kalakaua's schemes of huge loans and increased expenditures. The king had been turning more and more to the policies of Gibson, who was the leader of the native faction in the legislature.

A letter by Green to H. A. P. Carter in Washington, and one by Green to the editor of the *Advertiser* throw more light on the cabinet change. These letters also indicate that Gibson was brought to power, in part at least, by persons who did not favor his policies. These persons hoped to use him as a "front man." Because of his influence with the native Hawaiians he could help install a new cabinet that would be favorable to the Reciprocity Treaty but essentially conservative.

Green wrote to Carter on May 8, 1882, that he had already made up his mind to resign. Green said that he understood the Planters' Labor and Supply Company was not satisfied with the way things were going. The planters felt they should arrange a new ministry, for they felt that the one led by Green was "not American enough and not prepared to yield to such demands of the Americans as they might require in negotiating a new reciprocity treaty. The new cabinet talked of by these gentlemen comprises Mott Smith, Adams and Gibson. I believe they wanted Bishop for Foreign Affairs, but he declined." [17]

In a letter of May 25 to the *Advertiser,* Green wrote that an agent (not named) of the Planters' Labor and Supply Company had called on Gibson and urged him to take a cabinet post under certain conditions. Green did not spell out the conditions. Presumably one of them was that the planters would support Gibson if he, in turn, would support reciprocity. Gibson declined to take office under the conditions offered, but he

then saw that the game was in his own hands, for being the acknowledged leader of the native inhabitants, it was natural that His Majesty, when any change of Ministry became necessary, should desire to call to his councils

57

one who was the choice of both the native and foreign-born populations. The new Premier, however, when sent for by His Majesty selected his colleagues to suit the King and himself without consulting his would-be supporters who retire crest-fallen, and cry out . . . that the country is in danger! What! with the man of their choice at the head of affairs? If the country is in danger, which I don't believe, they have nobody but themselves to blame. . . .

I am aware that when Mr. Gibson declined to be made a tool in their hands the red hot Reciprocity party subsided, and would have been glad to see even the old Ministry patched up, but it was too late, for now a new set of performers had come upon the stage, and quick to take advantage of the situation, take up the cue and continue the game which the others had just thrown up.[18]

Although Kaai and Preston had a record of previous dealings with Spreckels, the most significant fact about the new cabinet was the emergence of Gibson as premier. For the next four years the Kalakaua-Gibson-Spreckels triumvirate substantially controlled the Hawaiian government. The cabinet led by Gibson was to pull the strings in a dramatic legislative fight over the Spreckels land bill.

CHAPTER VI

The Legislature of Many Luaus

P*remier* Walter Murray Gibson was the first to bring the Spreckels land bill to the attention of the legislature. He gave notice on July 11, 1882, that a measure would be offered "to authorize the Commissioners of Crown Lands to convey certain portions of such lands to Claus Spreckels in satisfaction of all claims he may have on such lands." [1] One week later Attorney General Edward Preston formally introduced the bill. Simon K. Kaai, minister of the interior, moved that the bill take first place over all other business. G. W. Pilipo,[2] the "Lion of North Kona," and J. W. Kalua deprecated undue haste. They moved for a postponement to July 20. The motion failed.

The assembly resolved itself into a committee of the whole with C. H. Judd, one of the commissioners of crown lands, as chairman. The legislators voted to take up the bill section by section. After the first section had been read, Pilipo moved for indefinite postponement. He said the bill should not make the assembly "joyous or lead them to conduct themselves as if they were in a theater." [3] Then he went on:

This is not a matter that will please the Hawaiian people. It really has no business before this Assembly. It should be considered in the courts. And I say now that I have no further confidence in the law adviser of this kingdom. There is something strange about this. The Minister of Foreign Affairs gave notice a few days ago of his intention of introducing the Bill, and now another Minister brings it in. Who is the cause of this? The person who is agent for a high chiefess of this kingdom. What are we to think of such a native Hawaiian, the same color as myself, whose duty is to watch over and protect the interests of the country? And who says, "We shall protect you in this." The Attorney-General and the Minister of Foreign Affairs, who has just gone out, a man whose mouth is full of *aloha* ["affection"] for Hawaiians, but whose actions are not. We must consider what a man does, and not what he says. This measure, of which rumors have been heard, has now assumed a definite shape. I hope that it will be indefinitely postponed. I think that taking crown lands away from the crown and giving them to another person is a step toward destroying the independence of the country.[4]

Chairman Judd halted Pilipo on a point of order which limited speeches to five minutes. This rule was temporarily suspended. Pilipo resumed:

I cannot understand the Ministry at all. This Minister of Foreign Affairs has said a great deal about upholding the dignity of this Act. I consider a bill of this kind like an attempt to undermine the King on his throne.

The Minister knocks at the door of the Members of this House and asks them to join him at a lunch at his home. I am informed that he said to those present that a conciliatory policy was best, that it is better to give this small tract of crown land to prevent trouble. Where will this trouble come from? Do not our Courts give just decisions?

The Ministers are frightened. If they cannot protect the dignity of the throne, they had best leave their seats. It makes me ashamed to see a Ministry who are afraid. Where is the danger? Is it from Great Britain, from Germany or the United States? No! It is from one man—a merchant. I don't think I can be blamed for saying what I feel. Perhaps one or two, or three or more of the Ministry are in the clutches of this man. Perhaps he holds their papers. If this bill pass, it will relieve them. The Attorney-General must have drafted this bill, therefore he is the mother of it. It has been hinted that the Attorney-General before his appointment gave an opinion on this matter. I am afraid of one like him. I fear that he will not do his duty. I said this Ministry was weak. I still say so; I still think it. They are the protectors of the King, and should defend him to the last. Now the order is reversed. It is for the Members to defend the throne. If they fear the consequences, they can stand behind us.

We may have all been unwise, but the Ministry has been more so than the rest of us. Last night, certain Members were driven in a flock to a room with the Minister of foreign affairs. When he gets them there, he begins feeling them and tickling them, and brings them around to his views. Is this the way for a strong Ministry to act? Why not bring the measures first before the House, and not feel around outside? The Ministers took oath that they would support the constitution of the Kingdom. Are they not violating that oath now? I can say unhesitatingly that the bringing in and supporting of this bill is a betrayal of their trust. It may be that the Ministry are doing what they are told to do by a higher power. Is it the King? What is the matter with our King? Is he in the power of the same man? [5]

Preston retorted that the ministers were the advisers to the king. They were responsible for, and were here to defend, their own actions. Pilipo answered he was glad to know that, as it removed the responsibility from the king. C. H. Judd ruled that Pilipo was out of order to speak of his majesty as he had. Thereupon the gentleman from North Kona resumed his assault upon the ministry. Pilipo said that with this bill, the ministers were asking the assembly to give in to one man to save trouble. Pilipo did not believe that the assembly had the right to act in the matter. Let Spreckels present his claim to the supreme court of the kingdom.

J. Kauhane said he was not sure about the right of the members to act on the bill. But here it was. The cabinet had brought it in, and surely "the law adviser to the Crown" would not have offered it "if it were not right and proper to be considered." [6] Kauhane did not think the cabinet would do wrong. He was not skilled in law, but he had waited patiently for Pilipo to quote some law in support of his stand.

In reply to Pilipo's charge that certain members of the legislature had gathered at Gibson's home, Kauhane admitted he had been "one of the flock." Although not invited, he had just dropped in. Nothing wrong had taken place. And if Pilipo had been present he would have been satisfied that they had met "without a desire to ruin the country." [7] On reflection, said Kauhane, he believed the legislature had the right to act on the land bill. The ministry should not be condemned for bringing it in, before their side of the story had been heard.

The whole morning had gone by in debate. After a noon recess Preston took the floor. He noted with regret that Pilipo was not yet in his seat, and then went on:

[Philipo] has attacked the Bill before waiting for an explanation. I am sorry that he has lost confidence in the Ministry and the Government. I believe the gentleman is conscientious; that he is doing what he thinks to be right and proper. I am sorry he thinks others cannot introduce a Bill unless from corrupt motives.

This Act has been introduced to settle a claim that might cause trouble for this country. I have been legal adviser for Mr. Spreckels, but I have no retainer from him or any other man in the Kingdom. In 1848, Kamehameha III executed a deed giving certain lands to the people and reserving a portion—about one fifth—for himself, his heirs, and successors for their own purposes exclusively. These reserved lands are what are known as crown lands. Kamehameha III dealt with them as his own, and sold or leased portions of them. These lands were devised to his successor, Kamehameha IV.[8]

Preston said that Princess Ruth claimed a half interest in the crown lands because she was a half sister to Kamehameha IV and Kamehameha V. This interest she sold to Spreckels. Spreckels had been "induced to forego his full demand and accept a compromise as proposed in this bill." [9] Under the compromise he would get 24,000 acres; if he went to court he might get title to a half interest in a million acres. The present bill, said Preston, had been brought in to settle title to the crown lands. It would save much court action, he thought, and he recommended it to the assembly.[10]

Pilipo and J. Nawahi came into the hall toward the end of Preston's speech. Nawahi arose to support the earlier arguments of Pilipo against the bill. Kaai next got the floor to defend himself against charges of betrayal of trust and of treason to the kingdom. He thought these charges were "on poor foundation when backed up by . . . indulgence in personalities." [11] He had simply done his duty. As far back as 1880 he was satisfied that the person he represented, Princess Ruth, had a good claim to a half interest in the crown lands.[12] Kaai said that the ministry was quite willing to test its strength with the bill before the house. It was the duty of the ministry to bring it in and the duty of the assembly to accept or reject it. "The ministry are not weak," said Kaai, "but just and honest, and fear not to do their duty." [13]

A. S. Cleghorn of the House of Nobles arose to give a simple, forthright explanation of the bill:

What is the origin of this matter? Mr. Spreckels leased land on Maui for thirty years, where he established mills, cane fields, etc. He was afterwards told the title was imperfect; that there were other claimants. He purchased Ruth Keelikolani's title. He is on good terms with the King, Government and people. He was told by the best legal authority that he has an undivided interest in the crown lands of the Kingdom, about 1,000,000 acres. He gives all this for a perfect title to the land in question. The present Ministry deserves credit for attempting to settle this question, which should have been disposed of long ago. Every one knows that I would not be willing to part with an inch of the crown lands if it were not for the benefit of the King and Country.[14]

When Cleghorn had finished, J. W. Kalua spoke bitterly against the bill, and called Spreckels a "land-grabber." Godfrey Rhodes spoke in favor of the measure. He regretted that appeals had been made to passion rather than to reason. He called attention to the motto of the kingdom: *Ua mau ke ea o ka aina i ka pono* ("The life of the land is preserved in righteousness"). A wrong had been done Princess Ruth by making crown lands of certain property which rightfully belonged to her. "Now we have gentlemen in the Cabinet who desire to right these wrongs and they deserve praise instead of censure." [15] "Hear! Hear!" cried most of the members.

The debate which had consumed most of the day was almost over. J. L. Kaulukou and G. E. Richardson spoke in favor of the bill; Pilipo and Nawahi made a last stand against it. At five o'clock a vote was taken on indefinite postponement of the bill. This was defeated 30 to 8.[16] The entire bill was then passed and placed on the calendar for a third reading on July 20.

When it came up on that day, Nawahi again moved for indefinite postponement. He claimed that Attorney General Preston had not given the legislature a legal opinion on the merits of the bill. Preston answered that he had made his explanations orally before the house, and he could not help it if Nawahi was not then in his seat.[17] The motion for indefinite postponement was defeated 25 to 9, and the bill then passed.[18] It was a short bill, as follows:

Whereas, Claus Spreckels claims to be entitled to an undivided moiety of the lands known as Crown Lands, by virtue of a conveyance from Her Highness Ruth Keelikolani; and

63

Whereas, it is expedient and advisable that such claims should be satisfied or compromised; therefore,

Be it enacted by the King and the Legislative Assembly of the Hawaiian Islands, in the Legislature of the Kingdom assembled:

Section 1. The Commissioners of Crown Lands are hereby authorized and empowered to make proper deeds of assurance to the said Claus Spreckels, of the several lands specified in the schedule hereto, in full satisfaction and discharge of all claims the said Claus Spreckels may have or claim in the said lands known as Crown Lands.

Section 2. Before receiving such deeds or assurances, the said Claus Spreckels shall, by proper assurance, convey, relinquish, and quitclaim to the said Commissioners of Crown Lands, all his right and interest in and to the residue of said Crown Lands.

Section 3. The Minister of the Interior is hereby authorized to prepare and deliver to the said Claus Spreckels a Royal Patent for the said land, to be conveyed to him.

The Schedule

The Ahupuaa of Wailuku, in the Island of Maui, with the Ilis therein or thereunto belonging, and estimated to contain Twenty-four Thousand Acres or thereabouts.[19]

King Kalakaua signed the bill next day, July 21. On the same day he appointed Gibson and Preston commissioners of crown lands to fill existing vacancies.[20] The king, in his speech at the close of the session on August 8, thanked the assembly for, among other things, "the settlement of certain claims against Crown lands." [21] The quitclaim specified in the bill was signed by Spreckels on August 11, and the commissioners authorized the issue of Royal Patent Number 3343 conveying the Maui lands to him.[22]

Those who voted against the Spreckels land bill in the legislature were all native Hawaiians. Those who voted for it included native Hawaiians and some of the outstanding *haole* citizens of Honolulu. As the *Pacific Commercial Advertiser* pointed out in a dispute with the *Hawaiian Gazette* a few years later, it could hardly be charged that such men as C. R. Bishop, A. S. Cleghorn, Godfrey Rhodes, J. Mott Smith, and Paul Isenberg were corruptly influenced by Spreckels.[23]

Apart from the ministers and their supporters, what motivated those persons who voted for the bill? They may have felt that (1) Spreckels had a good case, and the compromise offered was the best solution; (2) Spreckels had no case, but they feared the power of his money to hire the best lawyers and, one way or another, get title to half the crown lands; [24] (3) it was desirable to alienate the crown lands and free them for more productive use. Ceding of lands to Spreckels would be the opening wedge.[25] Besides these possible reasons, some of those who voted for the bill probably understood little of its merits. Having been entertained at Gibson's home, they were just going along with the crowd. Gibson and the other ministers had succeeded in whipping up sentiment for the bill.

After the bill passed, some of the newspapers charged treachery by the ministers, corruption in the legislature, and undue influence by Spreckels. *Ko Hawaii Pae Aina,* a Hawaiian language newspaper, deplored an alleged assumption of judicial power by the legislature:

On Tuesday last, the assembly of "half-educated pagan legislators" took out of the hands of the judges, and assumed to itself the power to settle up an estate; and jealously arrogating to itself the power belonging to another body, it constituted itself a high court, and proceeded to introduce a bill to dispose of land. We had supposed the legislature had power only to make laws. Lo! and behold, it also usurps the authority of the judiciary department of the government.

Is not this the work of empty-headed ignorant men? . . . It seems to us that the haste of the Cabinet in this important matter is suspicious, for if we look at the true inwardness of our cabinet, we shall find some curious coincidences, to wit: The Attorney-General is also the attorney for the one who asks for the land, the Minister of the Interior is the one who sold Keelikolani's interest in the (crown) lands; and the Minister of Foreign Relations was aided in his hour of deep trouble by this very petitioner.[26]

The same newspaper one week later denounced the "extreme folly" of the cabinet in "advising the King to make over to Mr. Spreckels, the millionaire of the plains of Kamaomao, the whole Ahupuaa of Wailuku." The editor also accused the cabinet of "leading the legislators over to the residence of a certain Cabinet Minister, where a certain number of the members gave their pledge to aid in . . . this mischievous piece of business." [27] The article ended with a call to the kingdom not to place its trust in the cabinet, but to test the land bill in the supreme court.[28]

65

Premier Gibson came under the heaviest attack. *Ko Hawaii Pae Aina* spoke of the "base-hearted treacherous cunning of the premier who has led astray our representatives and beguiled them into giving Wailuku to another." [29] Pilipo charged that Gibson was primarily responsible for the land transfer, and also for a $2,000,000 loan bill which had been passed. He alleged that part of the consideration for the land transfer was an agreement by Spreckels to take up this loan: "I [Pilipo] definitely heard that this millionaire said: 'I am the moneyed man of this kingdom who intends to take up this loan, but I will not loan any money until they first put the government under my thumb, then I will let them have my money.' " [30]

It was said that Spreckels had made a personal loan to Gibson, in addition to the charge that he was going to take up the government loan. *Ko Hawaii Pae Aina* said of Gibson: "His character is that of a malcontent, a revolutionist, a rebel. He is one . . . whom money has power to buy over to treason." [31] Reported the *Gazette:* "We learn that the Ministerial head of our Government has borrowed $37,000 in his own name, at six per cent interest. Perhaps that is his reward for a recent land grant." [32]

Gibson was the primary target, but there were many attacks on the ministry as a whole, and especially on Kaai: "This Cabinet has been paralyzed by the magnetic influence of the millionaire . . . that acts very like an epidemic. The Minister of the Interior [Kaai] has been robbed of his strength by the bright gilding of the $10,000." [33] By mid-August, 1882, Princess Ruth had evidently become suspicious of Kaai's handling of her affairs. She required that he deliver all cash into her hands. She took personal possession of the keys to a safe containing her private papers, and requested H. A. Widemann, a prominent Honolulu businessman, to go over the accounts in the presence of herself and Kaai.[34] A few months later Kaai had to step out of his position as manager of her interests. The *Gazette* commented: "Of the manner in which the estate has been managed it does not become us to speak; but public opinion is pretty unanimous on the subject." [35]

The newspaper attacks did not neglect the legislature. The *Gazette* said that "the representatives were captured with feeding and with offices; 24,000 acres of crown lands were given away by the treacherous legislature." [36] At the close of the session the same newspaper said: "The only thing that the legislature of 1882 may be handed down to ... history for is voracious appetite; it attended about a dozen luaus ["native feasts"] besides other forms of free amusement. ... Adieu, Legislature of many Luaus!" [37]

At a public meeting in October, 1882, condemning the Gibson ministry, Pilipo referred to the Wailuku land grant and said it was wholly a ministerial measure. The land given away was "much loved by the people. It was the place of sepulchre of the ancient chiefs. And yet not one dollar of consideration was received by the Crown." [38] He moved for a resolution asking the king to dismiss the cabinet:

Whereas, His Majesty's present Ministers have by their extravagant uses of public money, incompetency in the administration of Government affairs, the giving away of the Crown lands of Wailuku, forcing the country into debt, taking away the appointing power of District justices from the Supreme Court, and appointing their favorites in office, have lost the respect and confidence of all classes of His Majesty's subjects, and left the Government on the verge of trouble and danger of foreign interference, and the King to unfavorable criticism ... [39]

The meeting approved this resolution, but one of the signers, W. R. Castle, dissented in writing from the part concerning the crown lands of Wailuku. He could not support it because he had given Spreckels a private legal opinion that he had good title to half the crown lands.

The resolution was addressed to the king, but Gibson drafted and signed the reply. He said that though the ministers were members of the legislature, it was the assembly as a whole that had passed the acts about which there had been complaints. He also noted that two signers of the resolution were members of the legislature. Therefore, he said, "you should address your animadversion" to that body, not to the king:

One member of your Committee, an ex-Attorney General, has appended to his signature a withdrawal of censure from the act of transfer of certain crown lands. By his knowledge of law, he was satisfied of the propriety and legality of the measure.... Under the circumstances the allegations are an intrusion upon the attention of the sovereign.[40]

The petitioners led by Pilipo thus received no satisfaction and the matter was dropped.

In the battle over the Spreckels land bill, nevertheless, it is the figure of George Washington Pilipo, the old Hawaiian warrior, the Lion of North Kona, who stands out. He did not hesitate to fight against what he regarded as a throwing away of part of the Hawaiian heritage. A few years later, by the personal efforts of Kalakaua and by generous handouts of gin to the voters, Pilipo was defeated for re-election.[41]

The manner in which Spreckels obtained the Maui water rights —by ousting the cabinet in July, 1878—set the pattern for his political operations to gain economic goals. His purchase of the Maui lands, as told above, continued the pattern. With outright ownership of the land secured, Spreckels could develop his plantation without fears about a clouded title or the short period of a lease.

CHAPTER VII

Spreckelsville
Plantation

J*ared* G. Smith, the first head of the Hawaii Agricultural Experiment Station and later a prominent Honolulu journalist, made a visit to Maui in 1932. He climbed Puunene ("hill of the wild goose") where he could get a good view of the surrounding plain. About a quarter of a mile to the east he could see the swale where in 1879 Claus Spreckels had first planted sugar cane.

In his account of this visit, Smith recalled that before the Reciprocity Treaty of 1876 there were two widely separated plantation centers on Maui. One lay to the east, the other to the west. Each group included perhaps a score of little cane farms and water-driven sugar mills. "The great stretch of treeless plains between them, now occupied by the Hawaiian Commercial and Sugar Company, was a poor windswept pasture, considered utterly unsuited for any kind of farming because there were no running streams. It was ranch land, and not very good ranch land at that." [1]

We have already seen how Spreckels brought water to the plains and how he got title in fee to most of the land of his plantation. This chapter concerns the Spreckelsville plantation as a successful venture in agricultural and industrial capitalism. The next chapter concerns the Hawaiian Commercial and Sugar Company (which controlled the plantation) as a somewhat less successful venture in financial capitalism.[2]

In 1878 Spreckels had leased the Wailuku crown lands in central Maui. That same year he paid Henry Cornwell $20,000 for an undivided half interest in 16,000 acres of the adjoining Waikapu Commons.[3] He also bought lands on the island of Hawaii. These investments received favorable notice. With them, said the *Pacific Commercial Advertiser,* Spreckels was showing his own confidence in the economy of the kingdom.[4] The *Hawaiian Gazette* expressed wonder that there were not more enterprisers like Spreckels who were willing to invest in sugar, the "king in commerce in these islands." All that was needed was courage and pluck. Investors could double their money.[5]

In order to carry out his plans, Spreckels formed the Hawaiian Commercial Company in San Francisco on September 30, 1878. Authorized capital stock was $10,000,000, represented by 1,000 shares with a par value of $10,000 each. The original stockholders and their holdings were: Claus Spreckels, $5,200,000; Frederick F. Low, $100,000; William F. Babcock, $500,000; Hermann Schussler, $3,200,000; and Herman Bendel, $1,000,000.

The purposes of the company as set forth in the charter were to build and maintain irrigation ditches in the Hawaiian kingdom; cultivate, mill, and sell sugar; build mills, railroads, wharves, and other needed structures; acquire lands, leases, and water rights; and build or buy ships to sail between the Hawaiian Islands and other ports.[6]

After forming the Hawaiian Commercial Company, Spreckels acted quickly to make his plantation the most modern and productive in the kingdom. By completing the Spreckels and Waihee ditches he solved the major problem of irrigation. In 1879, 500 acres were planted to cane and the next year yielded a crop of about three thousand tons.[7]

In 1880, Spreckels engaged Joseph and Andrew Moore of the Risdon Iron Works, San Francisco, to build a mill with a capacity of 20 tons a day. Construction of three more mills of improved design, based on the experience with the first mill, was begun during the following year. These mills were completed in 1882 and capacity was thus increased to 100 tons a day. The crop for that year was estimated at 12,000 tons, a fourfold rise over the yield for 1880.[8]

As the physical development of the plantation went forward, a change took place in the controlling company. In 1882, the Hawaiian Commercial and Sugar Company was incorporated in San Francisco to take over the assets of the Hawaiian Commercial Company. Capital stock of the new company consisted of 100,000 shares of 100 par. Purposes of the company as stated in the charter were much the same as those of Hawaiian Commercial.[9] The reasons for the replacement of Hawaiian Commercial by the Hawaiian Commercial and Sugar Company are somewhat obscure. It may be that the Spreckels interests wanted to sell stock to the public. The new par of 100 (as compared with the old par of 10,000) would make the stock more attractive to buyers.

In the year the new company was incorporated the *Gazette* described the plantation as follows:

Claus Spreckels has certainly made out of what was once considered worthless land a waving plain of cane. One must ride through these acres and acres of cane to fairly understand how great the enterprise is: one must compare the sweep of bright green crops at the base of Haleakala with the few patches upon the lowlands of west Maui, to fully realize how much more has been done, how much more is still doing. If this is gathering wealth to the owners and projectors, it is also scattering money among the Hawaiian people.

We learned that during the construction of the mills the pay roll of the plantation rose as high as $39,000 per month; at present it is about $20,000 per month. A large portion of this must find its way into the pockets of the Maui people, native and foreign, another portion must come to Honolulu.[10]

The activity at Spreckelsville contributed to the development of the port of Kahului, and that of the whole island of Maui. As the largest producer of sugar, Spreckels was the best customer of Captain Hobron's railroad, incorporated in 1881 as the Kahului

Railroad Company.[11] Spreckels' intraplantation railroad, further described below, joined directly with the branch of the Kahului railroad that ran between Spreckelsville and Kahului.

Kahului had become a port of entry in 1878. Within five years it was the second port of the kingdom and its exports and imports were exceeded only by those of Honolulu.[12] At Kahului Spreckels had his own landings and storehouses; [13] here the ships of the Spreckels line made frequent visits; and the town was the center of a telephone system that included Paia, Wailuku, Spreckelsville, and other plantations.[14] Railroading, shipping, telephones—all reflected the prosperity of the port, and in turn hastened its further development.

Spreckels also had a large store at Kahului with a branch at Spreckelsville. In size, and in variety and amount of goods carried, the store equaled any in the much larger city of Honolulu. At the Spreckels store one could buy anything "from the traditional needle to an anchor or silver service." Even truffles were sold.[15] Among the goods sold were dry goods, clothing, hardware, luggage, saddlery, farm implements, groceries, and books. There were two gunpowder warehouses, an oil storage house, and bulk warehouses for flour, feed, lime, cement, and salt.[16] By 1884 it was one of the largest and best appointed stores in the islands and did a business of about $50,000 a month.[17]

Small planters also shared in the general economic development of Maui. Spreckels invited them to cultivate sugar on shares on his land and offered to lend money for this purpose at 7 per cent a year. At the time, the going rate was 9 to 12 per cent a year compounded quarterly. The *Gazette* expressed hope that his offer would help to reduce interest rates throughout the islands. Lower rates would stimulate new ventures.[18]

Not only did the Spreckelsville plantation hasten the progress of the port of Kahului and the island of Maui. In the sugar-based economy of the islands the largest plantation was obviously important in development of the entire kingdom. In 1892 the plantation was called the "largest sugar estate in the world." [19] It contained 40,000 acres, of which 25,000 were good cane land,

12,000 acres were under cultivation, and the mills had a capacity of 100 tons a day.[20]

Spreckels introduced many technological improvements into the Hawaiian sugar industry. The most important of these were the following.

FIVE-ROLLER MILL. One of the outstanding innovations at Spreckelsville, in 1881, was the five-roller mill in place of the three-roller mill of the time. Added rollers increased juice extraction from the cane.

At Spreckels' mills each carload of cane was weighed before milling. The trash (bagasse) was also weighed afterward, so that the percentage of juice extracted could be found. In the early 1880's other Hawaiian mills did not have equipment for weighing cane.[21] Joseph Moore of the Risdon Iron Works in San Francisco (he had designed the mills) with his son, Andrew Moore, set out in 1881 to determine how much sugar was lost by only one grinding in the three-roller mill. This he did by drying and weighing the trash after one grinding, and again after a second.

In this way he found that it would be profitable to add a second set of two rollers. Water was added to the trash after it passed through the first set of three rollers to dissolve additional sugar and thus increase the yield. Hydraulic pressure operated the second set of rollers. This left the bagasse so dry that it could be burned directly without being stored in trash houses. Other advantages claimed for the five-roller mill were that a greater quantity of cane could be put through in a given time than with a three-roller mill, and irregularity of feed did not result in imperfect grinding.[22]

Spreckels' plantation had the first five-roller mill in the islands, though this type of mill had been known earlier in Cuba. But it was believed that the hydraulic attachment to create pressure on the second set of rolls was first used at Spreckelsville.[23]

DIRECT BURNING OF GREEN TRASH. Direct burning of green trash saved coal and avoided delay in getting up steam at the mill. On other plantations which used bagasse for fuel, drying it in the trash houses was a problem, especially in wet weather. Delay in drying increased the cost of idle time, both of men and machines. In addition, the trash houses were a fire hazard.

An 1883 report of the committee on machinery of the Planters' Labor and Supply Company, stated that the best green trash burner in the islands was to be found at Spreckelsville. A large automatic conveyor carried the trash directly from the mill to the boiler house, and fed it onto smaller conveyors that led to the hoppers of each furnace. Automatic feed meant that a smaller work force could be used. The saving claimed at Spreckelsville in 1893 by the burning of bagasse instead of coal was $15,000 a year.[24]

ELECTRIC LIGHTS. The Spreckelsville mills were the first in the Hawaiian Islands to be lighted by electricity. In fact, the use of such lights there in 1881 preceded the lighting of Iolani Palace in Honolulu by five years.[25]

Electric lights were tried for the first time at Mill Number One on September 22, 1881. To satisfy the curiosity of persons anxious to see the "concentrated daylight," Captain Hobron ran a special train from Kahalui. "After an hour spent in examining the engine room and mill by the aid of the powerful lights, the party started homeward, much pleased with what they had seen." [26] On October 3, the mill started grinding on the new crop. With the help of the lights, work continued around the clock.[27]

At various times King Kalakaua, Dowager Queen Emma, and Princess Ruth Keelikolani inspected the mills and were intrigued with the marvel of the new lights. Their visits with their retinues were festive occasions. Queen Emma herself described one of these visits:

I must write & tell you of the very pleasant visit we are making here, everybody has been so extremely good & kind to us. Last night Mr. J. D. Spreckels called & invited me to go & see the electric light, which they use at the mill, so this evening we started by train with a party of nearly 600 people for Puunene where his mill stands. Everything is carried on on the most extensive scale, and the newest inventions are used of machinery, etc. Mr. Spreckels showed us the electric machines where electricity is made & conducted through wires to every part of the mill. You have seen the light no doubt, so can fancy how like unto day was the entire interior

74

& exterior of [the] building. It really was wonderfully grand, he explained the various process[es] of sugar making, giving scientific names & meanings of things, he was awfully patient with us. There was music, vocal & instrumental, wine & cake at his house & music in [the] train.[28]

RAILROAD HAULING. The Spreckelsville plantation was the first (1881) to use railroads for large-scale hauling of cane, replacing mules and oxen.

An ingenious system of permanent and portable track connected Spreckelsville with the branch of Captain Hobron's railroad that ran to the port of Kahului. Rails also radiated in all directions from the mill buildings and connected them with each other. Within the mills, a crane moving on rails could transport machinery or other heavy equipment.[29] Spreckels thus found a solution for intraplantation cane hauling, inter- and intramill transport, and for transporting his sugar directly to the wharf at Kahului.[30]

The laying of permanent track along the main roads of the plantation began in late 1880. Portable track could also be laid down in any part of the fields being harvested. At first, horses drew the cane cars because the locomotives had not yet arrived. Additional track, curves, and switches, and two locomotives arrived in the fall of 1881.[31]

Many other plantations gradually adopted cane-hauling by rail. The method continued on the islands until recent times. But even in the 1920's when railroads were dominant, trucks and trailers began to make their appearance and these became the chief means of hauling cane.[32]

CONTROLLED IRRIGATION. Spreckels claimed that his system of irrigation reduced the amount of labor needed. One man could irrigate up to thirty acres a day. With former systems, one or two acres was a good day's work for one man.[33]

Use of water, secured at great cost by the Spreckels ditch, was carefully controlled. Men were assigned to see that it was not wasted. They kept hourly records of the water level in various parts of the ditch, and reported each night to the plantation superintendent. The main ditch was tapped by means of field ditches, which in turn led to smaller water courses. Sluice gates about thirty feet apart controlled the flow of water to all parts of the plantation. A bookkeeper consolidated irrigation reports daily, checked them off on a map, and went over them each morning with the superintendent. The system aimed at distributing "a large amount of water in the least possible time . . . with the least possible waste." [34]

STEAM PLOW. The Spreckelsville plantation, in 1880, was the first in the Hawaiian Islands to use a steam plow. Among its advantages were that a greater area could be plowed per day than with oxen or mule teams, more effective plowing increased the sugar yield per acre, and there was a saving of manpower. One disadvantage was that the plow was not suited to stony soil where there was the added cost of removing rocks and stones. Moreover, the plow was suited only to land that was mostly level.[35]

In the autumn of 1882, two years after the plow was first used, an improved model made by John Fowler and Company, Leeds, England, was demonstrated at Spreckelsville. The test aroused great interest among the planters. Many of them from all islands were on hand. Spreckels and the other planters said they were well pleased with the work done by the plow, as well as by the cultivator and harrow attachments.[36] After the value of these plows had been proved at Spreckelsville, their use gradually spread to other plantations. Steam plows were still used in the islands into the late 1920's.[37]

FERTILIZERS AND SOIL ANALYSIS. Fertilizers were being tried at Spreckelsville at the personal suggestion of Spreckels, at a time when their use in Hawaii was by no means extensive. In a letter of 1883 to the committee on fertilizers and seed cane of the Planters' Labor and Supply Company, superintendent G. C. Williams of Spreckelsville reported on an experiment with superphosphate, boneblack dust, and dry coral sand.[38]

At the 1883 meeting of the Planters' company, the trustees were instructed to hire a competent agricultural chemist, but this was not done until 1885. In 1884 the Spreckelsville plantation became the first in the islands to hire a soil chemist, a Dr. G. Martin. He also opened an office in Honolulu and offered his services as a soil analyst.[39]

Some of the laborsaving devices, and assembly-line and continuous process techniques at Spreckelsville have been discussed above. Efficiency of management at the plantation and mill resulted in low-cost production. A visitor in August, 1883, gives an interesting picture of the place and of "the system or order and capable administration everywhere discernible":

> The hubbub and bustle that mark this gigantic enterprise on ordinary occasions seem to have departed with the finishing of the crop.... [The] interior [of the buildings] presents a picture of cleanliness and order that many smaller, less complicated works could profitably copy. Everything seems in its place, the bright portions of the machinery have been well cleaned, covered with rust preventives, and the most careful inspection even to the tubes of the many boilers failed to show anything for the most expert to cavil at. All the buildings are receiving a coat of paint, which vastly improves their external appearance, the grounds have been cleared of debris and covered by a thick coat of velvety grass, the trees ... add much to the beauty of the place. Networks of railroad tracks radiate from the buildings to all conceivable directions, diminishing not only the costs of transportation to a minimum, but likewise consolidating the different interests represented.[40]

Management and supervision at Spreckelsville were excellent at a time when not much attention had been generally given to scientific management. Records were kept for comparison with past performance and used as guides to current control.

The men were divided into five camps with a foreman at the head of each. Subforemen in charge of each work gang filled out a printed form, showing how each of the men was employed, where, and the number of hours. These forms went to the manager daily.[41]

The Spreckelsville plantation was one of the first to keep systematic records of cost. "The owner can tell ... the cost per pound at almost any stage of the crop, and not only upon the whole crop, but upon the produce of particular pieces of land." [42]

To this comment the editor of the *Gazette* added that after, say, a ten-year period such statistics would be valuable. They would be even more valuable if all plantations kept a record of the success of their planting and milling operations.[43]

With his efficient production, it was estimated that Spreckels could land his sugar in San Francisco at two cents a pound less than his competitors. This fact explains why he was somewhat indifferent to extension or renewal of the Reciprocity Treaty. Without the treaty, many Hawaiian planters could not survive. But Spreckels could. Commenting on the prospective 13,000-ton crop at Spreckelsville for 1886, a writer in the *Gazette* said: "Treaty or no treaty that plantation will be able to make money as it has facilities for cultivating, irrigation, portable and permanent track and rolling stock for conveyance of cane to the mills, and mills which yield a larger percentage of sugar than in former times." [44]

VERTICAL INTEGRATION. Apart from its size and productivity, the plantation was important as part of the pattern that Spreckels created for the Hawaiian sugar industry. He was the first planter in the islands to gain nearly complete control of his sugar from growing to marketing. In this he set the pattern that the Hawaiian sugar industry still follows.

The plantation, with its vast fields of cane watered by the Spreckels ditch, was the first component in the pattern of vertical integration. After the cane was processed in the mills, the raw sugar went directly by rail to the port of Kahului. There Spreckels had his own landings and warehouses.

The second component was the sugar agency of William G. Irwin and Company (Spreckels and Irwin), which acted as the agent for the Spreckelsville plantation and also for others.[45] In addition, the Irwin company served as agent for the Spreckels Oceanic line that carried the sugar to California. Oceanic thus formed the third part of the pattern.[46] The last part was the Spreckels refinery in San Francisco. Grower, agent, shipper, refiner—Spreckels was all of these and more.

The Spreckelsville plantation stands out as a truly pioneering venture. In this venture, the vision, the drive, and the optimism of Claus Spreckels himself are everywhere evident. In 1879 when the population of the Hawaiian kingdom was only about 60,000, he said that the islands were wonderfully productive of sugar and could support a million people.[47] No doubt this estimate was regarded as far-fetched. Today the population of the islands is over 700,000, and sugar is still the most important crop.

Spreckels envisioned in 1881 a 40,000-ton crop at Spreckelsville within four years, that is by 1885.[48] This yield was not reached until 1906, two years before his death, when the crop was about 44,000 tons.[49] He tried in 1890 to enlarge the plantation, already the largest in the islands, by consolidating with Wailuku, Paia, and Haiku plantations. This failed because at the time the Hawaiian Commercial and Sugar Company was heavily in debt and this debt was unattractive to the other plantations.[50] But over fifty years later the consolidation was achieved. Hence Spreckels envisioned the plantation at pretty much its present size, 55,000 acres, long before that size was reached.[51]

Between 1878 and 1893 Spreckels visited the plantation once or twice a year to make inspections, stir things up, and make new plans. Of one such visit in 1880 the *Gazette* said: "He usually makes things hum wherever he goes." [52] The *Bulletin* wrote about another visit in 1892, a year of depression in Hawaii: "He looks as hale, hearty, young and active as of yore, and does not seem to share the general gloomy view of things indulged in by most of the planters at the present time." [53] Spreckels was then sixty-four years old.

Spreckels' last trip to Spreckelsville was in August, 1893, when he was making plans for an electric power plant to operate pumping stations, which would enable him to increase the water supply and hence the acreage in cane.[54] He was making these plans despite the existing depression in Honolulu and despite the recent political defeats which he had suffered. But the project for increasing the water supply was not to be carried out by him. Several months later he found himself in a fight for control of Hawaiian Commercial and Sugar Company.

CHAPTER VIII

Hawaiian Commercial and Sugar Company

U*p* to now we have looked at the Spreckelsville plantation as an outstanding venture in agricultural and industrial capitalism. As a venture in financial capitalism the controlling company, Hawaiian Commercial and Sugar Company, presents a less glorious picture. Between 1882 and 1896 the company's stock rose and fell sharply in the San Francisco market. Indeed, the *Hawaiian Star* said in 1898 that the company had caused more sensations in the market than any other company. On public issue in 1882 the stock sold at around $60. By the autumn of 1884 the company was deep in debt. The price fell to 25 *cents*. A personal loan of $1,000,000 by Spreckels, and authorization of a bond issue by the directors moved the price up again. Good crop reports in 1885 reinforced this upward movement. By September of that year the price was around $10.[1]

The *San Francisco Chronicle* charged in many articles that the Spreckels interests were manipulating the stock.[2] After one such article in November, 1884, Adolph B. Spreckels, Claus's son, stormed over to the office of M. H. De Young, owner of the newspaper, and accused him of spreading lies. As the argument grew increasingly warm, Adolph suddenly drew a small pistol and shot De Young. The wound was not fatal. Adolph was tried on a charge of assault with intent to kill.[3]

At the trial, Claus Spreckels gave some testimony about the affairs of the Hawaiian Commercial and Sugar Company, since one of the issues was whether the articles published by the *Chronicle* were true. If the articles were untrue, there might have been provocation for the assault. Claus Spreckels swore that there was no truth in the articles: neither he nor any member of his family had ever manipulated the company's stock.[4]

One of the few humorous incidents of the trial, in which Adolph was acquitted, deserves mention because it throws some light on Claus Spreckels' attitude toward Hawaiian affairs. He was testifying about certain deeds of the trust that he had signed in 1882. Under these deeds his plantation land holdings were turned over to the Hawaiian Commercial and Sugar Company.

He was asked: "A foreign corporation cannot hold land there?"

He answered: "They could not hold real estate then, but a law has been passed in the Hawaiian Islands that a corporation [can] hold land. I had the law passed myself." [5]

From a low of 25 cents in 1884, the stock of the company gradually rose until it was about $34 in 1889.[6] Then it began to fall because of pending tariff bills in the United States Congress. These resulted in the McKinley Tariff of 1890. One effect of this law was to wipe out the two-cent a pound benefit to Hawaiian sugar producers under the Reciprocity Treaty. The Hawaiian Commercial and Sugar Company was therefore in trouble again. In 1893 when the stock was practically worthless, Claus Spreckels as chief bondholder tried to foreclose. His own sons, C. A. and Rudolph Spreckels, thwarted this attempt. They fought to get control of the company. As the stock rose after the end of the McKinley Tariff in 1894, the price was driven up even further when a Hawaiian syndicate moved to take control. These events are further considered below.

In the depression year of 1884 the Hawaiian Commercial and Sugar Company, as already mentioned, began to fall heavily into debt. To raise funds for the firm, Claus Spreckels endorsed a note of $1,000,000 to the Nevada National Bank of San Francisco.

He asked for security and there was some talk of a special assessment on all stock of the company to meet his request. Instead, the directors at a meeting of November 23, 1884, authorized a ten-year bond issue of $1,100,000 at 7 per cent. Spreckels, not then a director, was asked to give his views. He said: "I am willing that the stockholders should take as many of these bonds as they wish. If they do not want to, I will take the whole of them." This statement was applauded.[7]

On the strength of the loan by Spreckels and of the proposed bond issue, the stock rose in December, 1884, to $8.00 a share.[8] Spreckels took the entire bond issue dated April 1, 1885, to mature April 1, 1895. The issue was managed by A. Lilienthal and Meyer Ehrman of San Francisco, who also acted as trustees. Security for the bonds was all the property, real and personal, of the Hawaiian Commercial and Sugar Company.[9]

In the middle of another depression in 1892, the company again found itself in financial trouble. Under California law the directors levied a stock assessment of $5.00 a share. Unpaid assessments were to become delinquent January 24, 1893. The minority stockholders charged this was part of a scheme by Spreckels as chief bondholder to take over the company. He then held $700,000 of $900,000 in bonds still outstanding. The assessment was paid on only 2,450 shares of stock out of a total of 100,000 shares; the company declared the remaining 97,550 shares in default. The company bought up these shares at a public auction for practically nothing. Included in the 2,450 paid-up shares were enough held by the Spreckels interests for them to keep control. Other stockholders threatened legal action but nothing came of that.[10]

Claus Spreckels' control of the Hawaiian Commercial and Sugar Company was attacked several months later by his own son, C. A. (Gus) Spreckels, who filed a suit for $2,500,000. Named in the suit were Claus Spreckels, his sons John and Adolph, and the company. Rudolph, another son, sided with Gus against his father.

82

The immediate cause of the suit was a threat by Claus Spreckels to foreclose on his bonds after the company had failed to pay interest on October 1, 1893. Gus Spreckels charged that (1) the original issue of bonds in 1885 had been illegal because the stockholders had not approved, the secretary of the company had not signed the bonds, and the bonds had not been recorded in the county clerk's office; [11] (2) Claus Spreckels had caused the sugar agency of William G. Irwin and Company (Spreckels and Irwin) to withhold $38,000 due the Hawaiian Commercial and Sugar Company; (3) Claus had caused the latter company to keep $500,000 worth of sugar off the market to make the company seem poorer than it was.[12] Gus Spreckels also charged that 990 of the 2,450 shares of stock which had survived the assessment belonged to him, though only 40 were in his name. He claimed that 700 of the shares belonging to him were in the name of Claus Spreckels and 250 in the name of H. L. Dodge, president of the company. Gus's suit asked transfer of these shares to his name, an injunction to avoid foreclosure by the bondholders, and punitive damages of $2,500,000.[13]

An out-of-court settlement of the suit in January, 1894, gave Gus Spreckels control of the Hawaiian Commercial and Sugar Company. It is fairly obvious that Gus "had the goods" on his father, but just what the "goods" were never came out. Claus Spreckels and his sons John and Adolph were ousted from the company. The Honolulu sugar agency of Hackfeld and Company replaced Irwin and Company as agent for the Spreckelsville plantation.[14]

Control of the Hawaiian Commercial and Sugar Company and of the Spreckelsville plantation thus slipped from the hands of the elder Spreckels. But if Gus was inclined to gloat at all in the victory over his father, he did not gloat for long. Soon Gus and Rudolph Spreckels found themselves fighting a Hawaiian syndicate for control.

Despite ups and downs of the Hawaiian Commercial and Sugar stock in the San Francisco market, the Hawaiian planters well knew the worth of the Spreckelsville plantation. J. B. Castle, a descendant of a missionary family in Hawaii, quietly made an agreement in 1898 with Edward Pollitz, a San Francisco broker, to buy the stock. Pollitz was to deliver 51,000 shares for $1,900,000, slightly more than $37 a share. Castle was to pay $500,000 on delivery, $700,000 in January, 1900, and the balance of $700,000 in January, 1901.[15]

In September, 1898, Pollitz notified Castle that he was ready to deliver. Castle sought the help of the sugar agency of Alexander and Baldwin, a partnership, to pay for the stock. The firm agreed to advance $225,000 and to give Castle a one-fourth interest in the partnership. H. P. Baldwin was to become president of Hawaiian Commercial and Sugar Company, and the firm of Alexander and Baldwin was to be made agent for the Spreckelsville plantation. The 51,000 shares were to be pooled as follows: James B. Castle, 15,000; S. N. Castle estate, 15,000; William R. Castle, 6,000; Henry P. Baldwin, 8,000; and Samuel T. Alexander, 7,000.[16]

By October, 1898, Pollitz and his associates held 67,310 shares of the stock, including 51,000 shares on behalf of J. B. Castle. Pollitz had paid an average price of about $26 a share, or around $1,750,000. His gross profit on the 51,000 shares to be delivered to Castle was about $11 a share, or over $500,000.[17] Most of the stock had been sold by Gus and Rudolph Spreckels and their associates. Their profit was huge, because they had picked up the stock early in 1894 when it was practically worthless. It appears that they hoped to buy back the shares at a low figure. They put out a circular, bearish in tone, calling for an issue of more stock to be considered at the regular annual meeting on October 13, 1898.[18]

But the Spreckels brothers were too late. Under the bylaws of the company, Pollitz and associates called a special meeting of the stockholders on October 1. They ousted all the old directors including Gus and Rudolph Spreckels.[19] Pollitz replaced Gus Spreckels temporarily as president and general manager until the stockholders' meeting of October 13 when J. B. Castle and his associates took over. W. J. Lowrie, former manager of Ewa plantation on Oahu, became manager of the Spreckelsville plantation, replacing George Boote. The firm of Alexander and Baldwin became Honolulu agent for the plantation, replacing Hackfeld and Company.[20]

At the time of these events Claus Spreckels was seventy years old. In his declining years, then, he saw the magnificent plantation that he had founded slip not only from his grasp but from that of his family.

Twenty-eight years later, in December, 1926, the Hawaiian Commercial and Sugar Company was dissolved in California and incorporated in Hawaii.[21] Largely under the leadership of H. P. Baldwin and of his son, F. F. Baldwin, great changes have taken place in what was once the Spreckelsville plantation. It is still the largest and most productive in the islands.[22] This plantation was originally the dream and the vision of Claus Spreckels and is the most important reminder of his Hawaiian career.

CHAPTER IX

William G. Irwin:
The Man

As an entrepreneur, Claus Spreckels had the ability to select outstanding men to carry out his plans. He chose Hermann Schussler to solve the problem of getting water for his plantation, and Joseph and Andrew Moore to build the sugar mills. These men proved to be excellent choices.

Spreckels' most important decision on business associates in Hawaii was his selection in 1880 of William G. Irwin as a partner. William G. Irwin and Company, as the firm was known, became the leading sugar agency of the kingdom. Irwin acted as Spreckels' eyes and ears in Honolulu, the watchdog of his Hawaiian interests, as most of the time the sugar king himself was in San Francisco. The close association between the two men lasted for almost thirty years. Spreckels, the fiery Teuton, and Irwin, the staid Englishman, made a remarkable team.

William G. Irwin was born in England in 1843, the son of James and Mary Irwin. James had been a paymaster in the ordnance department of the British army. During the gold-rush days he set out with his wife and four children for California by way of Australia. When the ship put into Honolulu he heard about the privation and suffering among the California pioneers. He therefore decided to stay in Hawaii. It was his son William who was to find gold—not in the gold fields of California, but in the cane fields of Hawaii.

William G. Irwin received his education at Oahu College (now Punahou School) in Honolulu. When he was about twenty-one he went to work for Aldrich, Walker and Company, a sugar agency and merchandising firm. After it failed in 1866 he became a bookkeeper with a lumber company, Lewers and Dickson. He soon left to take a similar position with Walker, Allen and Company. There he resumed his education in the sugar business. In 1874 he formed a partnership with J. S. Walker and Z. S. Spalding to carry on a sugar agency and commission business under the name of William G. Irwin and Company. The firm was quite successful. All three partners later became prominent figures in the Hawaiian sugar industry. Claus Spreckels bought out Walker and Spalding in 1880; the firm of William G. Irwin and Company continued with Spreckels and Irwin as partners.[1]

Irwin also became a partner of F. F. Low and Claus Spreckels in the first bank of Spreckels and Company, founded in Honolulu early in 1884. When this partnership was dissolved several months later, William G. Irwin and Company continued the banking business until the second bank of Spreckels and Company opened in 1885. Spreckels and Irwin were partners in this venture.[2]

Irwin married Mrs. Ben (Fannie M.) Holladay in 1886 in San Francisco. The couple had one daughter, Helene, born in Honolulu in 1887. When she later married Templeton Crocker of San Francisco it was reported that Irwin gave her a check for $1,000,000 as a wedding gift.[3]

Irwin was known as a man of exceptional business shrewdness and managerial ability. The *Pacific Coast Commercial Record* further characterized him as follows:

This gentleman is of a very reserved and independent disposition. He is not given to indiscriminate social intercourse, and among those who are not well acquainted with him he has the reputation of being very distant in all matters, except those of a business nature. He is very outspoken and decided in his manner and address, and nobody need ever be at a loss to understand exactly what he means. Although abrupt and unceremonious in business matters, this gentleman is a very intelligent talker,

and among his friends and familiars he is a man of extremely entertaining
and pleasing manners and generous impulses.[4]

The esteem in which the Spreckels interests held Irwin was
shown when they named a barkentine in his honor.[5] The "William G. Irwin," owned by the San Francisco firm of J. D. Spreckels and Brothers, put into Honolulu in July, 1881, on her maiden
voyage. Irwin invited some of his fellow townsmen aboard for
lunch, and they drank toasts to the new vessel.

Henry Macfarlane said the youth of the town should look up
to Mr. Irwin as an example. Macfarlane did, and he too wished
he could find a rich backer. This caused some smiles; a toast was
proposed to Claus Spreckels. A. S. Hartwell, a lawyer, then said
they had all wanted capital to come to the islands, but now that
it had been brought in (by Spreckels) there was fear of monopoly. He himself had no such fears. Of Spreckels' partner, Irwin,
Hartwell said that they had never heard a word against him.
His one fault was that he did not run much to lawyers.[6]

Irwin thanked his friends. Then he said: "I bespeak for the
new clipper two qualities which I trust will never be character-
istic of her namesake, which are to be always *full* and *fast*." [7] The
two qualities that Irwin bespoke for the barkentine named after
him were amply realized in later years. For example, in 1897 the
ship made a run from San Francisco to Honolulu in eight days
and ten hours. This record for commercial sailing vessels still
stands.[8]

As a prominent citizen of Honolulu, Irwin was twice decorated by King Kalakaua. In August, 1885, the king made him
a Knight Commander of the Order of Kalakaua. "Mr. Irwin
[said the *Advertiser*] was a gentleman who had grown up in the
country, and from his youth had been identified with its active
business interests. By intelligence, enterprise, and probity he had
made his own business affairs eminently successful, and it gave
His Majesty pleasure to recognize these qualities which had distinguished Mr. Irwin throughout his ... career." [9] About a year
later King Kalakaua also made him a Knight Commander of
the Royal Order of Kapiolani.[10]

Irwin, though influential, was less prominent in politics than Spreckels, who was much given to political maneuvering for gaining economic goals. Irwin devoted himself mostly to business, but he was a member of the Privy Council of State under King Kalakaua and also under Queen Liliuokalani.

In a New York interview just after the overthrow of Queen Liliuokalani in 1893, Irwin said that he had tried to caution her against visionary schemes. He and a few other persons had gone to see the queen in November, 1892, to advise her to put in a better cabinet. This she did. Irwin added: "It appears that since I have been away from Honolulu she has turned things over again and got in some second rate men, who have evidently advised her so badly that . . . she has made a fatal mistake." [11]

After the fall of the monarchy, Irwin evidently favored annexation to the United States, but he soon deferred to Spreckels' views. Spreckels at first favored annexation, but later changed his mind and became an out-and-out royalist. In late May, 1893, the *Hawaiian Star* published an interview with Irwin headlined: "He leaves politics to Mr. Spreckels and attends to business." The *Star* had published a list of large taxpayers who, it claimed, were in favor of annexation. Irwin's name was on the list. A reporter asked him if he wanted to make any change. "When Mr. Spreckels is here," answered Irwin, "I leave all politics to him and I attend to business, and if anyone wants to talk or ask about politics, I send them to him."

"But you are in favor of annexation?" the reporter asked.

"Well, the Government has treated us very well," said Irwin. "We have nothing to complain of. I suppose the list is all right— but you must talk to Mr. Spreckels, he attends to the politics of the firm. I keep to the work." [12]

Spreckels was a skeptical man, inclined to be suspicious of almost everyone. But he trusted Irwin. However, toward the end of his life, Spreckels began to distrust even him although there seems to have been no grounds for it.

In 1907 Spreckels sent an accountant named Reynolds to examine the books of Irwin and Company and of the Spreckels and Company bank, in which Spreckels and Irwin were also partners. The examination was to be a personal one for the benefit of Spreckels, and not merely a routine audit. Irwin, who was then in San Francisco, wrote W. M. Giffard, vice-president of the Irwin company, to make all records available to Reynolds because there was nothing to hide.

The accountant, falling in love with the Hawaiian climate, decided to extend the engagement as long as possible. He called for huge volumes of records, going all the way back to the start of the Spreckels-Irwin partnership in July, 1880. He took up a great deal of Giffard's time for several months without uncovering anything of consequence. Giffard and Irwin felt that Reynolds was on a wild goose chase; he was pulling the "old gentleman's" (Spreckels') leg.[13]

Spreckels and Irwin were both excellent businessmen, but they are a study in contrasts. Spreckels was inclined to be bold and reckless. Irwin was moderate and levelheaded. Spreckels was violent in his likes and dislikes, and made many enemies while Irwin, less inclined to rub people the wrong way, made few enemies. Steady and reserved, Irwin was an effective counterweight to the irascible and volatile Spreckels. Irwin was friendly with the *kamaaina* ("old-timer") planters. He was accepted by them, he belonged. Spreckels was looked upon as an interloper, his name anathema to many of the very planters and businessmen who liked his partner.

Irwin was a citizen of Hawaii; Spreckels was not, though he maintained a home in the islands. As we have already seen, Irwin was not much interested in politics. Spreckels dealt in politics with a bold hand. As a former bookkeeper, Irwin seems to have taken much joy in the details of business. Spreckels was much less interested in detail. He was probably the more imaginative entrepreneur.

Regardless of these contrasts, or perhaps even because of them, the two men made a highly successful team. There can be little doubt that Irwin's presence in Honolulu lent stability and continuity to the ventures of the two partners in Hawaii.

The association of Spreckels and Irwin over a period of 28 years was broken on December 26, 1908, by the death of Spreckels in San Francisco. Unaccountably, the firm of Irwin and Company was not immediately notified. W. M. Giffard, a vice-president of the company, learned of the event from Associated Press cablegrams. He hung black crepe on the doors and closed for the day. On December 28, the day of the funeral, the Irwin firm remained closed and put their flag at half-mast.[14] Irwin himself, in San Francisco at the time, served as a pallbearer.

In his later years Irwin spent most of his time in San Francisco, where his wife had lived before their marriage. He became a director of the Mercantile National Bank, and was otherwise active in the commercial life of the city. He died in San Francisco on January 28, 1914, leaving a fortune estimated at fifteen million dollars. The *Pacific Commercial Advertiser* spoke of his death as "the cutting of one more of the few remaining links between the Honolulu of the monarchy days, when the foundation of many of today's fortunes were laid, and the Honolulu of the present." [15] All the sugar agencies and many other leading business houses in Honolulu closed for the day of his funeral.

CHAPTER X

William G. Irwin: The Company

William G. Irwin and Company was founded just a few years before Spreckels came to the kingdom in 1876. At the time, the distinctive Hawaiian sugar-agency system was already well established. Of today's "Big Five" agencies—American Factors (formerly H. Hackfeld and Company), C. Brewer, Castle and Cooke, Theo. H. Davies, and Alexander and Baldwin—all except the last-named were then in existence.

At first the main agency functions were to sell sugar on commission, arrange shipment, finance, and purchase supplies and equipment for the plantations. Through loans or direct investment, the agencies acquired a large measure of control over the plantations. The agency functions gradually broadened. Today these functions include, besides those already mentioned: (1) policy recommendations to plantation boards of directors; (2) technical consulting service in agriculture, engineering, land matters, taxation, public relations, and industrial relations; (3) leadership in co-operative action, through the Hawaiian Sugar Planters' Association, in matters affecting the sugar industry.

William G. Irwin and Company was launched without much fanfare in November, 1874, as a partnership of Irwin, J. S.

Walker, and Z. S. Spalding. The office was a small one on Kaahu-manu Street in Honolulu. A modest business card was the first advertisement: [1]

W. G. IRWIN & CO.
COMMISSION MERCHANTS
PLANTATION AND INSURANCE AGENTS
HONOLULU, H. I.

The editor of the *Pacific Commercial Advertiser* said of Irwin: "[He] has grown up from youth to manhood in this community and has earned for himself a reputation for probity and business habits that will commend him to the patronage of those in need of his services." [2]

At first the firm had the agency for only one plantation. Within a month another was added. [3] The timing of the business proved fortunate, for soon reciprocity was to provide an immense stimulus to the Hawaiian sugar industry. The growing company moved in 1879 to new offices at the corner of Queen and Fort streets. The *Hawaiian Gazette* congratulated the partnership on its move and added: "If industry, competency, and a courteous demeanor on all occasions, and business tact will suffice, the firm of W. G. Irwin & Co. must prosper." [4]

How did Claus Spreckels happen to choose William G. Irwin as a partner? J. D. Spreckels, Claus's son, had come to Hawaii in 1874 and worked at H. Hackfeld and Company, a large sugar agency, and also on one of their plantations. He later started J. D. Spreckels and Brothers, a San Francisco sugar agency and commission firm which bought island sugars for Claus Spreckels' California refinery. The Irwin company acted as Honolulu agent for the J. D. Spreckels firm, and represented it in both buying and shipping of sugar. Claus Spreckels acquired wide interests in Hawaii after his first visit in 1876 and looked for someone to represent him. Irwin, with his record as a representative of J. D. Spreckels and Brothers, was a natural choice. [5]

A notice of dissolution of the partnership of Walker, Spalding, and Irwin, doing business as Irwin and Company, appeared in the newspapers on June 30, 1880. Irwin alone was authorized to

93

wind up the firm's affairs, assume all liabilities, and collect indebtedness. On the same day a notice appeared of the Spreckels and Irwin partnership, with the previous firm name being continued. The purpose of the new partnership was to carry on business as "sugar factors and commission agents." [6] In a prophetic understatement, the editor of the *Gazette* said of the new agency: "From the well known business ability of its partners [it] will doubtless take a prominent position in business circles." [7]

Spreckels' riches and renown gave the firm a huge advantage over its competitors. It soon became one of the leading sugar factors of the kingdom.[8] Its growing affluence was reflected in December, 1884, in a move to handsome new offices on Fort Street near Merchant Street, across from its former location. The building, especially constructed for the firm on property owned by Spreckels, was two stories high, 123 feet long, 60 feet deep, and of fireproof brick construction. By present standards it was a modest structure, but at the time it caused admiring comment as a welcome addition to the growing business district of Honolulu.[9]

Spreckels and Irwin decided a few years later to incorporate. Prospective Irwin company shareholders held an organization meeting on July 31, 1890, to accept a charter from the Hawaiian kingdom.[10] The corporate name was William G. Irwin and Company, Limited. Officers were elected as follows: William G. Irwin, president and manager; Claus Spreckels, vice-president; W. M. Giffard, secretary and treasurer; T. C. Porter, auditor. Spreckels and Irwin kept most of the stock, but gave a small amount to old employees.[11] The corporation took over all assets and liabilities of the partnership. The only reason given for incorporation was that this was "a more convenient way of handling the large business." [12]

The purposes and powers of William G. Irwin and Company as set forth in the charter were:

To carry on business as commission merchants and factors, and to act as agents for ships, ship owners and companies engaged in shipping, both foreign and domestic, and to own ships and vessels and shares in the same, and to charter vessels and make contracts of affreightment, to import and export goods, wares and merchandise, and to do a general mercantile business on its own account or as agents for others, to be agents for sugar plantations, and to perform all business usually done by plantation agents and sugar factors, and to make advances and loans and to take and hold securities by way of mortgage or pledge to secure such advances and other debts, to acquire and hold such real and personal property, and to make such contracts and do such acts as may be incidental to said business.[13]

Corporate purposes and powers are often set forth in charters in much broader scope than the contemplated activities of the business. For the Irwin firm, however, the statement was a fairly accurate account of activities both before and after incorporation. If anything, later operations were more extensive than the charter indicated, unless the phrase "such acts as may be incidental to said business" be broadly interpreted.

SALES AGENTS. Irwin and Company acted as sales agents for sugar plantations that it owned wholly or in part, and also for others in which it had no ownership interest.[14] The company served as agent for the Spreckelsville plantation from its beginnings in 1878. (When Gus and Rudolph Spreckels got control of Hawaiian Commercial and Sugar Company in 1894, the agency for the Spreckelsville plantation was transferred from Irwin and Company to H. Hackfeld and Company, prominent Honolulu sugar factors.) Besides sugar plantations, Irwin and Company represented producers of coffee, pineapple, and other tropical fruits.[15]

PURCHASING AGENT. The company acted as a purchasing agent, on a commission basis, for plantation equipment and supplies.[16]

GENERAL MERCHANDISING. The merchandising activities of the firm might be likened to those of a country store on a wholesale scale. Newspaper advertisements from time to time reflected a vast variety of goods. One advertisement offered for sale "18 fine young mules, just received ex brig *Consuelo*."[17] Another offered sugar, tea, soap, salmon, flour, bread, lime, cement, manila and sisal cordage, blasting powder, and wheelbarrows.[18] The Irwin firm was sole agent in the islands for the Paraffine Paint Company, and for the Baldwin Locomotive Works, which manufactured equipment for railroad cane hauling.[19]

INVESTMENT IN PLANTATIONS. Spreckels and Irwin individually, and William G. Irwin and Company started or invested in many plantations for which the company became agent. The Hilea Sugar Company was incorporated in 1880 with Claus Spreckels as president, John S. Walker, vice-president, and William G. Irwin, secretary and treasurer. Among other plantations in which investments were made were Hutchinson, Hilo, west Maui, Paauhau, and Waimanalo.[20] Irwin and Company also secured effective control over many plantations in which they had no ownership interest by lending money on crops or on the plantations themselves. At times the loans outstanding amounted to $2,500,000.[21]

FINANCIAL AGENT FOR THE KINGDOM. Informal loans to the kingdom by the Irwin firm caused sharp debate in the legislature of 1886. The legislators spent much time in trying to get from the ministers a statement of the total indebtedness of the government, including amounts which did not appear in official reports. Premier Walter M. Gibson tried to explain the amount owed. As reported in the *Advertiser,* part of his explanation was as follows:

> Certain cash indebtedness does not appear. He [Gibson] would beg to inform the House that the Government had engaged Messrs. W. G. Irwin & Co. as its financial agent. That firm had been transacting business for the past two years for the Government. They had been making advances ... on immigration and other matters. At one time the Government was owing them $200,000. There is an open account with that firm.[22]

Sanford B. Dole charged several weeks later that under Gibson's ministry the minister of finance had unlawfully borrowed $80,000 from Irwin and Company. Dole introduced in the legislature a resolution of censure.

Gibson said there was ample precedent for such temporary borrowings in the public interest, whether they were lawful or not. During a temporary deficit in the treasury the Irwin company had advanced money to meet pressing needs, such as financing immigration of contract labor for the cane fields.[23] With his usual skill in diverting questions, Gibson pointed out that in 1880 a previous ministry had made a loan of $250,000 at 7 per cent to the Bishop bank. At the time, the treasury had a surplus and the planters were faced with a financial crisis. The Bishop bank, in turn, made loans to the planters at 12 per cent.

C. R. Bishop, a partner in the bank and also a member of the legislature, admitted that the loan by the government had been illegal. Representative Kaulukou thereupon asked: "Then how does the Hon. Noble [Bishop] account for his action in assenting to anything that was not law?" Bishop answered: "Because it was a matter of great public exigency." [24]

Gibson had evaded the question and, with Kaulukou's help, made his point: when it was in the "public interest" expediency might call for lending and borrowing that was not strictly legal, and this was the justification for borrowing from Irwin and Company. The resolution of censure was indefinitely postponed.

After the break between King Kalakaua and Spreckels in October, 1886,[25] the government paid off in full the account with Irwin and Company. Some years later the company again began making loans to the government. A loan for $95,000 was made shortly before the overthrow of Queen Liliuokalani in 1893. Irwin said of this loan:

I have no fears whatever for the peace of the islands or for the financial stability of the commercial institutions of the government. Everything will go on quietly, I am sure, pending the final decision [on annexation to the United States or restoration of the queen]. As a matter of fact, I lent the Government about $100,000 just before I came away. Some of the revenues had not come in and there was a little money needed to pay some salaries and for other expenses; so I lent the money. I have no fears at all but that I shall get it back all right.[26]

AGENT FOR IMMIGRATION. The Irwin firm acted as agent of the Hawaiian board of immigration in bringing in Japanese contract laborers and transporting them to their final destination.[27] The firm took applications for labor, processed the paper work, acted as a local distributing depot on arrival of the laborers, and occasionally advanced money to the government to cover the costs.

Amounts paid to the company became a subject of controversy in the 1886 legislature when an appropriation of $16,200 for the board of immigration was under discussion. Representative Brown noted that the Irwin company had received a bonus of $9,540 for Japanese immigration. He said that company "had nothing whatever to do with the introduction of Japanese into the country." [28] Representative Thurston failed to see the need for a private intermediary between the board and the Japanese government. "On its face it looks as if there had been a deliberate put-up job between Irwin & Co. and the Government [of Hawaii]." [29] Nothing came of these protests. It does not appear that the payments were for anything other than services rendered.

TRANSPORTATION. Even before Claus Spreckels became a partner in 1880, Irwin and Company was Honolulu agent for a fleet of sailing ships controlled by J. D. Spreckels and Brothers of San Francisco. From 1882 on, the Irwin firm was agent for the Oceanic Steamship Company, organized and controlled by the Spreckels interests. The steamship line, which succeeded the sailing fleet, dominated transportation between San Francisco and Hawaii during the last two decades of the nineteenth century. For part of that time contracts between the Spreckels sugar refinery, on the West Coast, and the island planters specified that the sugar had to be shipped by the Oceanic line.[30]

The Oceanic line received a subsidy from the Hawaiian government. Irwin and Company did not neglect its relations with the legislature. In the middle of the 1886 legislative session, the members and their families were invited to a reception aboard the Oceanic liner "Australia." Other prominent residents of Honolulu were also invited. The purpose was "to enable the members of the Assembly . . . to realize for themselves the great and unparalleled development of the shipping trade of this country under the stimulus of the Oceanic Co." [31]

Irwin and Company also acted as agent of the British government for the Australian-English mail. Oceanic carried the mail to San Francisco, and it then went by rail to New York where it was put aboard British ships. The route was four days shorter than by way of the Suez Canal.[32]

The Irwin company was also agent for the Matson Navigation Company in the formative years of that firm; the Pacific Oil Transportation Company, a line of oil tankers controlled by the Matson company; [33] the Japan-Seattle line, Nippon Yusen Kaisha; and the Union Steamship Company.[34]

BANKING. Between the dissolution of the first Claus Spreckels bank in November, 1884, and the opening of the second bank of the same name in May, 1885, William G. Irwin and Company conducted a banking business. One notable feature of this activity was that the company attempted to maintain confidence in silver by issuing 60-day drafts on San Francisco for silver at a discount of only 1 per cent.[35]

REAL ESTATE. The Irwin company dealt in real estate and also acted as real estate agents. For example, in 1882 the firm was appointed to collect rents for Samuel Parker, a wealthy land-holder and owner of the vast ranch on the island of Hawaii which still bears the family name.

INSURANCE. The company was the first to make fire insurance on growing crops available to Hawaiian planters. This was done through the agency of the Union Fire and Marine Insurance Company of New Zealand. Among other insurance companies represented by Irwin were Royal Fire, Swiss Lloyd's, Great Western, North Western, and California.[36]

In an interview in 1882, Irwin indicated that Irwin and Company represented 15 out of 60 sugar plantations in the islands, and that these 15 produced about 25,000 tons of the total 60,000-ton crop. Of this amount, 4,000 tons were produced by the Spreckelsville plantation. Irwin said that Spreckels had invested about $4,000,000 in Hawaiian plantations.

The reporter asked whether Spreckels' wealth did not enable him to monopolize the sugar market of the islands. "Yes, I suppose so," said Irwin. "He comes into the market and buys the

99

total crop, but the market is open to everyone else in the world who desires to do the same thing." [37] The interview continued:

Q. But no one can come in, as I understand it, to buy sugar.

A. Mr. Spreckels is a man of brains and business and he does the largest business in sugar with the planters. He purchases their crops from year to year, and ships them to his refinery in San Francisco.

.   .   .   .

Q. But the cry is that he monopolizes everything on the island, and gives nobody else a chance.

A. I suppose that he does monopolize the sugar trade, but each plantation is at liberty to sell to anybody else. The planter can deal with whom he pleases. [38]

The questioning touched also on the extent of Spreckels' political control. "I suppose that Spreckels is virtually the Government?" said the reporter.

Irwin said: "Mr. Spreckels naturally has something to say in the government of so small a country where he has so much invested." [39]

The interview then turned to the Reciprocity Treaty with the United States. To what extent had it stimulated the Hawaiian sugar industry? Was Spreckels the sole beneficiary of the treaty? Irwin admitted that the treaty had been an immense stimulus, but he pointed out that most of the island planters were by no means wealthy. Scarcity of labor and its high cost had kept many of them in debt. He thought that abolition of reciprocity would leave many of the plantations in a bad way.

He denied that abolition would hurt Spreckels very much. In spite of possible losses on plantations he would still profit from his West Coast sugar refining business. Irwin denied too that only Spreckels had benefited from the treaty:

The U. S. have profited by reciprocity. Through it the Islands have purchased all the agricultural and other machinery in this country. They have nine American built inter-island steamers constructed in San Francisco; and also some twenty-five sailing vessels for the island trade, which carry the sugars, machinery, etc. The English and French Governments would like to see reciprocity between the U. S. and the Islands abolished. These Islands are the key to the Pacific, and the U. S. should continue to control them. Nearly all important Government positions are held by Americans, and the Islands are really an American colony. [40]

Without denying the extent of Spreckels' control, Irwin had attempted to defend it. He was also aware that the Reciprocity Treaty which had helped to launch Spreckels' career in the islands was a matter of economic life and death to the other planters.[41]

In 1891 Irwin and Company marketed about 50,000 tons of sugar, slightly more than one-third of the 137,000-ton crop.[42] The extent of control at this time was somewhat less than that claimed by Irwin in 1882. Spreckels claimed in June, 1893, that the Irwin firm had direct control of 45,000 tons (presumably through plantations in which Spreckels and Irwin had an ownership interest), and were agents for 20,000 tons more, a total of 65,000 tons.[43] Since the 1892 crop was 131,000 tons, Spreckels was claiming control of about half of this for his firm.

By the opening years of the twentieth century, control by the Irwin firm had dwindled. In 1901 the company shipped 60,000 tons of the 360,000-ton crop, or one-sixth; in 1902, 50,000 of 356,000 tons, or about one-seventh; in 1905, 70,000 of 426,000 tons, about one-sixth.[44]

There were several reasons for this decline: after Spreckels' sons Rudolph and Gus took control of Hawaiian Commercial and Sugar Company in 1894, the agency for the Spreckelsville plantation was shifted from Irwin to Hackfeld and Company; Spreckels and Irwin were getting old and had made no provision to infuse young blood into the company; both men were spending more and more time in San Francisco, and active management of the company fell to W. M. Giffard who was conscientious but did not have the ability of Spreckels or Irwin; Spreckels had become more concerned with beet sugar in the United States than with Hawaiian affairs.

Before its decline, the Irwin company was an important link in Spreckels' control over Hawaiian sugar—control to an extent not since equaled or even closely approached by any one man or company. If the existing Big Five sugar agencies in Hawaii have ever deserved that title, then an appropriate title for Spreckels might be the "Big One." He was not so known though he was often referred to in Hawaii as the *'Ona Miliona* ("multi-millionaire").

One day in 1909 Irwin was having lunch at the Honolulu Pacific Club with George R. Carter of C. Brewer and Company, the oldest sugar agency in the islands. Irwin said that he would like to be relieved of some of the burdens of business. Carter then suggested a merger of the two companies.

Irwin answered: "I like the idea and am ready to talk about it." He soon left for San Francisco, and was followed by E. Faxon Bishop, a director of the Brewer company. They quietly worked out details of the change on the Coast.[45]

There were sound economic and other reasons for the merger. As already shown, the fortunes of the Irwin company were on the decline. Spreckels' interest in Hawaii had waned well before the end of the nineteenth century. Irwin was getting along in years—he was about sixty-five at the time of the merger—and had no son to succeed him. Absentee management from San Francisco was proving burdensome. W. M. Giffard, acting manager while Irwin was away, was also ready to retire.[46]

Brewer and Company doubtless thought it could breathe new life into the interests represented by Irwin and Company, and that the merger would yield economies of large-scale operation. Many of the plantations represented by the Irwin company adjoined those of Brewer and the merger doubled the amount of sugar marketed by Brewer, and gave that firm another outlet for its retained earnings in the form of investment in plantations previously controlled by Irwin.[47]

The effective date of the merger was January 1, 1910. The capital stock of Brewer was increased, and Irwin stockholders received shares in Brewer. As part of the merger agreement, Irwin insisted that all the employees be provided for. W. M. Giffard retired, but was to be "handsomely taken care of for the rest of his life, as a reward for many years of earnest, faithful service." [48] Practically all the other former employees of Irwin and Company were retained.

Brewer took over eight Irwin plantation agencies: Hutchinson Sugar Plantation Company, Hawaii; Hakalau Plantation Company, Hawaii; Paahau Sugar Plantation Company, Hawaii; Hilo Sugar Company, Hawaii; Olowalu Sugar Company, Maui; Waimanalo Sugar Company, Oahu; Honolulu Plantation Company, Oahu; and Kilauea Sugar Company, Kauai. The important agencies for the Oceanic Steamship Company and that for the Baldwin Locomotive Works were also taken over.

One aspect of the merger deserves special notice. The move was a final step toward unified control by the Hawaiian agencies and planters over refining of their sugar. Claus Spreckels had dominated the refining of Hawaiian sugar on the West Coast throughout the last quarter of the nineteenth and the opening years of the twentieth century. The planters had made sporadic, abortive attempts to break this control. When not being ground down by Spreckels, the planters found themselves crushed between *both* Spreckels and the United States sugar trust. Spreckels and the sugar trust joined forces in the 1890's; together, they operated the Western Sugar Refinery in San Francisco (formerly Spreckels' California Refinery).

By 1905, nevertheless, the planters had succeeded in establishing their own co-operative refinery at Crockett, California. Most of the Honolulu sugar agencies began sending their sugar to Crockett, but the Irwin firm continued to send its sugar to the Western Sugar Refinery. The merger of William G. Irwin and Company with C. Brewer and Company thus marked the end of an era—the Honolulu agencies had gained control of Hawaiian sugar refining.

CHAPTER XI

From Sails
to Steam

A glance at a map shows the strategic position of the Hawaiian Islands as a hub, or at least a way station, of trans-Pacific trade. During the early nineteenth century sandalwood days and the mid-century whaling days, the ports of Hawaii were busy with sailing vessels. Then in the 1870's came the first fairly regular calls of the Pacific Mail steamers. These ships stopped at Honolulu on the San Francisco–Australia route.

By 1883, even though sailing vessels were still the chief means of ocean transport, Honolulu also had a direct, semimonthly steamer service to San Francisco. The Oceanic Steamship Company, commonly known as the Spreckels line, started the service. The company dominated the San Francisco–Honolulu run through the waning years of the nineteenth century and into the early twentieth century.

At one time the Oceanic line played an important part in Claus Spreckels' Hawaiian sugar empire. The line began with a fleet of fast sailing vessels that J. D. Spreckels and Brothers of San Francisco ran between that city and Hawaiian ports, beginning in 1879.[1] The ships carried lumber and general merchandise from San Francisco and returned with cargoes of sugar and rice from the Hawaiian ports of Honolulu, Kahului, and Hilo.

Spreckels somewhat overshadowed his sons who ran the firm of Spreckels and Brothers. Appropriately enough, therefore, the first sailing ship of the fleet was named the "Claus Spreckels." This was a 247-ton vessel of 132-foot length and 32-foot beam, the largest two-masted schooner of the time in San Francisco harbor.[2] Launched on June 4, 1879, she set sail several days later for Kahului, Maui, the port that served the Spreckelsville plantation and arrived on June 27, 1879, after a trip of nine and one-half days—the fastest time made in several years.[3]

The *Hawaiian Gazette* said: "It seems as though the name . . . Spreckels carries with it some of the energy and perseverance for which its owner is so renowned, even when the same is applied to nothing more than wood and canvas."[4] After unloading at Kahului the schooner sailed to Honolulu where Irwin and Company, the agent for Spreckels and Brothers, advertised for "quick dispatch" for her return trip.[5] On her first voyage out of Honolulu, the "Claus Spreckels" took 681,865 pounds of sugar for San Francisco.[6]

Spreckels and Brothers launched the second ship of the line about six months later. This was the brigantine "John D. Spreckels" named after Claus Spreckels' eldest son who was the senior partner of the firm. The new ship was about 300 tons, and "one of the finest looking vessels of the Turner build."[7] The "John D. Spreckels" and the "Claus Spreckels" left San Francisco for the islands on the same day in February, 1880, the first bound for Honolulu and the second for Hilo, Hawaii. The race was on, and in the ocean-conscious islands there was much interest as to which ship would win. The *Gazette* said: " 'Sir Claus' will not permit himself to be beaten by the juniors of the family. All such [ships] are welcome, no more ancient tubs for us if you please."[8] Both vessels reached their destinations in the fast time of ten and one-half days, causing some speculation about which side of the San Francisco–Honolulu–Hilo triangle was shorter.[9] (The "J. D. Spreckels" had won, because the Hilo route is shorter.)

Other ships of the line soon followed: the "W. H. Dimond," honoring a San Francisco sugar broker who was a friend of Claus

Spreckels; the "Anna," named after Spreckels' wife; the "W. G. Irwin," named after Spreckels' Honolulu partner; the "Consuelo," the "Selina," the "Emma Augusta," and others. These ships had a well-deserved reputation for speed. In November, 1881, the "W. G. Irwin" made the fastest sailing time then on record between San Francisco and the Hawaiian Islands—8 days and 17 hours to the port of Kahului.[10] In December, 1882, the "W. H. Dimond" made one of the fastest trips on record from Kahului to San Francisco—11 days.[11]

The experience with these sailing ships gave the Spreckels interests a good base for starting the Oceanic steamship line. Pride in their sailing fleet did not blind them to the advantages of steam. As indicated below, there were many good reasons for starting such a line. Oceanic was not the first steamship line to touch at Honolulu, but it was the first to offer regular service exclusively on the Honolulu–San Francisco run. About 1875, an American line, the Pacific Mail Steamship Company, had started a service between San Francisco and Sydney, Australia. The ships also touched at Auckland, New Zealand, and at Honolulu.

Pacific Mail was primarily interested in the through business to Sydney and San Francisco. Although the company received a subsidy of $1,000 a month for carrying the Hawaiian mails, it regarded Honolulu merely as a way station. As trade rapidly expanded under the stimulus of reciprocity, the tiny Hawaiian kingdom felt some dissatisfaction with Pacific Mail. The *Pacific Commercial Advertiser* and the *Saturday Press* complained that the ships came and went as they pleased; the only money they left in Honolulu was the pilot's fee; and their "flying visits" were not long enough for passengers to spend money sight-seeing, or for business men to arrange freight shipments.[12]

Noting the great increase in exports because of reciprocity, the *Advertiser* in March, 1880, suggested a semimonthly steamer line to be owned in Hawaii or jointly in Hawaii and California. Such a line, argued the newspaper, would command ample cargo. With local control the ships would stay in port longer, and there would be enough time to do business.[13]

The *Saturday Press* proposed in June, 1881, that Hawaiian businessmen start a line with two steamers of 1,500 tons each. The editor said that increased trade between Hawaii and the United States, and the enlarged output of the sugar plantations would assure the line enough business. Such a "line being owned and worked here would give us a feeling of independence which we are far from enjoying at present." [14]

Spreckels acted with his usual speed and decisiveness to fill the need for steamer service.[15] In December, 1881, under his leadership and that of his sons, the Oceanic Steamship Company was incorporated in San Francisco. The company proposed to do a general freight and passenger business between San Francisco and the Hawaiian Islands. Later, service would be extended to other ports of the Pacific.[16] The organizers issued $2,500,000 worth of stock, 25,000 shares of par 100. The original subscribers and their holdings were: Claus Spreckels, 4,900 shares; C. A. (Gus) Spreckels, 9,600 (on behalf of J. D. Spreckels and Brothers); Charles Goodall, 6,500; James De Fremery, 500; E. L. G. Steele, 1,000; A. L. Tubbs, 250; Gustave Touchard, 250; and George A. Low, 2,000. All except Low were also directors of the line.

The sailing ships of Spreckels and Brothers were turned over to the new line, and continued in the Hawaiian trade well past the end of the century. Oceanic announced it would charter ships as soon as possible to get the steamer service started. Afterward, the company would buy or build ships to give Hawaii a semimonthly line. Besides freight, the company intended to give special attention to passengers by making the ships suitable for tropical voyages. It was "hoped thereby, to make Hawaii a pleasure resort more frequented by San Franciscans." [17]

The company soon carried out its announced plans. In January, 1882, it sent an agent to England looking for two vessels to charter.[18] The agent had some trouble in finding ships of the desired size and speed. However, Claus Spreckels announced, in April, 1882, that the 2,800-ton British steamer "Suez," formerly in the China trade, had been chartered for one year. She was to arrive at Honolulu in June.[19]

Oceanic's charter of the "Suez" was well timed. By April, 1882, sugar was coming in so fast at Spreckelsville that the Spreckels sailing ships could not take the sugar of other Maui planters for direct shipment to the coast. Many of these planters had to transship their sugar to Honolulu by interisland boats, store it there, and await space for shipment to San Francisco.[20] "The lack of freighting accommodations," said the *Advertiser*," is a serious drawback to commerce and is a powerful argument in favor of . . . lines of steamers." [21]

In the circumstances, Honolulu awaited the "Suez" with special interest. She arrived on June 14, 1882, the first steamer to serve the Honolulu–San Francisco run exclusively. "An event of importance," said the *Bulletin* (Honolulu). "The rapidly increasing trade on this route requires more and better accommodation than we now have." [22] The *Gazette* said: "The material benefits to be derived from this additional steamer are already manifest, and on the line being fully established with two first class steamers it will be still more advantageous for all concerned." [23]

On her first trip out of Honolulu, June 22, 1882, the "Suez" took a cargo valued at $223,919: 1,500 tons of sugar, 40 tons of rice, 1,339 bunches of bananas, dried fish, coffee, and goat and sheepskins.[24] The ship was scheduled to make trips leaving the islands on the twenty-second of each month. In May, 1883, she took what was then "probably the largest general cargo that [had] ever left the port" of Honolulu.[25] In the next month with her term of charter ended, the "Suez" left Honolulu for Hong Kong.[26]

Even before the "Suez" arrived in Honolulu on her first voyage, the Oceanic company had announced a contract with the shipyard of Cramp and Son, Philadelphia, for two steamers. E. L. G. Steele, the president of Oceanic, wrote to W. G. Irwin: "It is our intention to leave nothing undone to make these boats as complete and comfortable for this island trade as experience can suggest." [27] Steele emphasized that the new ships would probably bring a surge of tourists to the islands. "We do not doubt," he added, "that all such travel will tend to the material benefit of Hawaii." [28]

One year later, May, 1883, Honolulu heard that the two ships, the "Mariposa" and the "Alameda," had been completed. They would soon arrive in the islands.[29] This was good news to the steamer-conscious residents of Hawaii. The anticipated arrival of the ships infused new life and optimism into the commercial activity of the island. By the end of June the largest warehouse in Honolulu, which Oceanic had recently built, was filled with sugar, rice, and other domestic produce awaiting shipment.[30]

The arrival of the "Mariposa" marked a "steamer-day" that Honolulu would not soon forget. The lookout at Diamond Head Point telephoned at ten in the morning on July 31, 1883, that the ship had been sighted beyond Koko Head. The news spread quickly through town and brought masses of people to the waterfront. From his boathouse, King Kalakaua waved to the steamer as she passed. He then dispatched his carriage to the wharf to await Claus Spreckels.

With the Royal Hawaiian band aboard, the tug "Pele," decorated with bunting, steamed out to meet the "Mariposa." Governor J. O. Dominis of Oahu headed the welcoming party aboard the "Pele." Also on board were W. G. Irwin, Spreckels' Honolulu partner; G. W. Macfarlane, a close friend of and adviser to Kalakaua; A. S. Cleghorn, a member of the Hawaiian House of Nobles; J. H. Paty, a partner in the bank of Bishop and Company; H. P. Baldwin, a planter; H. Waterhouse, a merchant; other prominent citizens; and representatives of the *Gazette, Advertiser, Saturday Press,* and *Bulletin.* As the tug met the ship the band struck up a tune. The "Pele" had trouble coming around, so the "Mariposa" came in alone, with the tug trailing far behind and trying to catch up. The shore battery boomed a twelve-gun salute.

The reception committee aboard the "Pele" finally reached the dock and, by means of rope ladders, clambered up the sides of the "Mariposa." Among the distinguished passengers greeted were Mr. and Mrs. E. L. G. Steele, Senator and Mrs. J. F. Miller of California, and Mr. and Mrs. Claus Spreckels. As Sprec-

109

kels left the ship to enter the king's carriage, the Reformatory and Industrial School band, which was on the dock in addition to the Royal Hawaiian band, played "Hail to the Chief." [31]

Clearly, the arrival of the "Mariposa" was a festive event— but it was more than that. The record trip of 5 days and 21 hours—the fastest time made up to 1883 by any ship between San Francisco and Honolulu—was a foretaste of speedier transport between the islands and the United States. The *Advertiser* exulted: "Strains of music, the acclaim of a thousand voices and the booming of guns were just the proper announcements of an event which signalizes a complete revolution in our means of communication with the Coast." [32]

Kalakaua gave an elaborate dinner on August 2 at Iolani Palace in honor of the visitors who had arrived by the "Mariposa." After dinner Claus Spreckels proposed a toast to the king. Senator Miller then rose to praise the "Mariposa" as a "noble specimen of naval architecture." He extolled the Reciprocity Treaty and said this new ship was one result of that treaty.

E. L. G. Steele remarked that corporations were often said to have no souls, but Oceanic Steamship Company was an exception, for it had a "warm and animating soul" in Claus Spreckels. The new line was a "fruitful expression of the good will of Mr. Spreckels and his associates toward the islands."

Senator Miller added that he recognized Colonel Spreckels as "a benefactor to this Kingdom, a credit to the United States and a general benefactor of mankind." [33]

Spreckels modestly replied that he was no orator, but he told how he had enlightened the president of the United States about the benefits to that country of the Reciprocity Treaty. The president had thought, said Spreckels, that all the benefits of the treaty went to Hawaii. But Spreckels had pointed out to him that over $1,000,000 for the building of the "Mariposa" and the "Alameda" had been spent in Philadelphia. The United States, said Spreckels, benefited from the Hawaii-California carrying trade, and much of the Hawaiian profit on sugar was spent in America. That country was "receiving her full share of benefits in her relations with the Islands, and the President . . . and his Cabinet now appreciate as much." [34]

The next evening Spreckels gave a dinner at his Punahou home. Among the guests were Kalakaua, Senator Miller, E. L. G. Steele, J. D. Spreckels, Rudolph Spreckels, and prominent residents of Honolulu. The Royal Hawaiian band played during the dinner prepared by the chefs of the "Mariposa." The guests made selections from an ample menu of 32 items, including 6 entrees and 10 desserts. [35]

Celebration of the "Mariposa's" arrival continued with a shipboard reception on August 4 for several hundred guests. Proudly, Captain Howard showed Kalakaua around the ship. The king expressed his "pleasure that such a vessel should be so intimately connected with the Hawaiian Kingdom." [36] Two days later the king gave a *luau* at his boathouse. After an afternoon spent in feasting and observing native dancing to the music of the Royal Hawaiian band, the lei-bedecked guests went back to town. [37]

Greatly honored for a full week, the "Mariposa" made ready to sail on August 7. The band struck up "Sweet Lei Lehua" and ended with the "Star Spangled Banner." The band boys continued to play even while waving farewell to their friends. Vessels in the harbor, decked with flags and bunting, sounded their shrillest whistles as the shore battery fired a salute. Thousands of people lined the shore and the wharves, or swarmed on the decks of nearby ships. Kalakaua and Princess Likelike went aboard the "Mariposa" to bid departing passengers *aloha*. [38]

The sister ship of the line, the "Alameda," arrived a few months later, on October 22, 1883. [39] Her welcome was cordial, though not as enthusiastic as that given the "Mariposa." On a later trip, in March, 1884, the "Alameda" bulged with the largest cargo of freight that had ever been taken from the islands in one vessel: 2,990 tons, including 2,200 tons of sugar and rice. [40] With these twin ships, the "Mariposa" and the "Alameda," a semimonthly steamer service between Hawaii and San Francisco had begun—the first such service in ships built especially for the Hawaiian trade.

CHAPTER XII

Subsidy and Controversy

H*ailed* in its beginnings, the Oceanic line soon became the subject of much controversy. The Hawaiian government on August 18, 1883, through Premier Walter M. Gibson, had granted Pacific Mail Steamship Company the privilege of transporting Chinese immigrants to Hawaii to work on the sugar plantations. A few months later this privilege was suddenly revoked. As the *Hawaiian Gazette* said, "no reason [was] assigned further than the transfer of the monopoly to a monopolist of purest ray serene [Spreckels]." [1]

Gibson wrote letters on October 15, 1883, to Hackfeld and Company, the Honolulu agents for Pacific Mail, and to Williams, Dimond and Company, the San Francisco agents, telling them that the privilege had been revoked and transferred to Oceanic. At the same time Gibson wrote to Oceanic:

In the event of the Oceanic Steamship Co. placing in service, for the accommodation of Chinese and other Asiatic immigrant passengers to this Kingdom a superior line of vessels, which will be virtually a domestic Hawaiian line, ... His Majesty's Government will extend to your Co. all the opportunity for the transportation of such immigrant passengers as may be within the discretion of the Government, and such as will be justly warranted by the superiority of the accommodations and conditions which your company offers. [2]

112

H. A. P. Carter, the Hawaiian minister at Washington, was disturbed by these events. He said Pacific Mail had considerable influence in Washington. Earlier, the company had been in favor of the Reciprocity Treaty, now up for renewal. Pacific Mail expected competition from Spreckels, wrote Carter to Gibson, but objected to the Hawaiian government's favoring Oceanic, and this was especially true because Oceanic was planning to use British ships in the China trade.[3] Carter also said the transaction gave the impression that Oceanic, for some hidden consideration, had taken full control of Chinese immigration to Hawaii.[4]

Attorney Edward Lauterbach of Pacific Mail charged, in a strong letter to Carter, that the transfer of the privilege to Oceanic violated "every principle of equity and justice," and the spirit of the Reciprocity Treaty. He charged too that Claus Spreckels had instigated the transfer after making repeated threats of such action.

Lauterbach claimed that Oceanic had wanted Pacific Mail to give up the freight and passenger traffic on the Honolulu–San Francisco run and that Pacific Mail refused to do so. Pacific Mail argued, concerning transport of Chinese immigrants, that it was already calling at Chinese ports and Oceanic was not when given the concession. After getting the concession,

Mr. Spreckels plainly and bluntly stated to the Agents of this Company [Pacific Mail]...that if they would consent to avoid stopping the Australian vessels at the Islands, he would transfer his privileges to our Company, and the Occidental and Oriental Steamship Company, but if we would not so consent, he would give the privilege to the Occidental and Oriental Company alone, thus affording to British vessels exclusive rights, from the benefits of which our line of American steamships would be deprived.[5]

Lauterbach hinted that he might take the matter up with the government of the United States. To prevent such action, he requested Carter to intervene with the Hawaiian government.

Carter's main concern was the possible effect of the quarrel on the delicate negotiations to renew the Reciprocity Treaty. As a powerful American steamship line, Pacific Mail could presumably make its voice heard in Washington. Gibson defended his action in giving the concession to Oceanic. "Such a line will be in fact a notable extension of American enterprise and commerce in the Pacific." [6] Carter, on the basis of a note from United States Secretary of State Frelinghuysen, conveyed to Gibson the following impression: "Alleged contracts said to exist between merchants and planters at the islands and Mr. Spreckels . . . regarding the sale and freighting of Hawaiian sugars, are looked upon here [in Washington] as an unfortunate and unsatisfactory outgrowth of the [Reciprocity] Treaty." [7] Thus Spreckels' monopoly of sugar freight, in addition to the Pacific Mail–Oceanic controversy over transport of Chinese immigrants, gave ammunition to opponents of the treaty.

Pacific Mail sent David G. Adee to Hawaii in December, 1883, to protest the alleged favoritism of the Hawaiian government to Oceanic. The *Gazette* reported that Adee left "far from satisfied with the treatment he had received." The newspaper warned that it was a serious mistake to make an enemy of Pacific Mail when Hawaii needed support for the Reciprocity Treaty. [8] Gibson wrote Carter that Adee had brought a dispatch from the United States Secretary of State to Minister Resident Daggett in Hawaii, but he (Gibson) had no knowledge that Adee had any official status. [9]

Daggett took the stand that "so long as Chinese came as a spontaneous migration, paying their own passages, there should be no discrimination as to the vessels for their transportation." [10] Gibson claimed that with Pacific Mail in charge of the immigration it could not be properly regulated. Oceanic had offered to conduct the immigration in a manner satisfactory to the Hawaiian government. Gibson went on: "However, I discovered that the real grievance was that we had apparently engaged in too much business with one wealthy man [Spreckels], and that his alleged monopoly in the islands was regarded as objectionable—I think there is a good deal of misunderstanding on this subject in Washington." [11]

To counter Daggett's complaint that the Hawaiian government

had no right to discriminate in favor of Oceanic (because Chinese immigration was a voluntary matter not regulated by the government), Gibson issued regulations for the control of this immigration. He notified Daggett of the new regulations, and also wrote Carter that it was his (Gibson's) intention to propose laws on the subject to the 1884 legislature.[12]

The Pacific Mail–Oceanic quarrel also became a political issue in the campaign for election to the 1884 legislature. The Independent party candidates used the issue to discredit the cabinet and Spreckels' influence in the government. In a resolution at a mass meeting in December, 1883, the Independents: charged that the controversy was responsible for sentiment in Washington against the Reciprocity Treaty, condemned action of the cabinet in withdrawing from Pacific Mail the privilege of bringing in Chinese immigrants, expressed lack of confidence in the cabinet, and called for the election of Independent candidates to the legislature.[13]

Because of the furor that had been created, or for other reasons, Oceanic did not exercise its privilege of transporting Chinese immigrants. Spreckels' aim was to get Pacific Mail to drop the freight and passenger business on the Honolulu–San Francisco route, in favor of Oceanic. He achieved this aim. In April, 1884, Hackfeld and Company, the Honolulu agents for Pacific Mail, got instructions not to book freight or passengers on the Honolulu–San Francisco run. The same instructions went out to Williams, Dimond and Company, San Francisco agents. Under the arrangement, Pacific Mail, on the San Francisco–Australia route, continued to call at Honolulu for mail and for Honolulu-Sydney freight and passengers, but left the business between Honolulu and San Francisco to Oceanic.[14]

The *Pacific Commercial Advertiser* said the arrangement was "presumably the result of a negotiation between that company [Pacific Mail] and the owners of the competing line [Oceanic]."[15] The precise nature of the arrangement was not revealed. Former Governor F. F. Low of California had written to Carter in November, 1883, that Spreckels, in talks with an agent of Pacific

Mail, had offered to give up his concession for Chinese immigration if the company would discontinue calls at Honolulu. Pacific Mail refused to do this, wrote Low, unless Spreckels would pay them a subsidy.[16] Now some such solution had evidently been found. The *Advertiser* said that the arrangement was better than not having the Pacific Mail steamers call at Honolulu at all (as Spreckels had proposed). Nevertheless it was "a vexatious interference with what ought to be the rights of the people of this country." [17] The newspaper questioned whether mail subsidies should be given to companies making such agreements: "The public cannot view with complacency a vote of public funds to a Company [Pacific Mail] which refuses to carry cargo and passengers between this port and San Francisco, or to a Company [Oceanic] which uses its influence to deprive the country of facilities which it has long enjoyed." [18]

One irritating feature of the arrangement related to shipment of newspapers from the West Coast. These came down as freight, rather than as mail, to newsdealers in Honolulu. Under the agreement not to carry freight on the San Francisco–Honolulu run, the Pacific Mail steamer "City of Sydney" in May, 1884, brought no newspapers. Said the *Gazette:* "At the mere whim of a capitalist or two a whole nation of people have been debarred of what they had a right to. . . . That one man [Spreckels] or even half a dozen men have the power to act in such a manner should open the eyes of our citizens to the danger of submitting to monopoly. A slight pinch is felt now, but the toy whip will become in time a very scorpion scourge." [19] Spreckels' many-sided monopoly was attacked on all fronts: "What with depreciated monopoly silver, monopoly steamers, monopoly sugar market and monopoly adventurers to fill government places, Hawaii must begin to understand *slightly* the immense advantages which are being conferred upon the nation." [20]

The failure of Pacific Mail to bring newspapers irritated Honolulans. Finally, on representations by W. G. Irwin to Oceanic the arrangement was relaxed in April, 1885, permitting Pacific Mail to bring newspapers (as freight) in addition to the mail.[21]

The *Gazette* charged that the newsdealers had not been able to get their papers because Oceanic had a monopoly of the freight. Oceanic finally let Pacific Mail carry the papers as a favor, said the *Gazette*, but the people of Honoulu should have demanded this as a right.[22]

The Pacific Mail–Oceanic quarrel and the later agreement between the two companies became factors in a debate over the subsidy to Oceanic. In the 1882 legislative session, $50,000 had been appropriated for mail subsidies to "ocean steamship lines" for the biennium ending March 31, 1884. This amount had been divided between Pacific Mail and Oceanic with each receiving around $1,000 a month.[23]

From June, 1882, to June, 1883, Oceanic ran the "Suez" once a month. The subsidy therefore amounted to $1,000 a round trip. From October, 1883, the "Mariposa" and the "Alameda" were each making one round trip a month. The subsidy thus amounted to $500 a trip. In the 1884 legislature, Oceanic asked for $2,000 a trip ($4,000 a month). A bill to that effect was introduced in May.[24]

When the bill came up for the second reading in June, W. O. Smith argued against it as follows: Oceanic had caused Pacific Mail to refuse transport of freight and passengers to and from the Coast. The subsidy requested was too large—Oceanic wanted $4,000 a month, while Pacific Mail got only $1,000. Smith also said that Oceanic already had too many privileges, such as free wharfage.[25]

Kauhane spoke against the subsidy on grounds of monopoly. Oceanic had driven off great numbers of sailing vessels, he claimed, and the company wanted to be "king among steamship lines." [26]

Kaulukou favored the subsidy because, he said, Oceanic ships stayed in port longer than those of Pacific Mail, and therefore brought more money into the community.

H. A. Widemann claimed that the finances of the kingdom would not permit a payment of $96,000 for the biennium. He also said that favoring Oceanic might cause Hawaii to lose the Pacific Mail service to Australia. After the debate the bill was referred to a committee.[27]

Many arguments also appeared in the newspapers. The *Advertiser*, though in favor of the subsidy, argued that it should be only $3,000 instead of $4,000 a month. The bill should also provide against increase of freight and passenger rates. But Oceanic benefited the kingdom economically, said the editor. Under the stimulus of faster and more reliable shipping, banana exports had increased from 20,576 bunches in the period October 1, 1882, to July 1, 1883, to 47,113 bunches for the period October 1, 1883, to July 1, 1884. During the same period, tourists had increased from 1,409 to 2,241. It was estimated that two-thirds of them spent as much as $250 each. Moreover, Oceanic paid Hawaiian labor about $1,000 a trip for stevedoring.[28]

The *Bulletin* (Honolulu), on the other hand, claimed that $48,000 a year was "paying too dear for the whistle." There was not enough business for two calls a month by Oceanic, but there was enough for one. In effect then, the *Bulletin* argued for cutting the subsidy in half, whatever amount per trip might finally be decided on.

But that newspaper aimed its main guns at Claus Spreckels' monopoly. He dominated Oceanic, and nothing should be done that would increase his power. His pet argument, said the editor, was "Do what I say or I will ruin you." The attack went on: "We cannot afford to place any additional power in the hands of a man who already has the crushing power of a monopoly; who already says to us, you *shall* sell your sugar to *me,* and ship it in *my* ships . . . ; who is now the power behind the throne, overshadowing the lawful incumbent, and making and unmaking cabinets at will." [29]

The legislative committee on the subsidy brought in two reports: one by L. Aholo, J. M. Kapena, and J. K. Kaunamoto, in favor of a subsidy, but recommending only $1,500 instead of $2,000 a trip; and another by S. B. Dole, C. R. Bishop, and Godfrey Brown recommending against any subsidy whatever.[30]

The main spokesman for the opposition was Dole. He said the legislature was being "asked to put money in the coffers of a rich man." [31] He called the proposed subsidy "an act of jobbery" and also referred to the "mysterious influence" that Oceanic had in the government.

Gibson countered with a diversion. The founding of Oceanic was "the noblest and most important event that has accrued to this kingdom in the way of commercial enterprise." [32] Frank Brown moved for an amendment providing that freight and passenger rates should not be increased. The bill passed with this amendment and was placed on the calendar for the third reading on July 15.[33]

On the third reading, Dole, Bishop, and Smith made a last vain effort to scuttle the bill. Dole said "he was informed" that Oceanic had agreed to pay Pacific Mail for the exclusive privilege of carrying freight and passengers on the San Francisco–Honolulu run. If the legislators voted a subsidy to Oceanic they were only paying money to hurt themselves. "[The subsidy bill] shows what immense influence this Oceanic Steamship Company has over our Government and the Legislature." [34] After some further argument the bill passed, providing $1,500 a round trip from July 19, 1884, to March 31, 1886. Freight and passenger rates were not to be increased. The mails were to be carried by steam vessels of at least 1,900 tons register.[35]

Perhaps the most notable feature of the debate had been the way the shadow of Spreckels hung over it. What was the subject of debate, the subsidy or Spreckels' monopoly and influence in government? It was hard to tell at times.

When Oceanic got the concession for Chinese immigration in October, 1883, there had been much talk of extending the steamer service to Chinese ports. Oceanic announced in February, 1884, that it would extend operations to all important Pacific ports.[36] J. D. Spreckels went to New York and Philadelphia to see about building or buying two ships.[37] In an interview in Philadelphia he said that Oceanic had two steamships ("Mariposa" and "Alameda") and nine sailing ships in the Hawaiian trade. General cargo was taken on the outward trip, and primarily sugar on the return trip from Hawaii. He also said the line was doing "remarkably well" both as to passengers and freight.

J. D. Spreckels indicated Oceanic might make an offer for some American Line ships if they were suitable.[38] However, he did not buy or contract for any ships on this trip. Possibly the Spreckels interests dropped the idea temporarily because of the agreement made about April, 1884, by which Pacific Mail agreed to leave the Honolulu–San Francisco business to Oceanic.

The extension of Oceanic service came over a year later—not to China but to Australia. Together with the Union Steamship Company of New Zealand, Oceanic in the autumn of 1885 received the colonial mail contract. This contract, formerly held by Pacific Mail, provided for carrying the mails on the Australia–New Zealand–Honolulu–San Francisco route. Under the new arrangement it was contemplated that the "Zealandia" and "Australia," formerly run by Pacific Mail, would be chartered from the owners of the ships, Elder and Company, of Glasgow. The pivotal and transfer point of the service was to be Honolulu. Union would operate between that point and Australia, and Oceanic between Honolulu and San Francisco. Honolulans were jubilant. In effect, their city would be the headquarters and terminus of the two lines, with a resulting increase of tourist and other business.[39]

The New South Wales government and the Sydney merchants insisted that Sydney and San Francisco be the terminal points, with no transshipment at Honolulu, though the ships would touch there. Other problems also arose. At the last minute Elder and Company decided not to charter the "Zealandia" and the "Australia" to Union-Oceanic. Instead, Elder decided to use the two steamers in an opposition line on the Sydney–San Francisco run. This move, it was charged, was at the instigation of Sydney merchants.[40]

Honolulu merchants, unfriendly to Spreckels, guaranteed the Elder line 700 tons of sugar every second trip on the Honolulu–San Francisco part of the run. The *Advertiser* charged that shipping of sugar by the Elder and Company (British) ships threw Honolulu stevedores out of work. The newspaper also said that use of British ships endangered the Reciprocity Treaty, because one of the claimed benefits of the treaty was to the American carrying trade. "Are the planters prepared to shoulder this responsibility to gratify the business rivals of Colonel Spreckels?" [41]

Elder and Company's refusal to let Union-Oceanic charter the "Zealandia" and the "Australia" meant the possible loss of the colonial mail contract. Oceanic acted to prevent this loss by putting the "Alameda" and the "Mariposa" on the Australian run, for which the "Mararoa" of the Union line was also available. But the shift of the "Alameda" and the "Mariposa" meant a temporary upset of the Honolulu–San Francisco steamer service. In place of the steamers, the brigantine "W. G. Irwin" made the mail run to San Francisco in December, 1885. The *Gazette* said this violated the 1884 subsidy law which provided that the mails should be carried in steamers of at least 1,900 tons register.[42] To meet this objection, Oceanic immediately chartered the steamer "St. Paul" of the Alaska line. The "St. Paul" ran temporarily between Honolulu and San Francisco.[43]

Oceanic began to fight the Elder line, first by slashing rates.[44] Oceanic also set out to prove that the "Zealandia" and the "Australia," though fast steamers, were no match for the "Alameda" and the "Mariposa." In January, 1886, Honolulu stirred to an account of the "Great Ocean Race." [45] The "Alameda" left San Francisco well after the "Zealandia," gained 52 hours on her, and arrived in Sydney 13 hours ahead of her. Elder prudently withdrew from the Australian service the very next month, and sold the "Zealandia" and the "Australia" to Oceanic.[46] Oceanic announced it would register the two ships under the Hawaiian flag.[47] Union and Oceanic together now had the "Alameda" and the "Mariposa" under the American flag, the "Zealandia" and the "Australia" to come under the Hawaiian flag, and the "Mararoa" under the British flag.[48]

In early April, 1886, Honolulu celebrated the first departure of the "Zealandia" under the Hawaiian flag. According to the *Advertiser:* "It was no ordinary occasion. One of the largest steamships sailing the Pacific Ocean had been added to the Hawaiian register. . . . It was the inauguration of practically a new steamer service with the Coast." [49]

In his speech at the opening of the legislature, April 30, 1886, Kalakaua took notice of the Hawaiian registry of the "Australia" and the "Zealandia"—the first ocean-going steamers (other than interisland) so registered. He also implied his support of a continuing subsidy to Oceanic: "It is a source of satisfaction to me that ocean steam communication under the Hawaiian flag has become an established undertaking. My Ministers will recommend for your consideration measures for the encouragement and expansion of an enterprise so essential to the progress and prosperity of the Kingdom." [50]

On May 31, 1886, William G. Irwin and Company gave a large party on board the "Australia" to celebrate her transfer to Hawaiian registry. Kalakaua headed a distinguished guest list that included members of the Hawaiian cabinet and legislature, consular officials, and many other prominent residents. Colored lanterns brightened the waterfront. The Royal Hawaiian band entertained the guests.

After dinner Captain Webber of the "Australia" offered a toast to Kalakaua, and congratulated him on having two of the finest ships in the Pacific under the flag of his kingdom. This, said Captain Webber, was due to "the energy and enterprise of the gentleman who had founded the Oceanic Steamship Company, and who had done so much to develop the trade and industries of this Kingdom, Colonel Spreckels." [51]

Kalakaua thanked Webber. The king said he was gratified to note "evidence of commercial and industrial progress . . . and to see the Hawaiian flag flying on such splendid steamships." These ships, he said, were important to the trade of the Pacific and connected Hawaii "with the great and energetic people of the Pacific Coast."

Paul Neumann, attorney general, said Claus Spreckels had been "instrumental, above all others, in promoting everything that could advance the interests of these Islands." Neumann also said he "never knew a man who could be so staunch a friend and so uncompromising an enemy. . . . However Colonel Spreckels [has] judgment in his friendships and justice in his enemies."

Spreckels thanked Neumann for his remarks, and then reviewed his own accomplishments in the Hawaiian Islands as an example of what could be accomplished by economy and attention to business. He recalled how he had first come to the islands in 1876, with his wife and daughter, on the very ship that brought news of the Reciprocity Treaty. From the beginning he had loved these islands, and he made up his mind to invest in them. He recalled how poor the means of interisland travel were then, and how they had since improved. He had gone to Maui and made of barren plains a plantation second to none in the world. He had built a home in Honolulu. He had started a bank. He was also "identified with the islands in mercantile and shipping pursuits." When he gave advice, therefore, said Spreckels, it was as a person having a large stake in Hawaii.

United States Minister Resident Merrill reviewed the progress of Hawaii during the past 20 years. The islands had "risen from canoes and schooners, in which voyages were taken to other islands, to steamships flying the Hawaiian flag, which [are] capable of carrying the trade of the Pacific, connecting the Pacific Coast . . . with Australia, and stopping . . . to serve this by no means insignificant Hawaiian Kingdom." [52]

William G. Irwin noted that the arrival of the "Australia" was an important event not only in the history of Oceanic Steamship Company but also in that of the Hawaiian kingdom.[53] The *Advertiser* said the party aboard the "Australia" was "well chosen to enable the members of the legislative assembly to realize for themselves the great and unparalleled development of the shipping trade of this country under the stimulus of the Oceanic Company." [54] In the midst of all the oratory, Samuel G. Wilder struck a practical note. He said that Oceanic was entitled to a subsidy. "Subsidy" was just "another word for fair pay for valuable services rendered." [55]

With some changes, the battle over the subsidy during the 1886 legislature was like that of the 1884 session. Spreckels was again either the hero or the villain, depending on whether one read the *Advertiser* or the *Gazette*. S. B. Dole was still his main adversary, the champion of either righteousness or retrogression, depending on one's point of view.

Minister of Finance Kapena, in early June, introduced a bill for renewing the $3,000 a month subsidy to Oceanic. The *Gazette* sneered: "Since their feed [aboard the "Australia"] a certain set of the Legislature like the O. S. S. Co. very much." [56] The newspaper complained that the company had violated the last subsidy bill without penalty, by using the sailing ship "W. G. Irwin" to carry the mails. The *Gazette* also complained of irregular sailings on the Honolulu–San Francisco run while the Australian service was being started. The editor said that these interruptions of service to the coast had injured the fruitgrowers. "Had the Hawaiian Government, instead of being a pocket borough, been a strong Government whose suffrage the O. S. S. Co. wished to obtain instead of to command, there would have been no letup on the regular mails." [57]

On the other hand, the *Advertiser* said of Oceanic: "Without its breezy and invigorating influence, Honolulu would be a stagnant pool of commercial inactivity today. Yet there are members of this community . . . who lose no opportunity of attacking the founder of the Oceanic Company and other great enterprises for the development of the resources and trade of the Kingdom, because he is an innovator, and tramples upon their business traditions." [58]

As the newspapers divided on the intertwined issues of Spreckels and the Oceanic subsidy, so also did the members of the legislature. In late June the banana growers of the kingdom petitioned that the subsidy bill should limit freight on bananas to 50 cents a bunch. After some argument, S. K. Kaai said he thought "the petition should be referred to Colonel Spreckels." [59] The petition was tabled, to be considered later with the committee report on the subsidy bill.

This committee presented two reports in August. The majority report by G. W. Macfarlane, S. G. Wilder, E. K. Lilikalani, and J. T. Baker favored the subsidy: Mail, freight, and passenger service of Oceanic had "become an actual necessity to the commerce . . . of the islands"; steamships were to Hawaii "what railroads are to other countries"; abandonment of the subsidy, with possible loss of the steamer service, "would remove the Kingdom from the world's highways of commerce and travel, and retard the prosperity of the nation indefinitely." [60]

S. B. Dole presented a minority report against the subsidy: (1) The financial position of the government would not permit $1,500 a trip; (2) two round trips a month between Honolulu and San Francisco were too many. One trip touching Honolulu on dates between those of the through steamers would be enough; (3) Spreckels in fact had said he would be satisfied with $1,000 a trip.[61]

The bill came up for the second reading on August 26. Frank Brown moved for $1,000 a trip, since Spreckels had said that was all he wanted. Kaulukou answered that perhaps Spreckels had changed his mind: "Changes often take place. Once Mr. Brown was a little babe, but [he is] now changed into a handsome man." [62] Thurston also said that $1,000 was enough. He did not admire the way the government operated in relationship to Spreckels. Macfarlane explained that Spreckels had offered to accept $1,000 a trip only if the government would also economize in other ways.

Thurston retorted: "If that is not cheek, I don't know what it is."

Dole said the subsidy should be no more than Spreckels had offered to take. "The freight paid so well that Mr. Spreckels was able to subsidize the other company [Pacific Mail] not to take any freight from Honolulu." [63]

The subsidy bill passed a few days later at $1,500 a trip ($3,000 a month, or $72,000 for the biennium ending March 31, 1888). Under the law, freight rates were not to be increased. The banana growers got their special rate of 50 cents per bunch into the law. This provision was unwise, said the *Advertiser,* because it was "an attempt to regulate international freight in the interest of one class of shippers." [64]

Kalakaua said, in his speech at the end of the legislative session, October 16, 1886: "The subsidy you have voted for Ocean Steam Service will secure for the country that regular and frequent communication with America which is of vital importance to the commercial and agricultural interests of the Kingdom." [65]

Spreckels' years of greatest power in Hawaii saw the start of regular semimonthly steamer service between Honolulu and San Francisco (1883) and extension of the service to Australia (1885). The remaining history of Oceanic may be briefly told.

Perhaps the most important event before Spreckels' death in 1908 was the arrival of the steamship "Sierra" in 1900. Soon her sister ships "Sonoma" and "Ventura" also arrived in Honolulu. Annexation of Hawaii by the United States in 1898 prevented the use of foreign-built ships in the California-Hawaii trade, which was considered "coastal" shipping, restricted to American-built ships. Oceanic had therefore withdrawn the "Australia" and the "Zealandia" from the Honolulu–San Francisco run. Both ships saw duty as transports to the Philippines during the Spanish-American War.[66]

The "Sierra," a 6,000-ton ship built at Cramp's shipyard in Philadelphia, arrived in Honolulu on its maiden voyage December 20, 1900. She was "hailed with delight by hundreds of people who swarmed about [her] decks, admiring the many beautiful furnishings and fixtures of the cabins." [67] The "Sierra" was 425 feet long, had a 50-foot beam, and could carry 400 passengers. [68] In January, 1901, the "Sonoma" arrived, and the following month the "Ventura." The ships offered a three-week service between San Francisco and Australia by way of Honolulu, in place of the previous four-week service. And so the growing demands for greater speed, better passenger service, more cargo space, and more frequent trips were met.[69]

As mentioned earlier, the sugar firm of William G. Irwin and Company (Spreckels and Irwin), which had been Honolulu agent for Oceanic, merged in 1910 with C. Brewer and Company. In the merger Brewer got the Honolulu agency for the Oceanic Steamship Company. One newspaper report on the event shows that the quarter century of control which Spreckels, through Oceanic, had held over the shipping of Hawaiian sugar had not been forgotten:

The *Bulletin* believes it is not far from predicting the future accurately when it suggests that as Hawaii's industry develops and we have more courageous and ambitious men who have made their fortunes here and intend to spend them for the further development of the islands, the time will come and is not so very far distant when Hawaii will send its sugars to its own refineries in ships that are controlled in Hawaii and that respond to general demands of Hawaii's community interests as well as· the specific needs of the sugar industry. Without prejudice to anything that now is or has gone before, that will be a happy day for this city and the Territory.[70]

The *Bulletin*'s predictions were soon realized. The California and Hawaiian Sugar Refinery became dominant in refining of Hawaiian sugar, and Matson Navigation Company in shipping. California and Hawaiian Sugar Refinery, founded in 1905, was (and still is) controlled by the Hawaiian sugar agencies. The agencies also have had large holdings of stock in Matson and have maintained close working relationships with that company. During the twentieth century Matson has replaced Oceanic as the chief carrier in the California-Hawaii trade.[71] Vertical integration of the Hawaiian sugar industry, including shipping, has therefore been largely achieved. This pattern for control of sugar from growing to marketing was first set by Claus Spreckels.

CHAPTER XIII

King Kalakaua's Coins

Whose *is* this image and superscription?—Mark 12:16

T*he* Hawaiian silver coinage of 1883, generally known as the Kalakaua coinage, satisfied diverse ambitions of King Kalakaua, the merry monarch; Walter Murray Gibson, the king's chief minister; and Claus Spreckels, the financial angel of the government. At the time, this trio controlled the kingdom.

Kalakaua took pride in having his image and superscription on a national coinage. He also thought this enhanced his stature as an independent monarch. Premier Gibson got money to run the government in a way that the more conservative members of the community thought corrupt and extravagant. In effect, the coinage represented a loan to the government by Spreckels. As the most down-to-earth member of the trio, he pocketed the profit, variously estimated at $100,000 to $200,000. The loan aspect of the coinage also further obligated the kingdom to him. He could thus press for additional political favors which would bring him economic gain.

The coinage resulted in much controversy, including a celebrated lawsuit and also attacks by the newspapers, by the Honolulu Chamber of Commerce, and by some members of the legislature of 1884. The controversy nevertheless directed needed attention to the monetary problems of the kingdom, and produced the much-debated Gold Law of 1884. In the furor over the coinage we can see echoes of similar battles over the silver question which occurred in the United States.

Before the silver coinage of 1883, a variety of foreign coins circulated in the islands. As the *Pacific Commercial Advertiser* said:

> Honolulu has long been a mine of great resources for devotees of numismatics. Let an American land from one of the steamers or a trading vessel ... and go out to make a few trifling purchases, ... when he returns to his vessel he will have a pocketful of rare and quaintly beautiful specimens of foreign coin from every part of the world. ... Mexican, Chinese, Danish, Swedish, English and American coins pass current. A piece of the size and approximate weight of a quarter is a quarter to all intents and purposes.[1]

Under the Legal Tender Act of 1876, gold coins of the United States were the standard and legal tender at face value for all debts.[2] Silver coins of the United States were legal tender up to $50, and also for varying proportions of larger debts.

Foreign coins other than those of the United States were not legal tender at face value, but only at values fixed by the government from time to time.[3] To discourage the import of silver coins, the Legal Tender Act provided a duty of 10 per cent on such imports. Import duties on all goods were payable only "in gold coin of the United States or its equivalent." All these provisions of the 1876 law are pertinent to later battles over the Kalakaua silver.

Little had been done before 1883 about a national coinage. In 1847 the kingdom issued $1,000 worth of copper pennies bearing the head of Kamehameha III. In 1881, after a trip around the world which seems to have stirred his interest in a national coinage, King Kalakaua had some five-cent pieces struck off, with his portrait on one side. These coins found no favor with the Hawaiians because the motto of the kingdom was misspelled.[4]

The Kalakaua coinage of 1883 resulted from an adroit combination of two apparently unrelated laws: the Coinage Act of 1880[5] and the National Loan Act of 1882.[6] The Coinage Act provided that the minister of finance could buy gold and silver bullion "with any moneys which may from time to time be in the Treasury." With the bullion he could have gold coins minted of certain specified denominations, and "Silver Coins of the value of One Dollar, Fifty Cents, Twenty-five Cents and Twelve and one-half Cents." All coins were to be equal in weight and fineness to coins of the United States.[7]

The National Loan Act provided for a loan of $2,000,000 for specific purposes. Among the most important were encouragement of immigration and agriculture, and construction of roads, bridges, and government buildings. Under the law, none of the proceeds was to be used for current expenses of the government. Bonds under the Loan Act were to be issued at not less than par and at an interest rate of not more than 6 per cent. Principal and interest were to be payable "in United States gold coin or its equivalent."

Shortly after the Loan Act was signed on August 5, 1882, there were rumors that Spreckels would take all the bonds. This was "denied authoritatively."[8] Emphasizing the kingdom's lack of credit, the *Bulletin* (Honolulu) said: "The ways and means of floating the Two Million Loan were being discussed on the beach the other day and nearly everyone decried it as impossible."[9] For several months requests for tenders up to $500,000 were published in the Honolulu newspapers. Nothing happened. The government also made vain efforts to float part of the loan in San Francisco.[10]

Just when Gibson hit on the combination of the coinage and loan acts as a solution to the financial troubles of the government is not entirely clear. Despite official denials, the thought that Spreckels would lend the money was an early one. Even before the Loan Act passed, Gibson wrote to E. H. Allen in July, 1882: "You will see our appropriation bill is rather large, but we propose to provide for all the estimate over estimated revenue by loan. What we propose to borrow . . . will not exceed one million dollars, and this is promised by Spreckels & Co.; or rather Wm. G. Irwin & Co."[11]

On September 20, 1882, the Cabinet Council passed a resolution offered by Gibson that "the Minister of Finance be authorized to enter into an agreement with Claus Spreckels or other parties for the coinage of a sum of gold and silver not to exceed $150,000." [12] About the same time Gibson got a long letter from J. Mott Smith on the possibility of minting the coins in the United States. Mott Smith reported on an interview with E. F. Burton, superintendent of the San Francisco mint. Under a law of 1874, the United States could execute coinage for a foreign country "according to the legally prescribed standards and devices of such country." Mott Smith indicated that the profit to Hawaii should be 10 to 15 per cent. He also wrote: "Mr. Severance, your consul [at San Francisco], can do the business just as well as anybody else, and you can make your own terms with him." [13]

Mott Smith's implied advice to arrange the coinage through regular consular channels was ignored. It soon became clear that Spreckels was to have the coins minted in the United States, that he was to receive Hawaiian government bonds in exchange for the money, and that Gibson was behind the scheme. On March 6, 1883, the Cabinet Council passed the following resolution: "That the Minister of Finance [J. M. Kapena], in concurrence with the Premier [Walter M. Gibson] be authorized to conclude a negotiation with Mr. Claus Spreckels for the coinage of Hawaiian money to be exchanged for Government six per cent bonds, as initiated by the Premier." [14]

Spreckels received a commission dated May 18, 1883, as Hawaii's agent for the coinage. The document set forth that the minting could be done more cheaply in the United States than in the kingdom, and that it was not convenient for the minister of finance to leave his post to superintend the transaction. The document continued:

I, John M. Kapena, ... do ... authorize and empower Claus Spreckels, Esq. to make all necessary arrangements for the purchase of Silver bullion sufficient to make One Million dollars in value of silver coins of the denominations of One Dollar, Fifty Cents, Twenty-five Cents and Twelve and one-half Cents ... and said Claus Spreckels is authorized to enter into Contracts with the government of the United States for the purchasation [*sic*] of the proper dies and the execution of the coinage at any of the Mints of the United States, said coins to be of the same standard of fineness and weight as coins of the same denominations issued by the government of the United States.[15]

H. A. P. Carter, the Hawaiian minister at Washington, wrote many letters to Gibson and Kapena about the proposed coinage. Carter also wrote to and had interviews with the United States Department of State and the Treasury. In June, 1883, he wrote to Kapena: "The laws of the U. S. are very strict in regard to the coinage, they telegraphed to San Francisco about it. They regard the whole arrangement as very queer—They said that they would have bought your bullion and turned out the money for simple cash." [16] Carter also said he hoped the estimated $150,-000 profit on the minting (from the difference between face and bullion value of the coins) would go to the Hawaiian kingdom.

Long before the first installment of the silver arrived, three of the four English-language newspapers in Honolulu—the *Hawaiian Gazette,* the *Saturday Press,* and the *Bulletin*—undertook a vigorous campaign against it. This campaign reflected one aspect of the opposition of most of the Honolulu business community to the Kalakaua-Gibson-Spreckels regime.[17] In May, 1883, the *Gazette* predicted that there would be some difficulty with the coinage. It would not be worth par. "It rests therefore entirely with the people whether they will accept it or not. . . . We are quite prepared to find that the people of this country will refuse to take the depreciated silver which the present cabinet are so anxious to palm off on them." [18]

On May 21, 1883, Thomas G. Thrum, publisher of the *Saturday Press,* addressed the following letter to Premier Gibson. The letter was also published in the *Press* on May 26:

The rumors of the proposed Hawaiian Coinage causing grave apprehension and alarm in the public mind, I would be obliged for such information on the subject as you may have, calculated to relieve this apprehension —upon the following points:

1st. Is the proposed coinage to be entirely a silver one, or if both gold and silver, in what proportions?

2nd. Of what intrinsic values will the coin or coins be?

3rd. What amount is it proposed to coin?

4th. Is the amount of coinage to be issued to be settled for by accepted bonds under the loan act?

5th. Is it proposed to put this coinage in circulation, or hold it in the treasury as a deposit and issue certificates therefor? or,

6th. Is it proposed to make the Hawaiian coinage supersede all other but that of the United States?

Although the letter was addressed to Premier Gibson, Finance Minister Kapena replied on May 22, as follows: He denied that any apprehension or alarm existed; any decisions on the coinage would be promptly made public; the coin would be circulated with a minimum of disturbance, the amount issued depending on how much the community could absorb; and the issue would be paid for according to law.[19]

Hardly a day went by that the newspapers did not raise objections to the coinage. Among these were the following:

1. *The general financial policy of the government.* "In any other matter, the mischief a set of ignorant men may do can be repaired, but a mess in national finance is a very serious thing, and in their supreme self-conceit the cabinet appear to have blundered egregiously."[20] The loss on the coinage was "the premium which the country had to pay for its present cabinet." The scheme "meant that Hawaiian securities could be sold . . . at any price, at the caprice of venal or weak ministers."[21]

2. *Anxiety among businessmen.* "There is not a businessman in town who does not feel the gravest fears that a terrible blunder has been made."[22]

3. *United States coinage preferable.* The *Bulletin* said a Hawaiian coinage might "pander to national vanity" but it would be simpler and "save all trouble and expense" to use coins of the United States or England, preferably the former because United States coins were already in common use.[23]

4. *Legality.* The loan was to be made in silver coin worth 85 cents on the dollar, but principal and interest were payable in gold coin of the United States. The *Gazette* claimed the coinage

136

was illegal under the Coinage Act of 1880 and the Loan Act of 1882.[24]

5. *Debasement of monetary system.* The *Bulletin* speculated that if $1,000,000 in Hawaiian silver was brought in, it would depreciate and prices would rise.[25] The editor of the same newspaper had earlier raised a precisely opposite question. He estimated that there was $2,000,000 in foreign coin (including that of the United States) in the kingdom. Would this coin depreciate on introduction of Hawaiian coin as legal tender? [26]

6. *Foreign exchange problems.* The *Gazette* said that Hawaiian coins would not be worth face value in San Francisco, but only bullion value, about 85 cents.[27] With an excess of silver and a nonexportable coinage, exchange in San Francisco would be high. The Kalakaua coins would displace United States silver coins in Hawaii because the latter were acceptable at par in San Francisco.[28]

7. *Profit to Spreckels.* The profit would go to an individual although it should have gone to the government.[29]

About the time the first shipment of the coin arrived, $130,000 in half dollars on December 9, 1883, persons opposed to various actions of the government held a political mass meeting. Those present expressed a lack of confidence in the ministry, and also criticized the Kalakaua silver. Sanford B. Dole claimed it was debased coin, "not worth one hundred cents on the dollar." It was being paid for illegally with bonds, he said. Certain persons were making a profit, and this profit was coming out of the pockets of the people.[30]

The editor of the *Gazette* complained about the inability of the government to meet its bills. Somewhat inconsistently he complained too that the new silver was being used to meet them. "It [the first shipment of $130,000] has arrived just in the nick of time . . . for the Treasury has been . . . almost as bare as Mother Hubbard's well known cupboard." [31] The editor said there were so many unpaid bills and hungry creditors that there would not be much left of the $130,000. He claimed the kingdom was practically bankrupt.

Three days after the first shipment of coin arrived, W. R. Castle, S. B. Dole, and W. O. Smith, all lawyers and leaders in the opposition to the "palace party" and to Spreckels, filed a petition for writ of mandamus with the supreme court of the kingdom.[32] Their object was to compel Finance Minister Kapena to issue bonds at par under the Loan Act, and only for United States gold coin or its equivalent.

In his reply to the petition, Kapena did not deny that he was about to issue bonds for the silver coin. He tried to prove that this would be the same as an issue at par for United States gold. After hearing the reply, Chief Justice A. F. Judd allowed a temporary writ of mandamus to stand. He held that citizens, "as taxpayers, have the right to endeavor to prevent a public officer from doing what is an injury to the public good." [33] He also held that the proposed issue of bonds for silver coin was not equivalent to an issue for gold coin of the United States.

In reply to the attorney general's complaint that the mandamus action would ruin the credit of the kingdom, the chief justice said that his decision would not hamper government operations. Under the law, proceeds of the loan were to be used for certain extraordinary items and not for current expenses.[34] The chief justice also criticized the government on two more counts. Under the Coinage Act, he said, the government could coin money only by buying bullion "with any moneys which . . . may be in the Treasury." He thought this did not permit paying for the coin with bonds. He also said that Article 70 of the Constitution permitted the court to give the government an advance opinion on important questions of law. The court's opinion had not been sought in the contemplated issue of bonds for silver.[35]

The government at once gave notice of appeal to the full court from the decision of the chief justice. The day after the mandamus suit was filed, Paul Neumann, a friend of Spreckels, had joined the ministry as attorney general. Five persons were also appointed to the Privy Council, among them Paul Neumann and Samuel Parker,[36] the latter also reputedly a Spreckels man. The government was grouping its forces for battle.

With Kalakaua himself presiding, the Privy Council was hurriedly called into session. The council passed a resolution, introduced by Gibson, that the Hawaiian silver coins would be legal tender in the same manner as silver coins of the United States.[37] The government probably hoped this action would somehow help in the lawsuit. Just how it could have helped is not clear. Under the Legal Tender Act of 1876, United States *silver* coins were legal tender up to $50 (and in certain specified proportions of larger debts). The action of the Privy Council could hardly meet the objection of Chief Justice Judd that an issue of bonds for the Kalakaua coinage was not an issue for United States *gold* coin.

Many columns of newspaper space reflected the great interest of the community in the lawsuit. The *Advertiser* noted that the suit was brought at the last minute when the bonds were about to be issued, though the arrangement had been a subject of "street talk" for months.[38] (There was little merit in this complaint, as the chief justice had pointed out, because legal action was not possible until the act complained of was about to be done.) The *Advertiser* also noted the opinion of some segments of the community that the suit would upset business and damage the kingdom's credit.[39] The *Gazette* replied: "The credit of the country has been damaged not by these gentlemen [Dole, Castle, and Smith], who acted in strict accord with their legal rights, but . . . by a cabinet which, to prop its failing fortunes, is willing to commit any illegal act rather than lose its hold on the power it misuses." [40]

On appeal, the full court discharged the temporary writ of mandamus on a technicality. The court said that the proper petition was one for injunction. In its dicta on the dismissal of the mandamus writ, the court emphasized once more that: "Under the Loan Act of 1882 . . . it is illegal to issue the bonds for Hawaiian silver half dollars of less intrinsic value than their face value in United States gold coin." [41]

In accordance with this decision, Dole, Castle, and Smith now petitioned for an injunction. Kapena denied in his reply that he was "now or at any time or ever or at all about to issue ... any number of Hawaiian Government Bonds ... for certain silver coin." He denied too that he was "about to issue any of the bonds ... for any other moneys than is prescribed by law, to wit: 'not below par' and for gold coin of the United States or its equivalent." [42]

The petitioners objected that Kapena's reply was evasive; he should be required to produce a certain contract (with Spreckels); the reply was inconsistent with the government's answer in the mandamus case. The court nevertheless rejected the petition for injunction, and held:

> The respondent denies absolutely that he intends to issue bonds for certain or any silver coin not of value of U. S. gold coin or its equivalent, or that he is now or at any time or at all about to issue bonds except as authorized by law.
>
> .   .   .   .
>
> The statement of the respondent is "at least credible." There is no "extreme improbability" in it. The Court will take the answer as declaring in good faith that the respondent is not about to issue bonds "in any other manner, or for any other moneys, than as provided for by law," as construed by the Court.[43]

The editor of the *Gazette* seemed mystified by the decision and predicted a "speedy issue of the bonds." [44]

Just after the writ of mandamus had been issued in the early stages of the lawsuit, Gibson wrote to Carter at Washington that a special session of the legislature might be needed to solve the troubles over the coinage.[45] The government in fact took a much simpler course. It issued $500,000 in bonds to Spreckels, probably in return for a like amount of Kalakaua silver, and merely ignored the dicta of the court about the illegality of such issue.

It should be noted that most writers merely assume that Spreckels paid $500,000 in Kalakaua coin for the gold bonds. Firsthand evidence of what he paid for the bonds is not available; however, there are at least three possible hypotheses: He paid $500,000 in Kalakaua silver; somewhat more in Kalakaua silver, to equal in value $500,000 in U. S. gold coin; or he paid $500,000 in gold coin. A knowledge of the character of Spreckels and of the entire background of the coinage probably makes the first hypothesis the most tenable.[46]

In April, 1884, a few months after the unsuccessful suit in which Dole had taken part, Carter wrote to Dole: "The most damaging thing now in our currency is that a Gov't can, as a favor to a private individual, permit him without legal sanction to flood us with whatever he pleases and make it legal tender, and make $150,000 out of it. What limit is there to such proceedings? There was not a shadow of warrant for it in the coinage act. Probably the next move will be to declare photographs of Mr. Spreckels legal tender to any amount." [47]

A perceptive criticism of the legal opposition by Dole and others to the coinage appeared in the latter part of 1884. For the first $500,000, as indicated above, Spreckels probably was given bonds. For at least part of the balance he received silver certificates.[48] Anyone could get such certificates by turning silver coin into the treasury. But by the Gold Law of 1884 [49] silver certificates of other than ten-dollar denomination became exchangeable for gold coin of the United States. "This opposition [those who opposed the issue of bonds to Spreckels, and who also pushed the gold law through the legislature] would not allow Mr. Spreckels to get gold bonds payable in twenty-five years for his silver, but right away give him for it certificates payable in gold on demand." [50]

The first Kalakaua half dollar known to have been in circulation was found on the evening of January 10, 1884, in the receipts of the Honolulu Music Hall.[51] Another half dollar was displayed on January 12 in the window of Wiseman and Ashley, general business agents, and attracted much attention.[52] Two days later the coins entered into general circulation. On the same day the Spreckels and Company bank opened for business. Both the bank and the treasury made the coin available, and there was "a great demand at both places for it." [53] By June 9, 1884, a total of $1,000,000 in Hawaiian silver had been received, as follows:

Dollars (*akahi dala*)..$500,000

Half dollars (*hapalua*)...................................... 350,000

Quarter dollars (*hapaha*)................................. 125,000

Dimes (*umi keneta*).. 25,000 [54]

All the coins were of the same weight and fineness as coins of the United States. They had a profile view of Kalakaua's head on one side. On the reverse side was the Hawaiian coat of arms (except on the dime, which showed a wreath), and the motto of the Hawaiian kingdom, *Ua mau ke ea o ka aina i ka pono* ("The life of the land is preserved in righteousness").

Early reaction to the silver was mixed. The *Gazette:* "The new coins have entered quietly into circulation and have been accepted without a murmur, although there is an undercurrent of hostile feeling to their usurping the place of American half- and quarter-dollars, and this feeling may find expression in the near future." [55] The *Bulletin:* "The coins, so the ladies say, make very nice brooches and ornaments. Business men say what a pity they do not contain more silver." [56] The *Advertiser:* "The new coins are pretty to look at and smile out upon one from among the dingier ones which have seen more service as pleasantly as if they had never been the cause of heart-burnings and controversy and political plots." [57]

But more "heart-burnings and controversy" were yet to come. Argument over the coinage continued in the newspapers, occupied a great many meetings of the Chamber of Commerce, and raged in the legislature of 1884.

In reply to complaints about an excess of silver, the *Advertiser* claimed that there had really been a serious shortage of change and the Kalakaua coins were therefore a boon to retailers.[58] Both the *Advertiser* and the *Gazette* noted the disappearance of the United States half dollars and quarters, in favor of the Hawaiian silver. But they interpreted this differently. The *Advertiser* thought it was a sign of the acceptability of the new coins. The *Gazette* referred to Gresham's law and jibed: "Here is an opportunity for [the *Advertiser*] to start a new financial theory." [59] The *Gazette* derisively referred to the coins as *kimo-ai-luau* [60] ("cheap") coins and noted that British sovereigns were at a premium of 16 per cent as compared with the Hawaiian silver. "Merchants in Wailuku have put up the prices of staples from 6 to 10 per cent on account of the advance in exchange. People are beginning to feel the effects of the foolishness of the silver coinage." [61]

Spreckels' influence in the government also came under heavy attack. The *Gazette* said the coinage was the price paid by the government to keep the support of Spreckels.[62] A "pliant Ministry," hoping to make use of Spreckels' influence, had allowed him to introduce the coinage at a personal profit.[63] The editor of the *Planters' Monthly* charged that the Spreckels interests and Gibson were in collusion "to force upon the country this enormous and ruinous flood of short silver, which is now deranging our finances and driving up the price of exchange." [64] The *Bulletin* described a cartoon in the Hawaiian language newspaper, *Pae Aina,* in which Spreckels was pictured as having a club full of coin, driving the four members of the cabinet before him. In the background Kamehameha the Great, first ruler of the islands to know the foreigners, was asking: "Is this the way that you now govern the country?" [65]

In a letter to the minister of finance on January 9, 1884, the Chamber of Commerce expressed its concern over introduction of the silver. The chamber claimed it would be difficult to enforce the Legal Tender Act of 1876 because silver would fall in value relative to gold. The chamber recommended that further imports of silver be limited, and that all silver coins other than those of Hawaii and the United States be withdrawn at the expense of the treasury. The government thanked the chamber for its interest and said its views would be seriously considered.[66]

Attacks on the coinage began early in the legislative session of 1884, and increased in force as the session progressed. J. Nawahi, on April 30, introduced a resolution calling on Kapena to explain when the Hawaiian silver had become legal tender. This was a mild enough beginning, but the *Bulletin* called the resolution "a slight shred of cloud prognostic of coming thunder." Kapena explained that the coin had been made legal tender by the Privy Council on a date he had forgotten.[67]

On May 7, S. B. Dole moved that a duty of 10 per cent be paid on the Hawaiian coin in accordance with the Legal Tender Act requiring payment of duty on *foreign* silver coin. Gibson answered: "The Coin was ordered, consigned and delivered to the Hawaiian Government, in accordance with an act passed in 1880 [the Coinage Act], and the Government will not levy a duty on its own importations." [68] He dramatically held up three plantation coins: [69] one stamped "Wailuku plantation," another stamped "Haiku plantation," and a third with "T" (Torbert). These, he said, were practically worthless, but Hawaiian coins were as good as those of the United States. Nawahi retorted: "The Ministers remind me of a lot of new beginners in a primary school, they knew nothing when they started, but they picked it up" as they went along.[70] After more discussion, Dole's motion to require duty on the coin was tabled.

On May 23, in response to a resolution of the legislature, Kapena produced documents relating to the coinage.[71] Not satisfied with these, W. O. Smith moved that Gibson, the minister of foreign affairs, be required to produce all his papers on the transaction. Smith said that the first shipments of the coin had been consigned to the government but that later shipments had been consigned to William G. Irwin and Company. "The manipulating of the coin was more through the Foreign Office than through the Finance Office." [72] Representative Richardson amended the resolution to require the production of all "Cabinet supply papers," not only those of the foreign office. Gibson said he had "the honor to second the resolution offered by the Hon. Member from Wailuku." He would be happy "to give all information in his power relating to this matter." [73] During the rest of the session there was something of a game of hide-and-seek during which Gibson and the documents remained elusive.

S. B. Dole next took up the question of how much profit Spreckels had made. On May 27, he asked what salary had been paid to Spreckels for acting as agent for the coinage. Gibson replied that he understood "from Mr. Spreckels that he had a bill of charges to present," and that he (Gibson) would soon lay this bill before the house. "It included nine months' interest on bullion, seignorage of the United States, and insurance and freight." [74]

About a month later no bill by Spreckels had yet come in. Dole said the coinage had been illegal and had been given to Spreckels without regard to what this would cost the kingdom. In the mandamus case, said Dole, the minister of finance said he was about to issue the bonds for Hawaiian silver. In the injunction case he swore he never intended to issue the bonds for silver. "The Minister may say that the answers were only a matter of form, yet they were both sworn to, and both cannot be true." [75] After all this, the minister went ahead and issued bonds for the silver. Spreckels "pockets the net profit of $150,000. He also imports coin on which duties are waived, giving him $100,000." [76]

Gibson denied there had been any loss on the coinage. The government, he pointed out, had advertised its bonds but no one with the exception of Spreckels had been willing to take them. Part of the funds from the coinage was used to pay for Portuguese immigration in accordance with the Loan Act. If the government had suspended this operation, said Gibson, it "would have been blamed for so doing. . . . Through the Loan Bill and the Coinage Act, the Government saw a way to obtain funds to carry out their object." [77] Dole accused the ministers of dishonoring the throne by their unlawful actions. Gibson said that such a charge was not warranted. "His Majesty, in his intelligence, will not allow anyone to dishonor the throne by unlawful actions." [78]

Still trying to get information about the profit to Spreckels, Dole, on August 15, introduced a resolution that Gibson be required to report on the matter. The resolution passed.[79] Gibson denied that on May 27 he had said that Spreckels' bill of charges was yet to come in, although his remarks to that effect had been published in four different newspapers.[80] Gibson said that perhaps the newspapers were mistaken.[81] Nevertheless, he made his report on August 29. He remarked that the report had been in his pocket for several days and he might have forgotten it if someone had not asked for it:

> No payment has been made or promised to Mr. Spreckels . . . and as to the profit . . . I cannot say precisely, but Mr. F. F. Low submitted a statement to me . . . showing that the cost of the bullion assayed and refined for the Hawaiian Coinage was $87.40 per dollar [*sic*], added to 1.75 per cent seignorage of the U. S. Government, half of one per cent cost of dies, and then estimate for interest on bullion, cost of transportation, insurance, exchange, and minor expenses properly chargeable to the coinage, the cost of the coinage would be about 97 cents to the dollar.[82]

The legislature voted to accept the report and to publish it in the newspapers.

Gibson had been fairly successful in dodging and parrying the thrusts on the floor of the legislature, but in one area the opposition scored solidly, namely in the report of the finance committee. The report, evidently based on some deep and competent digging, charged that the minister of finance had violated the Coinage Act and the Loan Act. The Coinage Act authorized him to buy gold and silver bullion with money in the treasury. "He bought no bullion to be coined into gold and silver coins but agreed with Mr. Spreckels to take $1,000,000, in silver Hawaiian coins in exchange for U. S. Gold Bonds of the Hawaiian Government." [83] Dole said the cabinet should be called the turkey cabinet, as it had shown such a desire to gobble up public funds.[84]

Ten-cent pieces were brought in, continued the report, although the coinage act authorized 12½-cent pieces. The dollars were worth only 81½ cents as compared with gold coin of the United States, and two half dollars were worth only 79 cents. The report also charged that, in accord with Gresham's law, Hawaiian silver was driving British and American gold coins and American standard silver dollars out of circulation.[85]

The opposition held a mass meeting at the Lyceum on June 23 which resulted in a general indictment of the ministry and its action on the Kalakaua coinage. Leaders pictured the meeting as nonpolitical, but only views of the opposition found expression. J. O. Carter, who spoke for over an hour, said:

[The report of the finance committee] presents a startling condition of affairs to every tax-paying citizen of the Kingdom.

.   .   .   .

We want an honest, economical administration for this Government. The present aspect of affairs is a serious one. Are we to go on paying taxes to a set of men who seem determined to use Government money at their own sweet will? I hope this meeting will so express itself, without any hesitation, that His Majesty will understand we are doing that which is our last resort. There is nothing beyond this but force, and none of us wish to see force brought into play.[86]

Those present passed a resolution of no confidence in the ministry and called for its resignation. Item four of the resolution stated: "The Coinage Act of 1880 has been violated and as a result the Kingdom has a silver coinage in excess of its needs, upon which by the neglect of the Ministry, the Treasury has lost and an individual has made a large profit." [87]

A few days after this meeting Dole introduced in the legislature a formal motion of no confidence. Speaking in favor of the motion, W. O. Smith said:

This self-styled Premier [Gibson] and his colleagues stand before the country a miserable failure; the administration is despised at home and distrusted abroad; our national bonds have been hawked in foreign markets and our credit impaired; our currency is confused, our financial market thrown into disorder; ... the national debt has been largely augmented ... loyal men who have developed and built up the country have been denounced as its worst enemies; fawning, cringing sycophants have proclaimed themselves the only friends of the throne and the nation.[88]

Next day the motion was tabled 25 to 21. All four ministers voted to table. Except for their votes, permitted under Hawaiian law, there would have been a tie.

The downfall of the ministry might well have meant withdrawal of the Kalakaua coinage and upheaval in the monetary affairs of the kingdom—for better or for worse. It would have put the hard money men in the saddle, as opposed to the easy money Spreckels crowd. More conflict between these two forces was still to come.

CHAPTER XIV

Fight Over
Gold Law

The struggle over the Kalakaua silver focused attention on the coinage and currency problems of the kingdom. One important result was the Gold Law of 1884, signed on July 17. Spreckels and the government forces at first opposed this law. The conservative businessmen of the community, including the Chamber of Commerce and those who had fought the Kalakaua coinage, supported it. Essentially the argument was one of easy money versus hard money. "Gold is the only currency!" became the battle cry of those who backed the Gold Law.

Even before the Hawaiian coin went into general circulation, the *Pacific Commercial Advertiser* asked what was to be done eventually with English, French, Spanish, Mexican, and Italian coins. These had been passing as dollars and quarters. "If we are to have a coinage of our own, and if we are to make the coins of the U. S. legal tender here permanently, the day must come when all other coins must be deprived of that currency which the law gives to some and custom gives to others." [1] The *Advertiser* called for the ultimate redemption of foreign coins other than those of the United States. There should be no loss to the holders and the government should bear the cost of redemption.

It will be recalled that on January 9, 1884, the Chamber of Commerce had made similar recommendations. In addition, the chamber called for a limit on further imports of silver. In May, a committee of the chamber complained that the government had not heeded these recommendations. The committee also said that refusal of the government to receive silver in payment of customs would cause it to fall in value. "Your committee are at a loss to know how the circulation of silver coinage at par, and the demand for U. S. gold at the Custom House can co-exist." [2] The committee asked the chamber to sponsor a law which would bring the Legal Tender Act of 1876 "into harmony with the requirements of commerce," put the kingdom on a gold basis, provide for redeeming and shipping excess silver at treasury expense, and reduce the legal tender limit of silver from $50 to $20.[3]

A. S. Hartwell, who had been the Castle-Dole-Smith attorney in the coinage suit, wrote a long letter to the *Bulletin* (Honolulu) in favor of a gold law. "Gold is the least fluctuating in value," he wrote, "and the best kind of money." Gold, he argued, would prevent foreign exchange from going above 1¼ to 1½ per cent. He recommended that Hawaiian silver be made legal tender only up to five dollars.[4] The editor of the *Bulletin* also advocated a legal limit of five dollars on silver, and argued against that of ten dollars contained in the draft of a gold law by J. Mott Smith. The newspaper also complained that the Mott Smith bill provided only for calling in foreign silver (estimated at $500,000) other than that of the United States. This would leave Hawaiian and American silver (estimated at $1,200,000) outstanding. There would be too much silver, said the *Bulletin*. With a legal limit of only ten dollars, silver would fall in value and gold would be at a premium.[5]

As passed in mid-July, the Gold Law, entitled an "Act to Regulate the Currency," made both Hawaiian and American silver coins legal tender up to ten dollars. Other important provisions of the act, generally effective December 1, 1884, were:

Section 1. Gold coins of the United States were made the standard, and legal tender for all debts.

Section 3. Foreign coins (other than those of the United States) could be used only at bullion value for payments due the government.

Section 4. Whenever "equilibrium" between gold and silver coins in circulation was disturbed, the government was to replace sufficient silver with gold coins of the United States.

Section 5. All foreign silver coins (other than those of the United States) were to be exchanged at the treasury at par for Hawaiian silver coins within 60 days.[6] Redeemed coins were to be sold for gold.

Section 7. The treasury was to bear the loss on conversion of foreign silver.

Section 8. Silver certificates, except those of ten-dollar denomination, were redeemable at the treasury for *gold* coin of the United States. Redeemed certificates were to be canceled.

Section 10. The Coinage Act of 1880 and the Legal Tender Act of 1876 were repealed.[7]

A few days before passage of the gold law, Claus Spreckels, at his own request, addressed a meeting of the Chamber of Commerce on currency matters. He acknowledged that this was the first time he had ever spoken in public. "So please excuse all the mistakes," [8] he said. It was a rambling speech, followed by much spirited discussion. Spreckels' main purpose was to explain why he opposed the gold law. He hardly qualified as a monetary theorist but, considering the hard times in Honolulu, there were some germs of good sense in his remarks. He made it clear that he was an "easy" money man rather than a "sound" money man. He felt that the gold law, by contracting the money supply, would deepen the existing depression. He denied that the Kalakaua coinage had produced an excess of silver. He also denied the coinage was responsible for high exchange rates. Referring vaguely to the "law of supply and demand," he implied that the low price of sugar was an important factor in the foreign exchange problems.

Concerning the money supply and possible adverse effects of

getting on a gold basis, Spreckels said: "You have not got coin enough in this country. There are some who are crying about silver who would be very glad to get it to pay off their hands. Now, Gentlemen, are you doing a wise thing, upsetting the country and creating a panic as you certainly will. Look out that you do not knock somebody down and with him make someone fall who was leaning on him." [9] He did not favor the legal tender limit of ten dollars on Hawaiian and American silver dollars. He thought that these should be legal tender for any amount, although a limit of five or ten dollars should be placed on half dollars, quarters, and dimes.

Spreckels entered into a heated exchange with P. C. Jones of C. Brewer and Company, prominent sugar factors:

Mr. Jones. We have talked the matter over, and the Chamber of Commerce has decided it is better to run on a gold basis. If gold is demanded, we must sell the silver to buy gold.

Mr. Spreckels. I am sorry that you can't understand me better but as there is a touch of Dutch in the tongue, I suppose you can't. But I am going to get rid of you now, right here. By G-d, there is nothing but fair dealing in Claus Spreckels. Jones, my boy, you are looking out for your percentage when the gold is gone.[10]

A. F. Judd, chief justice of the supreme court, asked Spreckels if he was a bimetallist. Spreckels said: "I have no idea what I am, Judge, only I know I don't want to swamp the ship. You say that you want one million gold and one million silver, and I see that you are going to run the ship ashore." [11] Spreckels also had a verbal encounter with Theophilus H. Davies, head of a large British sugar agency in Hawaii.

Mr. Davies. Those people who have not got the gold will have to make provision for exchange. The point is, if the people have confidence enough there will be no serious difficulty. The law of legal tender does not change the ownership of money. . . . If I own $1,000,000 in gold, no law except a confiscatory law can take it out of my hands to pay other people's debts—unless I am willing to part with it.

Mr. Spreckels. Why Mr. Davies, you are becoming a monopolist; I did not think that of you, I thought you were a Christian.[12]

Toward the end of the meeting Spreckels, though still unconvinced of the merit of the gold law, indicated he would not oppose it. "I can see plainly," he added, "that I am not in accord with you but rest assured you will find that time will tell that the old man was right." [13] The meeting adjourned on a motion by C. R. Bishop, the banker. Little had been accomplished, except perhaps a catharsis of some of the bitter feeling for and against the gold law. The *Hawaiian Gazette* said of the meeting: "The solvers of the financial question of the day and the oracle which *was* to speak parted leaving a dim impression that they, as well as the question, were yet open to more convincing argument." [14]

The conservative hard money men in the community hoped to find a solution to the kingdom's monetary problems in the Gold Law. After passage of this law, however, controversy over the coinage continued. It had been charged that introduction of the Kalakaua coinage produced an excess of silver. Even after redemption of foreign silver many persons thought there was still an excess. The businessmen also charged the government with failure to carry out the Gold Law. There was ample justification for this charge, as will be seen below.

J. Mott Smith, on July 15, 1884, had made the following estimate of coin in the kingdom:

Silver in treasury and in banks (including $541,300 in Hawaiian silver)	$ 888,800
Hawaiian silver in circulation	458,700
Mixed coins in circulation	500,000
Total silver	$1,847,500
Gold in treasury, bank, and in circulation	$ 380,300
Total silver and gold	$2,227,800[15]

By December 31, 1884, approximately $525,000 in foreign silver had been redeemed, leaving $322,000 outstanding.[16]

A great difference of opinion developed about the amount of silver that should be kept in circulation. In early December, the Chamber of Commerce appointed a committee to recommend that the government reduce silver currency to $350,000 by converting part of the Hawaiian silver to gold.[17] This request was based on section 4 of the Gold Law. P. C. Jones, a prominent financier, thought that $400,000 would be about the right amount of silver. A "planter" was reported as saying that $600,000 would not be too much.[18]

The chamber memorial to the government calling for conversion of a large amount of Hawaiian silver into gold "was hardly practical," said the *Bulletin*, "since not a half-dozen merchants can be found of one mind as to what would be a sufficiency of silver to retain." [19] The *Gazette* said "a competent authority who has given much study to the question and knows its practical bearings" believed, as did Jones, that only $400,000 in silver should be in circulation. The editor added:

> It is all very well to complain that the "gold law" is at the bottom of the trouble—but that is complaining very much after the fashion of the sufferer from the gout, who having brought on his disease by high living, blames the medicine he takes as the cause of all his discomfort. Without thought for the future the Minister of Foreign Affairs greedily borrowed $1,000,000 in silver coin. We know perfectly well what was the result until the "gold law" medicine was taken; exchange ran up to eight and a half per cent, and there was still an upward tendency: directly the gold law came into operation down went exchange to a reasonable price. Unless steps are taken, exchange will go up again, for as long as we have so much silver in the country, it is bound to drive out the valuable coin.[20]

To settle the question whether there was too much silver, the *Bulletin* proposed that the government buy and sell silver coin freely at par for gold.[21] This the government was apparently either unwilling to do, or unable to do because it could not get enough gold in its coffers.

The Chamber of Commerce also complained about the government's failure to carry out the Gold Law. The chamber had resolved that effective December 1 (effective date of the Gold Law), its members "agree to receive and pay out [treasury] certificates of Deposit for all amounts over ten dollars as gold in all transactions among themselves and where practicable with others." [22] The *Bulletin* praised this action because it would "prevent an injurious run for the gold forming the security for our convenient paper currency." [23]

153

In mid-February, 1885, the chamber revoked this agreement, explaining its decision as follows:

1. At the end of November, 1884, there was $949,000 in certificates in circulation, backed by $600,000 in gold coin of the United States and $349,000 in mixed silver coin in the treasury.

2. Now, in mid-February, the certificates in circulation amounted to $584,000, backed by only $90,000 in gold coin of the United States, $456,000 in Hawaiian silver coin, and the balance in "uncanceled certificates."

3. The government had not taken any steps to convert Hawaiian silver to gold coin of the United States, in accordance with section 4 of the Gold Law.

4. The proportion of silver to gold in special deposits (backing the certificates) had so increased "as to make the redemption of certificates in U. S. gold as contemplated by the Currency Act of 1884 [Gold Law] impossible."

5. Certificates of deposit amounting to $75,000 had been redeemed with gold coin of the United States and reissued for silver coin, contrary to the Gold Law.[24]

The government also made payments in silver which under the law should have been in gold. This example of "law breaking," said the *Gazette*, was harmful to the small merchant or wage earner, since such persons were more or less compelled to accept silver, though they had to pay their large debts in gold. If they paid in silver this was acceptable only at a discount. "No one," the *Gazette* went on, "is to blame for this state of things save the Government and their patron. It is Mr. Spreckels' policy, it is their policy, to force . . . the 80¢ dollar on the community and put what profit they can into the monopolist's pocket." [25]

Besides paying out silver when it should have paid out gold, the government refused to accept silver. Post offices in Honolulu would not take the Kalakaua dollars for foreign money orders and country post offices would not accept the silver for drafts on Honolulu.[26] The *Bulletin* said it would support a movement to send the Kalakaua silver out of the country, and added: "The

secret of the whole difficulty is that we have a silver coinage current, bearing the image and superscription of the sovereign, which
is repudiated at the national treasury, because it is not worth as
much as it is marked . . . on the face." [27] It is clear that the government did not take appropriate action to establish the Hawaiian
silver at par. Continuing newspaper attacks also undermined confidence in the coinage.

Despite indecision by the government, not all persons were
convinced that the monetary troubles could be attributed solely
to the government or to Spreckels. A letter to the *Bulletin* signed
"Rellaw Rex" made some incisive comments on newspaper
statements that the Hawaiian silver was not worth face value:

> For the 30 years or more previous to this beautiful Gold Law, every coin
> —say French dollars, Bolivian (very bad) and Chile, South America, etc.,
> were taken and no word said, no growl raised, although everyone knew
> their [intrinsic] value was only 75 cents to 84 cents each. All at once it is
> discovered that U. S. gold coin was the only standard.
>
> .   .   .   .
>
> Is it not somewhat strange that so much objection is now made to our
> silver coins, which are exactly the same weight and fineness as the U. S.
> silver coins, when for all the 30 or 40 years before not a word was said about
> the coins of every kind that used to pass? It looks to me very like jealousy
> because the Hon. Claus Spreckels had something to do with it.[28]

Both the Claus Spreckels and Company bank [29] and William G.
Irwin and Company accepted the Kalakaua silver freely at par.
Moreover, they sold 60-day drafts on San Francisco for such
silver at a charge of only 1 per cent. The Bank of Bishop and
Company discounted silver at 20 per cent.

In San Francisco, Spreckels offered 95 cents for the Kalakaua
dollar. The *Gazette* said that, assuming a cost of 2 cents to bring
the coins back to Honolulu, Spreckels would still make a profit
of 3 cents on the transaction. This was an admission that the
coin could be circulated at par in Honolulu. Earlier, the *Gazette*
had denied this. On the Spreckels price of 95 cents in San Francisco, in the face of its claim that the coin was worth only 80
cents there, the newspaper said: " 'It is an ill bird that fouls its
own nest.' . . . We do not think that anyone can consider the

155

price paid by this firm as a criterion of the value of the Kalakaua dollar." [30] Some persons also thought that the action of the Spreckels bank and the Irwin company in accepting silver freely would hinder going onto a gold basis.[31]

The *Bulletin* said Spreckels' free acceptance of silver was a partial substitute for its recommendation that the government buy and sell silver freely at par.[32] That newspaper also called Spreckels' action "an act of relief in the present unhappy condition of the currency." [33] The *Advertiser* said: "[Spreckels] has faith in the country and . . . sees that the silver question is being made a handle of by the 'malignants' for party purposes and means of wounding the feelings of the King and hurting the reputation of his Ministers. . . . 'Give me your silver' he says, in effect. 'I am not afraid of it. You do not know what you are talking about when you tell me there is more silver money here than is needed.' " [34]

Whatever Spreckels' motives, his show of confidence in the silver boosted the confidence of wage earners and small merchants in it. They knew they could get rid of it for full value at Spreckels' bank or at Irwin Company. The *Advertiser* thought Spreckels was entitled to the thanks of the community for stepping in when other persons were creating something of a panic over the alleged excess of silver. "A certain number of persons look upon Mr. Gibson and the Colonel [Spreckels] as twin incarnations of Mephistopheles . . . and are momentarily expecting to find the gold in their own pockets and safes turned into Kalakaua dollars." [35]

As the temporary depression in Honolulu lifted, and the price of sugar gradually rose easing foreign exchange problems, controversy over the coinage died down. The silver remained in general circulation through the last years of the monarchy and through the regimes of the Provisional Government (1893–1894) and the Republic of Hawaii (1894–1898). In 1898, S. M. Damon, minister of finance of the Republic of Hawaii, reminded the Annexation Commission of the problem of the Hawaiian coinage.

He suggested "its withdrawal from circulation and substitution by a coin that would be legal tender in all parts of the United States." [36]

Despite this reminder, the Congress of the United States failed to act until 1903. Hawaii thus remained for a few years the only part of the United States where silver other than American circulated widely at par.[37] In 1903 A. N. Kepoikai, treasurer of the Territory of Hawaii, published a notice that "after the 1st day of January, 1904, the Silver Coins ... will, under an Act of Congress ... entitled 'An Act relating to Silver Coinage and Silver Certificates,' cease to be a legal tender in the Territory of Hawaii." [38]

Approximately $815,000 was redeemed at par for coins of the United States.[39] The balance of $185,000 had disappeared. Some of the coins were probably melted down in a large Chinatown fire in Honolulu in 1900. Others were taken away by tourists, went into the hands of collectors, or were used in the manufacture of brooches, pendants, cuff links, belt buckles, and other items. Jewelers invested in several thousand dollars worth of coin after the call for its redemption.[40]

The value of the Kalakaua silver to collectors has increased with passage of time. A complete set (dollar, half dollar, quarter, and dime), with a face value of $1.85 is worth about $100.00. King Kalakaua, once criticized for allowing his image and superscription on this "debased" coin, might well smile from his grave.

Finally, attention may be turned to an analysis of Spreckels' role in the coinage. The transaction was essentially a loan by him at a large discount. For about $500,000 in Kalakaua silver he received gold bonds of the kingdom. For much of the rest he received silver certificates.

How much merit was there in the objection that the profit on the transaction went to Spreckels? The credit of the government had been undermined, as already seen, by its own extravagance, and to a further extent by newspaper attacks and by the attacks of many businessmen. The government had to have money to meet current expenses. Failure to get the money would have further undermined the national credit. Floating a loan at par either at home or abroad was out of the question. Spreckels, the shrewd entrepreneur, merely took advantage of a market situation that his opponents had to a large extent created. Even in getting the loan at a discount, the kingdom could meet the practical problems of keeping the government going.

Only by a look at the earlier history of the Kalakaua regime can the violence of the attacks on the coinage be understood. When Kalakaua was elected in 1874 he had the support of the Honolulu business community. Its most prominent members were the secular descendants of the missionaries. The American segment of the community felt that Kalakaua was favorable to them and that he could be "controlled."

But the king acted with more force and independence than had been expected. Aligning himself with Gibson, he led a resurgence of Hawaiian nationalism. The businessmen (chiefly American and English) felt that this threatened their economic and political position. Although Spreckels had no particular interest in Hawaiian nationalism, he joined forces with Kalakaua and Gibson. He became the chief financial backer of the government. Spreckels' interests were mainly economic—the price of his financial backing was political favor that he could in turn use for economic ends. Though a businessman and a planter, he could remain largely independent of the rest of the Honolulu businessmen and of the planters. The reason for this was quite simple—he was a rich man.

Apart from certain legitimate objections to the Kalakaua coinage, the furor over it reflected the antipathy of the businessmen to Hawaiian nationalism, and also their general aversion to the Kalakaua-Gibson-Spreckels regime.

CHAPTER XV

Bank Bill
Shenanigans

When Spreckels first came to the Hawaiian Islands in 1876 he found only one bank, that of Bishop and Company. From time to time after it was started in 1858 there had been talk of another bank. Such talk grew during periods of depression and also after the Reciprocity Treaty, which stimulated the entire economy and increased the need for money and credit. In May, 1879, the *Hawaiian Gazette* reported rumors that San Francisco capitalists would start a new bank. Spreckels' name was not mentioned in these rumors.[1]

The *Gazette* said that a million dollars of additional banking capital could be profitably used in Honolulu. There was room enough for two banks. Bishop and Company was well managed but, with limited capital, it did not offer all the money needed. A new bank would help to enlarge the resources of the kingdom.[2]

For large financial needs Hawaiian planters often turned to San Francisco. In autumn, 1879, a group of capitalists from that city visited Honolulu. The planters arranged advances of $1,000,-000 on the current sugar crop of about 40,000 tons valued at $5,000,000. After this visit came more reports that another bank would soon be started in Honolulu.[3] Hope for relief from the tight money market lent credence to these reports. In April, 1883,

159

the *Gazette* reported the probable founding of another Honolulu bank under the auspices of the Anglo-California Bank of San Francisco. The president of that bank was F. F. Low, the former governor of California.[4]

Though there had been much talk of starting a new bank, the event occurred with unexpected suddenness in the midst of controversy over the Kalakaua coinage. On January 14, 1884, the day that the coin was first circulated, the bank of Claus Spreckels and Company opened as a partnership of Spreckels, Irwin, and Low.[5] One purpose of the company was to help circulate the new coin.

The first advertisement of the bank indicated that it would carry on a general banking and exchange business in the Hawaiian kingdom. Specific purposes were to make loans, buy and sell foreign exchange, receive deposits (both commercial and savings), and make collections. Offices of William G. Irwin and Company would house the bank until a new building could be erected. Irwin was to be the provisional manager.[6]

Reaction to the new firm was mixed but generally favorable. Kalakaua's attitude was probably expressed in a serenade to the bank by the Royal Hawaiian (government) band. A day after the opening the band played at the steamer "Mariposa's" departure. The band boys then marched from the Oceanic wharf to the offices of Irwin and Company, only a few blocks away. There was some speech making and toasts to the new bank. After playing a spirited number, the band boys were invited inside for some beer. Irwin also presented them with one hundred shiny Kalakaua half dollars. They accepted these with thanks and cheers.[7]

The stature of the partners in the firm got favorable notice in the newspapers. The combination of Spreckels, Irwin, and Low was a strong one, combining "financial experience, ability, and capital." Low and Spreckels would attract capital to Hawaii through their San Francisco connections. Low came in for special praise. Since he was president and manager of the Anglo-California Bank of San Francisco, his participation was "an earnest that the new venture is started on a basis that is commercially safe as well as financially sound." [8]

Not all comments on the Spreckels bank were favorable. The *Gazette* said the public would not be likely to benefit at once from the new bank. Nor would businessmen find the tight money market eased.[9] A few months later the *Bulletin* (Honolulu) said with doubtful logic: "The terrible shrinkage in the value of our staple product, the reduced income of the nation as a whole, and of most of the individuals comprised in it, is, singularly enough, coincident with the establishment of a new bank." [10] The editor also implied that the bank was flooding the country with cheap silver.

Spreckels' bank was a modest venture, but it whetted his appetite. After conferring with his friend Low, Spreckels decided to seek a charter in Hawaii for a national bank having the power to issue circulating notes. Drawn up by Spreckels and Low in San Francisco, the proposal was intended to provide a bank charter for the special benefit of the Spreckels group. Several prominent Honolulu businessmen, including the sugar king's partner, William G. Irwin, were induced to join in the scheme. Low brought the bill to Honolulu to help steer it through the legislature.[11] As a former governor of California he knew something of the ways of lobbyists. Moreover, he was the only member of the group with much banking experience.

The bill to charter the Hawaiian National Banking Corporation came to the attention of the legislature on May 20, 1884, when Cecil Brown announced he would introduce it. Brown was an active member of the opposition,[12] and thus presumably not one of the Spreckels crowd. The means used to get him to introduce the bill never came to light.

In the bill, the chief sections that were later attacked were these:

1. The proposed incorporators were named: Claus Spreckels, William G. Irwin, Frederick F. Low, Samuel Parker, James Campbell, Samuel G. Wilder, and Thomas R. Foster.[13]

4. Initial capital was to be $1,000,000, with the privilege of later doubling it. The charter was to be effective when $250,000, or 25 per cent of the capital, had been paid in.

6. Under this section the bank could issue circulating notes redeemable on demand, and could carry on many nonbanking activities. The company could acquire ships, lands, buildings, plants, machinery, and stock-in-trade, in Hawaii or elsewhere.

7. Bonds of the Hawaiian kingdom were to be deposited with the government up to the amount of the paid-in capital. The bonds were to serve as security for redemption of the circulating notes.

10. The notes were to circulate as money. They were to be legal tender for all debts, public and private, except for customs duties and principal and interest on the public debt.

14. The bank could redeem bonds deposited as security by surrendering a like amount of circulating notes.

17. The bank was to be exempt from tax, except for 1 per cent a year on the average amount of circulating notes outstanding, and except for taxes on real estate.

18. The bank could be designated as a government depositary and fiscal agent.

20. The government could use the pledged bonds to redeem circulating notes in case of default by the bank (failure for 90 days to redeem the notes), or sell such bonds for "lawful money." [14]

On May 31, Kalakaua, his chamberlain, Colonel Judd, and eight legislators were entertained aboard Spreckels' Oceanic liner "Alameda." These persons, the *Bulletin* charged, were shown the bank bill under an electric light "through a champagne lens." [15] The editor also reported rumors that Paul Neumann, attorney general, was to be attorney for the proposed national bank and was already drawing a salary from Spreckels. If he were attorney for Spreckels, asked the editor, how could he as attorney general give safe advice to the government? [16]

The *Gazette* said that the arch of monopoly had been raised; the keystone was to be the national bank. Now, not only would the refining and ocean transport of sugar be controlled, but inter-island traffic and all internal commerce would come under Spreckels' control. One man would dominate government finance and appointments to government offices. "We shall simply live here on sufferance at the pleasure of a monopoly with Claus Spreckels at its head." [17]

The *Pacific Commercial Advertiser* defended Spreckels. The sugar king had invested over $3,000,000 in the Spreckelsville plantation. By his investments he had given employment to thousands of persons in sugar. The editor also denied that Spreckels had kept other investors from coming in. "Who has held back the crowds of friendly investors who would come to these shores to invest their capital and compete with the crushing 'monopolist'? Surely not he who has provided the only class of superior and costly conveyance [Oceanic line] that is calculated to tempt the man of surplus means to come to our islands." [18]

The Honolulu Chamber of Commerce took the lead in official protests against the bank bill. Early in June the Chamber unanimously adopted a statement against the measure, and ordered it to be published. Among the objections were these: (1) The scope of the bank's business was too broad. (2) The circulating notes would become irredeemable paper currency. (3) Government bonds were not good backing for the notes. (4) The bank could lend at home or abroad without taking proper security. (5) Deposit of public funds in the bank would not be safe. (6) Directors did not have to be residents of the kingdom.[19]

Soon afterward the chamber got a detailed legal opinion on the bill from Edward Preston, a former attorney general. Among other things, Preston said that since the bank would be largely exempt from tax, the loss of revenue might force a higher general tax levy. Moreover, "the powers asked for might cause the formation of a monopoly of so dangerous a character as to prevent all outside competition." [20]

With Preston's opinion in hand, the chamber drew up a report condemning the proposal, and setting forth what a proper bank incorporation law should include. The business should be confined to banking, and the bank should not have the right to issue circulating notes. No tax preferences should be given. The bank should not serve as a government depositary. The term of the charter should be limited. Provision should be made for proper examination of the books, and semiannual statements should be published.[21]

The chamber resolved that the legal opinion and the report should be made the basis for a petition to the legislature. "Passage of the Bank Charter Bill," said the chamber, "would be fatal to our financial credit abroad, to our commercial prosperity at home, and ultimately to the national independence." [22] James I. Dowsett, a member of the Chamber of Commerce and also of the Hawaiian House of Nobles, read the petition on June 9 in the legislature.[23]

John T. Waterhouse, Sr., a well-known merchant, published in early June an open invitation to attend meetings at the Honolulu Lyceum to protest the bank bill. The sponsoring organization was given as the "Citizens Committee for Mutual Protection." The invitation stated that the bill was unconstitutional and would cause a revolution with loss of life and property. It was not really a charter for a bank, but for a "Universal Finance and Comprehensive Credit Company." It was contrived in San Francisco and was worse than the old South Sea Bubble.[24]

An overflow crowd came to the first meeting, at the Lyceum on June 7. Many persons stood in the halls or at the entrance. John Nott, the chairman, said he hoped the speakers would stick to the subject and not get personal. He called first on A. S. Hartwell. Hartwell said that money matters hit close to home for everyone. He did not believe in paper money and would oppose a bank issuing circulating notes "even in the hands of our trusted, conservative townsman, Mr. Bishop." "I believe in the hard coin," Hartwell went on, "and that of the best kind which for us is U. S. gold." [25]

As he sat down there were loud cries for Theophilus H. Davies, who "responded to the call." He said that once a bank charter were granted, no power in the kingdom could ever take it away.

Once in his school days, he said, he had played at banking with two of his chums. The currency was pins, and against this the boys issued notes. When they had taken all the pins, the boys shut up shop and divided them among themselves. That was the kind of thing that would happen if Honolulu permitted a bank to issue circulating notes.

Clarence Ashford next took the floor. He quickly brushed aside the chair's warning not to get personal. He said the monopolists behind the bank bill were "residents of California with a few local partners sufficient to give a sugar coating to the pill . . . but the pill is altogether too large and the coating too thin. They say 'You misjudge our motives,' but with one hand on your throat and another in your pocket, there is no time to ask what their motives are."

Ashford said the projectors of the bank bill were "veritable scoundrels," determined to push it through the legislature. "They do not carry their arguments in their heads, but in canvas bags, and we all know the result when the contents of those bags are spread before the legislators." [26] As Ashford sat down, loud cheers and stamping of feet rocked the building.

Representative Nawahi then spoke in Hawaiian, with William Halstead acting as interpreter. "If we want gold," said Nawahi, "we can have gold this night." The intruders behind the bill wanted to deprive the country of gold. They should be trussed up. He hoped that King David Kalakaua would act like the David of old in getting rid of these adventurers. All must help in the trouble about to come. G. W. Pilipo, the "Lion of North Kona," said everyone would suffer if the bank charter bill should pass. Even the throne would not escape.

Among the resolutions adopted at the meeting was one "that the proposed banking act has no public convenience or necessity in its favor, and is alike hostile to the Government and the people." [27] A committee was appointed to carry the resolutions about town for signature.

Another meeting at the Lyceum on June 23, 1884, resulted in a general indictment of the government. Charges of financial maladministration received special attention. A petition was drawn up requesting the king to dismiss the cabinet. The petition also charged that "a number of members of the Legislative Assembly . . . seem to have been so wrought upon by hidden influences that the will and voice of the people cannot find expression." [28]

At this meeting, J. O. Carter said that onlookers often see more of the play than those on stage. He was not fully aware of what was going on until he had "received two letters from California that the Bank Charter Bill has got to pass in its entirety, and that a gentleman at present in Honolulu [former governor, F. F. Low] carries enough votes in his pocket to pass it." Carter also said he had a letter from another writer in California that such a bill would be held unconstitutional there. To that writer it was really a bill to "confiscate the Hawaiian Islands." It had many provisions like those of "the Royal Charters of England which cost that country millions in money and much bloodshed."

Carter said it was up to the people to say whether the bank bill should pass. On this and other matters much of the language of the meeting hinted at revolution. Carter adjourned the meeting with the exhortation that there must be no shirking—"every man ought to stand up to the music and march to it." [29]

The *Bulletin* called on all persons to sign the petition, drawn up at the meeting, that the cabinet should be dismissed. If it were not, all the power of the government would be thrown behind the bank charter or behind a general government banking bill to accomplish the same purpose. "The whole strength of an unscrupulous administration will be given in favor of whatever its master, Claus Spreckels, chooses to direct. The cabinet must go." [30]

But the cabinet did not go. A motion of no confidence failed in the legislature. With their own votes, the ministers helped to keep themselves in office.[31] The petitioners were politely told that since there had been no vote of lack of confidence the king would not dismiss the ministry.

The bank bill, however, was already dying. Many other petitions against it appeared in the legislature.[32] On June 26, the bill was killed (technically, it was indefinitely postponed) by a vote of 35 to 2. So loud had been the outcries against it that even members of the cabinet dared not vote for it. All four of them— Gibson, Gulick, Kapena, and Neumann—voted to kill it.[33]

Even the *Advertiser*, which had earlier claimed that attacks on the bill were political and personal, said: "It was of so sweeping a nature, so thoroughly monopolistic, that no one with a spark of independence could have supported it." [34] The *Gazette* said: "The thing had so stank in the nostrils of the community that even the present brazen fore-headed Ministry, however much they might favor the measure, dared not, in the face of public opinion, countenance this iniquitous measure, so poor thing it died a very ignominious death." [35]

Before defeat of the bill, Governor Low, who had been trying to shepherd it through the legislature,[36] returned to San Francisco. On arrival, he told Spreckels the outlook for the scheme was dark. Spreckels told Low not to worry, "the bill was in good hands." The next steamer brought the news that it was already dead. This caused Spreckels to curse for half an hour. Then he took the next ship for Honolulu.

Spreckels reached Honolulu on July 8, in the middle of a fight over a second bank bill that had been drawn up and submitted to the legislature by the cabinet. This was labeled a General Banking Bill. Even while the first proposal was dying, the Spreckels forces cut loose from it. They pinned their hopes on this second bill. In fact, on the day the first proposal was indefinitely postponed (June 26), there had been a motion that it be considered together with a bill that the cabinet intended to introduce.[37]

The *Bulletin* charged that the same persons that had been behind the first bill were behind the second. They were merely shifting ground and pretending they would be satisfied with a general banking law permitting any group of persons to enter the banking business. A law coming from the same source as the old one would require "closest scrutiny." [38]

Reports came at the beginning of July that the cabinet bill would soon make its appearance. Minister of Finance Kapena introduced it on July 3 as "A Bill for the Establishment and Regulation of National Banks." By mid-July copies of the bill were available from the printing committee of the legislature. Free copies were also made available through Thrum's bookstore. The *Bulletin,* urging its readers to get copies, said it was the same "old iniquitous bill over again with the names left out, and a few changes made in the wording." [39] The *Gazette* charged that the hands behind the bill "are the hands of Esau [the cabinet], but the voice sounds uncommonly like that of Jacob [Spreckels]." [40]

With respect to note issue, deposit of government bonds as security, tax exemption, and service as a government depositary, the second bill was actually much the same as the first. Some attempt had been made, however, to meet objections to the first bill. The powers to engage in nonbanking business were somewhat less broad. Section 1 provided that charters under the act could be granted to *any* qualified group of not less than five persons. Sections 4 and 6 set forth a minimum capital stock of $500,000 of which 30 per cent had to be paid in at the start of business. Sections 32 and 34 provided for quarterly reports to the government and for examination of the bank by the government. Section 38 required that a majority of the directors be residents and citizens of the Hawaiian Islands.[41]

Attacks on the proposed measure echoed many of the objections to the first one. Especially vigorous was the assault on the provision for circulating notes. The *Bulletin* said that the people of Hawaii wanted a bank for issuing paper money about as much as residents of the nether regions wanted a powder magazine.[42] A. S. Hartwell, in a letter detailing objections to the bill, said that to permit a bank to issue paper money would be ruinous. No one wanted such money except the persons behind this bank.

Experience in the United States with wildcat banks should be a warning against note issue.[43]

Another objection was that the minimum capital of $500,000 was too high. Although the bill claimed to be a general one, only the moneyed Spreckels crowd, said Hartwell, would be able to qualify. He pointed out that the United States National Bank Act required a minimum capital of $100,000, or $200,000 in districts of over 50,000 population.[44]

As already mentioned, Spreckels arrived in Honolulu early in July, after introduction of this second bank bill. Soon after his arrival the *Gazette* criticized the Spreckels monopoly, his meddling in government, and the man himself. The editor charged that Spreckels had intended to reduce all interests in the kingdom to subservience to his own with his national bank bill. He kept in office "a weak, not to say corrupt Ministry, against the expressed wishes and interests of the vast majority of the best people in the country." [45] The editor continued: "He has found most people with whom he comes in contact either weak or corrupt, and always selfish. He uses them to suit his purposes, which is all that they are good for. Those who approach him with hypercritical, high-toned professions get their measure taken every time. They have their price, and are either purchased and used, or kicked to one side." [46]

It did not take Spreckels long to realize it would not profit him much to support the cabinet bank bill. With his large investments in Hawaii, he did not want to antagonize merchants, planters, and other potential customers of his bank further.[47]

Members of the Chamber of Commerce handled the situation rather cleverly by allowing the sugar magnate to save face. They invited him to address the chamber on July 11 on currency matters. At the meeting Spreckels said he had not known that the national bank bill (the first one) was so bad. He had read it over only once.[48] At another meeting of the chamber on July 16, Spreckels said he would not support the government bank bill (the second one), but would yield to the wishes of the chamber. Theo. H. Davies, Paul Isenberg, C. R. Bishop, and Spreckels were appointed to draw up a new proposal (the third one).[49] The chamber accepted the bill drawn up by this committee and made plans to present it to the legislature. The bill did not provide for banks to issue circulating notes or to act as public depositaries.[50]

Spreckels thus left the ministers in the lurch. They had drawn up the government bill as a face-saving gesture for him when it became clear that the first measure was doomed. Now they had this second bill, which they had recommended, on their hands. It had no chance of passing because of the action by the chamber and by Spreckels. Of him the *Bulletin* now said: "A foreigner, who is not even a voter, comes down here, and dictates who shall rule over us and what laws shall be made for us. Mr. Spreckels makes the statement in public that 'I can make Cabinets and I can break Cabinets,' and the worst of it is that it is true." [51]

Paul Isenberg, a member of the House of Nobles, introduced the chamber bill on July 23. The title was amended to read "An Act to Provide for the Incorporation of Banking Companies." The government bill was largely ignored and indefinitely postponed.[52] After some minor amendments, the chamber measure was passed in final form on August 4 and Kalakaua signed it one week later. [53]

Generally known as the "Banking Law of 1884," the act met most of the objections to the two earlier bills. It also met most of the requirements set forth in the chamber petition of early June. The law did not sanction circulating note issue. Any bank incorporated under it could not serve as a government depositary. Significantly, in view of the earlier controversy, section 26 said: "The corporation shall not undertake . . . any commercial, agricultural, manufacturing or common carrier business." [54]

So ended the battle of the bank bills. The Banking Law of 1884 became a long-lived law. Both of the largest banks in the islands today were incorporated under its provisions: the Bank of Hawaii in 1897 and the Bank of Bishop and Company (now First National Bank of Hawaii) in 1919.[55] Though amended from time to time, the 1884 law was not superseded until the Hawaii Bank Act of 1931 was passed.

Spreckels himself turned his back on the 1884 law that he had helped to spawn. It regulated incorporation of banks but did not *require* that banks incorporate. As we shall see, Spreckels and Irwin in 1885 opened the second bank of Spreckels and Company as a partnership rather than a corporation.

The national bank bill recalls the wildcat banks of a somewhat earlier period in the United States. Wide discussion of the bill focused attention on the money and banking problems of the kingdom. During the controversy it became clear that there was a shortage of bank credit. The controversy produced a banking law that served Hawaii for 47 years. The national bank bill also showed the magnitude of Spreckels' design for power in Hawaii. The resulting furor directed attention to the extent of his monopoly and of his influence in government. It aroused fears that this monopoly and influence would be enlarged. Much of the latent enmity to Spreckels as a mainland interloper came out into the open. With defeat of the bill, Spreckels suffered the first serious setback in his climb to power in the kingdom.

CHAPTER XVI

The Second
Spreckels Bank

The national bank bill controversy did little to endear the Spreckels bank to the Honolulu community. After defeat in that struggle, there were rumors that Spreckels, Irwin, and Low would not continue with the bank they had founded as a partnership early in 1884. The Hawaiian *Gazette* reported that the new building, under construction on Fort Street between Queen and Merchant streets, would be occupied solely by William G. Irwin and Company.[1] Noting that the front of the building was being painted green, the *Bulletin* (Honolulu) said: "Having been denied the privilege of putting forth greenbacks [by defeat of the bank bill] the new bank has put on a green front."[2]

Expectations that the firm of Spreckels and Company would close its doors increased with the reports in late October, 1884, that Low, one of the partners, had sailed from San Francisco for China on a proposed one-year trip around the world.[3] It was also reported he was in failing health and had been forced to give up all business matters for the time being.

The following notice of dissolution soon appeared:

BANKING NOTICE

The firm heretofore existing under the name of Spreckels & Co. is dissolved by mutual consent.

The banking business will hereafter be conducted by Wm. G. Irwin & Co.

Claus Spreckels
F. F. Low
Wm. G. Irwin[4]

Honolulu November 1, 1884

In effect, the business was merely continued with Spreckels and Irwin as partners. In its interim operation of the bank, Irwin and Company assisted the government in carrying out the Gold Law of 1884. The firm helped to avoid a run on gold by accepting Kalakaua silver and government silver certificates at par. It also sold foreign exchange on San Francisco at a discount of only 1 per cent for silver and aided the government in calling in silver coins other than those of Hawaii and the United States, as required by the Gold Law.[5]

In December, 1884, Irwin and Company moved to its new quarters on Fort Street, across from its former location. Part of the new building was given over to banking operations. In fact, this was the building that would have been the "Hawaiian National Bank" if the Spreckels bank bill had passed.

The interim operation of the bank by Irwin and Company, a sugar agency, was clearly a somewhat makeshift arrangement. In its review of the year 1884, the *Pacific Commercial Advertiser* complained that because of the bank bill fight, "in which quite a number of our businessmen were led by their noses by a few interested parties and cliques of demagogues," Spreckels and Company had not continued their bank and many people had thereby been inconvenienced.[6] There can be little question that a new bank was needed.

In late January, 1885, there were rumors that a combination of British and local interests would found a bank. These rumors reflected a continuing awareness of the shortage of bank credit and a hope that the shortage would soon be ended. "As the trade of the Kingdom has about trebled within the past three years," said the *Bulletin*, "there is room for another banking house. It certainly does not look as if financial despondency had seized the community, when many of its leading capitalists are ready . . . to embark in an enterprise of so great financial responsibility." [7] Any hope, however, that a bank would be started by other than the Spreckels interests was not to be fulfilled.

Soon came reports that Spreckels and Company would be back in business. It would open on April 15, 1885, with deposits secured by a pledge of bonds with the government and it was said that Paul Neumann would be legal adviser to the new firm.[8] The bank did not open on April 15 as expected but a notice appeared that it would open on May 4.[9]

The reopening of the bank was hailed as "the beginning of a new era of progress and development in Honolulu"; an "important signal advance upon existing banking facilities." [10] Establishment of the firm in the midst of business depression would tend to restore confidence among all classes in the community.[11] In what was clearly intended as a comment on earlier conservative banking practices in Honolulu, the *Advertiser* said:

Banks are at once the servants and directors of commerce. Without their aid and friendly co-operation, it would be impossible to initiate and successfully carry out any of the great enterprises which form so marked a feature of modern industrial development. . . . But there is quite as much evil to be apprehended from a narrow and exclusive banking policy as there is in speculative banking. In the latter case the evil soon cures itself, and the injury is apparent. In the former case the evil is not disclosed in any special way. . . . This kind of banking produces what may be described as commercial mildew, which can only be removed by the attrition produced through healthy competition and a more discriminating intelligence. It is as bad for a bank as it is for a community in which it does business, to be hide-bound by prejudice or paralyzed by timidity.[12]

As security for deposits, the partners of Spreckels and Company pledged $200,000 in Hawaiian government bonds with the minister of finance. The bonds were to be returned whenever the bank ceased to do business and 90 per cent of the deposits had been repaid.[13] Interest at 5 per cent a year was allowed on savings up to $2,000. Larger amounts were subject to special agreement. Interest was payable only on amounts left with the bank for at least three months. Savings were repayable in either gold or silver, depending on the original deposit. Commercial deposits, on which checks could be drawn, were accepted, and these too were re-corded in separate gold and silver accounts.[14]

The *Advertiser* greeted the opening of the new bank thus:

Monday, May 4, 1885, should be a Red Letter day in Hawaiian chronology. It was a day of financial emancipation and deliverance. For the first time in the history of the Kingdom every man had a banking option; that is, every one was in a position to decide for himself how he should dispose of his money, outside the barren and unprofitable recourse of "burying it in a napkin." This had been their only recourse of late years [because the bank of Bishop and Company did not pay interest on savings deposits].

. . . .

The new bank has given sufficient security to depositors. . . . It is by means of just such institutions that all new countries are built up, but uninterrupted expansion is impossible under the banking system heretofore in vogue here.

The large number of depositors in the savings department of the new bank yesterday proved that the people appreciated the opportunity for profitable and secure investment presented to them. Their Majesties the King and Queen were the first depositors, and having inspected the spacious banking premises they left full of expressions of good will toward the new institution. But it was not royalty alone who marked their appreciation of what had been done. Every class and rank in society had its representatives among the depositors. . . . Henceforward "old stocking banking" is at an end in Honolulu.[15]

The *Gazette* greeted the new bank somewhat less enthusiastically. "The new savings bank, . . . which is so elaborately advertised in the editorial columns of a contemporary, opened its doors for business on May 4." The editor noted that "the long promised (or threatened) bank" was not established under the Banking Law of 1884. It was only a partnership, whereas that law regulated incorporation of banks. Another criticism was that the new institution was not in harmony with the public interest because its projectors were not in favor of a gold currency. "Self respect will not allow us to abate one jot or tittle of our deliberated judgment that a silver currency is not for the public welfare." [16]

In reply to attacks by the *Advertiser* on the previous monopoly of the Bishop bank and characterization of its methods as "old stocking banking," the *Gazette* said: "When it comes to the question of whether the bank of Messrs. Bishop & Co. has been of great service to the community in times of its direct need, there we do not hesitate to join in the common expression of highest appreciation of its services." [17]

The *Saturday Press* derided Spreckels and Company's deposit of $200,000 in bonds with the government as a trick to deceive depositors. If this were so, retorted the editor of the *Advertiser*, let the Bishop bank play the same trick by making a similar pledge of bonds. If Bishop did not do so, the public could draw its own conclusions.[18]

The opening of the Spreckels bank forced the Bishop bank to resume payment of interest on savings accounts. On May 13, Bishop and Company published a notice that interest would be paid at the rate of 5 per cent a year on individual savings accounts of $500 or less. Interest would be paid only on amounts continuously on deposit for at least three months. On deposits over $500 the rate of interest would be subject to special agreement.[19]

Competition between the two banks brought about lower interest rates on loans and reduced exchange charges. The *Advertiser* said that Spreckels had killed "twelve per cent interest" on loans. The Bishop bank had sold exchange on San Francisco for silver at a discount of 20 per cent.[20] The new bank sold such exchange at par for Hawaiian silver or silver certificates. Some in the community complained that this free acceptance of silver would hinder getting on a gold basis.[21]

In the political campaign for the legislature of 1886, J. O. Carter of the Independents (opposition) charged that $500,000 to $1,000,000 had left the country because its owners had no faith in the government. The *Advertiser* retorted that this was only a half-truth. "He [Carter] did not say it was money his 'twelve per cent' friends could not any longer put out at usury . . . because the much-abused 'great man from San Francisco' had introduced millions which the people could borrow at living rates." He had freed the people "from the grinding tyranny of usury . . . —12 per cent compounded quarterly." [22]

There can be little doubt that by pursuing bold policies the Spreckels bank forced the conservative, well-managed Bishop bank to adopt bold policies to meet the competition. This created a banking atmosphere suitable to Hawaii's expanding economy in the postreciprocity boom. Despite the boom, the years 1884 and 1885 were years of temporary depression. The Spreckels bank helped to restore business optimism because it brought hope of outside capital during these depression years, and because it reflected the confidence of Spreckels himself in Hawaii's future.

In later years, the memories of the bitter controversy over the Spreckels bank, and over the Kalakaua coinage and the national bank bill, became dim. The firm established itself solidly in the financial and commercial life of Honolulu. As a partnership of Spreckels and Irwin, the bank carried on through the last years of the monarchy and through the early years of Hawaii as a territory of the United States. In 1908, 23 years after its founding, the partnership of Claus Spreckels and Company was automatically dissolved by the death of Spreckels in San Francisco.

Irwin bought out the Spreckels' interest from his estate, and continued the bank as sole owner through May, 1910.[23] On June 1, 1910, the bank was incorporated as the Bank of Honolulu, Ltd. Capital stock of $600,000 was issued, 6,000 shares of par 100. Irwin held 5,920 shares and the following persons 10 shares each: E. I. Spalding, G. C. Potter, W. M. Giffard, R. Ivers, J. M. Dowsett, Paul Muhlendorf, H. F. Lewis, and J. D. McInerny.[24]

Irwin, the nominal manager of Claus Spreckels and Company throughout its existence, became president of the Bank of Honolulu. Its location was the same as that of the Spreckels bank, on Fort Street and few changes were made, either in personnel or mode of operation. The name of Claus Spreckels and Company was scraped from the windows and replaced by that of the Bank of Honolulu.[25] Another reminder of Spreckels' once great power in Hawaiian affairs had passed from the scene.

A few years later, in 1914, Irwin died in San Francisco. His estate continued as the main stockholder in the Bank of Honolulu until 1919. The stock was then sold to a group of Honolulans:

J. M. Dowsett, Jno. Waterhouse, E. H. Wodehouse, H. Holmes, and A. N. Campbell.[26] On March 31, 1920, the Bank of Bishop and Company, Ltd., bought the assets of the Bank of Honolulu which had been dissolved. The firm which, as Claus Spreckels and Company, had been started 35 years before to compete with the only existing bank, Bishop and Company, was thus taken over by that very bank.

CHAPTER XVII

London Loan:
Original Loan Act

Toward the end of 1885, candidates for the Hawaiian legislature were waging a no-holds-barred campaign. The Independents, opponents of the "palace party," charged corruption and extravagance in government. Among the chief targets were Spreckels and Gibson, and the cabinet controlled by them. Spreckels' alleged baleful influence in the government came under a heavy barrage.

William Kinney of the Independents said it was "one man beyond the sea" who was the real issue of the coming (1886) session: "He placed himself here some years ago like a tree and at first overshadowed a few merchants, but since that time the tree has grown until it now overshadows the Kingdom, the Government and the throne itself." [1] Kinney recalled how Spreckels ousted the cabinet in 1878 over the Maui water rights, how he secured the passage of an act in 1882 to alienate the crown lands of Wailuku, and how he got the contract for the silver coinage in 1884. Kinney said that the bank charter act which Spreckels had failed to push through the legislature of 1884 "was in fact a prison house for this kingdom." [2]

Lorrin A. Thurston, also a candidate on the Independent ticket, said that Kinney had presented the big question of the times:

"Are we to act for ourselves and make our own laws, or are we to be led like swine with rings in our noses, at the will of a man who cares for nothing but his own interest?" [3] He claimed he had heard Spreckels boast he could buy any legislature that could be elected and called for the election of candidates who could not be bought.

At a political meeting in mid-January, 1886, Thurston compared the interference of Spreckels in the government with that of a genie let out of a bottle by the greed of the finder. "When let out of the bottle he filled the whole land and his exactions were interminable." [4] He also referred to the 1878 midnight cabinet dismissal over the Maui water rights; to Spreckels' acquisition of the plains of Wailuku, though this, said Thurston, had been properly a judicial matter; to abetments of Spreckels by Gibson "and the pay Gibson had had thereof"; and to the "nefarious National Bank Bill . . . which would have been the grave of the Hawaiian people." He urged the people to be ever watchful of Spreckels' "encroachments and machinations." [5]

Reports of the sugar king's influence in Hawaii also had some international repercussions. In March, 1886, hearings were being held in Washington on a resolution to abrogate the Reciprocity Treaty between Hawaii and the United States. At these hearings, the adventurer Celso C. Moreno, who had been practically ejected from Hawaii in 1880, made a wild and distorted statement about Hawaiian affairs. Nevertheless, as far as his assessment of Spreckels' role in the kingdom was concerned, the statement contained some truth. Moreno said that Spreckels was virtually the ruler of Hawaii. [6]

Hawaiian Minister H. A. P. Carter testified at the same hearings. Congressman Mills of Texas asked him what influence Spreckels had in the Hawaiian government. "None whatever," [7] answered Carter. He knew that reports of Spreckels' role in Hawaii were giving the opponents of reciprocity a powerful argument for doing away with the treaty. His statement was that of a diplomat trying to serve his country, but it was too much for the *Hawaiian Gazette*. "It surely must have been a reporter's error which makes Mr. Carter say that Claus Spreckels wields no influence over the Hawaiian cabinet," said the editor. "He wields and has wielded a very powerful influence, and it is not possible to deny the fact." [8] J. H. Wodehouse, British commissioner at Honolulu, wrote it was common knowledge that Spreckels was a kind of dictator to the Hawaiian government. He said the Carter statement that Spreckels had no influence was "extraordinary."[9]

Spreckels' influence in the Hawaiian cabinet rested mainly on his relationship with Premier Gibson. He held a $35,000 mortgage on Gibson's Lanai ranch.[10] More broadly, his influence in the government was based on loans to King Kalakaua and to the kingdom. It will be recalled that Spreckels had launched his Hawaiian career with a $40,000 loan to Kalakaua at the time the Maui water rights were granted. By the beginning of 1886 Spreckels was the chief creditor of the kingdom and held $700,000 of the total public debt of $1,300,000.

Kalakaua, tiring of Spreckels' dictation, sought a loan in London to pay him off. Kalakaua also felt that creditors at so great a distance would not trouble themselves about the internal affairs of the kingdom.[11] Gibson soon found himself in a cross fire between Kalakaua and Spreckels over the proposed London loan. The premier was anxious to avoid the king's displeasure; however, he was also under obligation to Spreckels and felt he needed his continued support. Spreckels, with extensive business interests in Hawaii, wanted a stable and solvent government and therefore urged economy on Kalakaua. If this failed, Spreckels wanted at least to prevent loans from any source except himself.

In his speech at the opening of the legislative session on April 30, 1886, Kalakaua indicated he was in favor of a loan. He said that estimated revenues would be sufficient to meet current operating expenses, but added: "At the same time there will be presented for your consideration enterprises of an exceptional and important character, such as immigration and works of national importance, which can only be properly carried out by the use of the credit of the nation." [12] The king made no mention of possible sources from which the loan might come.

Referring to the king's speech, Gibson on May 4 gave notice of the government's intention to introduce a loan bill for the following purposes:

Immigration	$350,000
Waterworks	200,000
Sewage system	100,000
Wharves	100,000
Dredging Honolulu harbor	50,000
Roads and Bridges	75,000
Total	$875,000

At this time nothing was said of provision for redemption or refunding of outstanding debt, which was around $1,300,000.[13] As introduced by Gibson about ten days later, the bill provided for borrowing not more than $2,000,000: $900,000 for immigration and public improvements, and an unspecified sum to redeem or refund the outstanding debt, presumably not more than $1,100,-000 for this purpose.[14] The loan bill came up for second reading early in June, and was referred to a special committee on a motion by Thurston.[15]

Behind the scenes there was to be a lot of pulling and hauling over the question of a loan. Spreckels gave an elaborate party aboard the Oceanic liner "Australia" at the end of May.[16] It is reasonably clear that the purpose of this party was to create the proper mood for Spreckels to make his wishes known to the legislators on the proposed loan and also on other matters. For example, the contributions of Spreckels' Oceanic steamship line to the prosperity of Hawaii were extolled. The subsidy paid to the line by the Hawaiian government would soon be up for debate in the legislature.

At this party, Spreckels made one of the few public speeches he ever made in Honolulu. His theme was "economy." He said he "liked the country, the climate, and the people. The people are mild, generous, and open. But they have one fault—they are extravagant. Take my advice—practice economy, be independent, have money in the bank, and care for nobody."[17] Hardly anyone could have missed the point. Spreckels' plea for economy in general was an indirect but unmistakable call for economy in the government.

The point of the speech was not lost, even on the king. On June 21, Kalakaua sent a special message to the legislature: "Impressed with the necessities of the economical carrying out of the expenditures of the Kingdom, and for prudential considerations of State, it is My earnest desire that your honorable body take every step toward retrenchment of public expenditures."[18] It is doubtful that the king had his heart in this message. It was sent under pressure from Spreckels.[19]

On June 29 the Hawaiian cabinet suddenly resigned. It was replaced the next day by another in which Gibson was the only holdover member. The change was as follows: Walter M. Gibson, Premier and Minister of the Interior, vice Charles T. Gulick; Robert J. Creighton, Minister of Foreign Affairs, vice Walter M. Gibson; Paul P. Kanoa, Minister of Finance, vice J. M. Kapena; John T. Dare, Attorney General, vice Paul Neumann.[20] Creighton and Dare were recently arrived California friends of Spreckels.

The newspapers expressed strong dissatisfaction with both the suddenness of the change and the failure of the government to explain it. The old cabinet had a majority, none of their measures had been defeated in the legislature, there had been no vote of lack of confidence. Said the *Bulletin* (Honolulu): "The people being kept in the dark are naturally dissatisfied and suspicious of covert designs."[21] One Spreckels cabinet had indeed been replaced by another.

It was widely rumored, but never proved, that the reason for the cabinet shift was that Spreckels wanted to get control of the waterworks, wharves, harbor, and other public utilities by means of long-term leases. These would serve as security for outstanding loans and also as a condition precedent to new loans by him.

Though largely under his influence, the former cabinet was said to have demurred.[22]

It was charged that the cabinet shift had been dictated by Spreckels in advance. Creighton had come to the islands at Spreckels' behest, and was whiling away his time as editor of the *Pacific Commercial Advertiser* until he should be called to the cabinet post. He had taken out "letters of denization" on June 29, the day before the shift.[23] The *Gazette* said that Dare, too, had come to Honolulu with the promise by Spreckels of a cabinet post. He had not come as a tourist, and yet as a lawyer he had no apparent business in the courts of Honolulu. Spreckels as the man who pulled the strings "had arranged this little shuffle of the knaves in the pack to suit himself." Then he left for Maui so he could say the change took place while he was away minding his own business.[24]

Hawaiians and long-time foreign residents could hardly rejoice about the appointment of two newcomers. As the *Gazette* said: "Why should aliens be imported to rule over us? . . . Why should we have the sweepings . . . of Mr. Spreckels' sugar refinery? This Cabinet is not made for the good of the country, but to please him and help him get back his money. . . . Let us squarely confess that a foreigner can do as he pleases with the Cabinet, and let the Hawaiians . . . acknowledge that an alien master of an alien cabinet is to rule their destinies." [25]

Charges like these, implying that Spreckels was the real ruler of the islands, must have been more and more disturbing to Kalakaua. These things had been said before, but hardly so openly and so bluntly. British Commissioner Wodehouse wrote to the foreign office: "It is useless now for Mr. Gibson to talk about the independence of the . . . Kingdom. The King is no longer a free agent but entirely in the hands of Mr. Gibson and Mr. Spreckles [*sic*]. Mr. Spreckels goes about saying he is the real King as the Govt. owe him money which they cannot apparently pay, and that he has a right to remove Ministers if he chooses. If he is not a King Maker he is certainly a Cabinet Maker." [26]

Rumors that Spreckels was trying to get control of certain

public utilities, as security for loans made by him, became so insistent that Representative Kalua introduced a resolution asking Gibson to report on the truth of these rumors.[27] Representative Dole said the resolution was not complete. One of the most intelligent men in town had told him that Spreckels was also trying to get a 99-year lease of Honolulu harbor. This might be incredible, said Dole, but "where there was a great deal of smoke there must be a little fire." [28]

Representative Kaulukou disagreed with Dole: "It appeared that the name of Spreckels was a great bugbear, the mention of which was as the mention of some evil spirit. Everybody seemed to be afraid of Mr. Spreckels and to regard him as having a large mouth that gobbled up everything." The two main planks of the Independents at the recent election had been "the bad qualities of Mr. Spreckels and the bad qualities of Mr. Gibson." Much of this, thought Kaulukou, was just jealousy.[29]

Gibson said he was sorry to see the time of the house taken up with matters such as this. Calling the rumors ridiculous, he argued against any formal action on the resolution. The resolution was indefinitely postponed.[30]

The Independents continued to criticize Creighton and Dare. These two persons became convenient targets for indirect attacks on Spreckels. Thurston charged that Dare wore Spreckels' collar, and that he had been Spreckels' attorney in both California and Hawaii.[31] A few days later Dare admitted on the floor of the legislature that he had been so employed.[32] Of Creighton, Thurston said he worshipped the dirt on which Spreckels walked.[33] The *Gazette* called Creighton "a twenty-four hour denizen manufactured to order." [34]

On August 12, Gibson defended the selection of Creighton and Dare. At the same time, he felt it necessary to extol the abilities of the Hawaiians, because he had always claimed to be their champion. He pointed out that more and more of them were getting public offices and said that one day he hoped to see a Hawaiian on the supreme court of the kingdom.

If Gibson had such love for the Hawaiians, asked Representative Dickey, why had he appointed two newcomers to the posts of minister of foreign affairs and attorney general? Gibson answered that the cabinet choices were his in name only. Really, Kalakaua had made the selection, but he "heartily concurred in His Majesty's choice." [35]

Thurston asked if Gibson meant "His Majesty Kalakaua or His Majesty Spreckels." Gibson said this was an insulting remark. Mr. Spreckels was an honorable gentleman and had nothing to do with the selection of the cabinet.[36]

Claus Spreckels himself, the subject of so much controversy in the legislature and elsewhere, left on July 31 for San Francisco by the steamer "Australia." Apparently the sugar king was undisturbed by the gathering storm over his own alleged malevolent influence and over the loan act. On the surface all was well. King Kalakaua, Princess Liliuokalani, Governor Dominis, Creighton, and Gibson came down to the wharf to see the ship off. "Wreaths of flowers and sweet-scented leaves entwined . . . the necks and shoulders of most of the passengers. . . . The Royal Hawaiian Band . . . played the steamer off in lively style." [37]

As Spreckels left he probably felt reasonably secure about Hawaiian affairs. He had induced Kalakaua to send an economy message to the legislature. He had the assurance of Gibson that a loan would not be made.[38] He had three of his henchmen—Gibson, Creighton, and Dare—in the cabinet.

Spreckels' departure was an act of confidence, but he may have suspected that there was going to be trouble. Before he left, he said to an unnamed gentleman: "You are glad at the idea of getting rid of me, but you will probably very soon wish me back again." [39] Wodehouse wrote the foreign office in London that, in the absence of Spreckels, the king and Gibson would likely go back to their free-spending ways if they could raise the money.[40]

It appears that Spreckels' departure was a great tactical blunder in his campaign for economy in government and for preventing loans from anyone except himself. As his steamer headed for San Francisco, another bearing H. R. Armstrong was on its way to

Honolulu. Armstrong was a member of a London syndicate that hoped to float a Hawaiian loan. The ships passed each other in mid-ocean.

In Hawaii, the idea of borrowing in London had been under consideration late in 1885, and possibly earlier. Gibson wrote to Abraham Hoffnung in March, 1886, replying to his letters of November 18, 1885, and January 9, 1886 (Hoffnung was a member of the London firm of A. Hoffnung and Company which had acted as Hawaii's agent for Portuguese immigration):

"Your suggestions as to putting a loan for this country on the London Market have received consideration on the part of my colleagues and will have their due weight in influencing the decisions that may be come to. ... In view of the present strength of the Government and the manifest approval by the people of its policy we contemplate more than one new and important departure." [41]

In July, Hoffnung wrote Gibson that H. R. Armstong would soon visit Hawaii for a conference about the proposed loan. Armstrong was a partner in the firm of Skinner and Company, successors to A. Hoffnung and Company. Hoffnung wrote to Gibson:

"You are aware ... that I have had this loan undertaking in view for some time. Messrs. Skinner & Co. and I in conjunction with others who are themselves wealthy and have great influence in the financial world now believe that the time is ripe." Hoffnung wrote further of Armstrong: "You will be in experienced and intelligent hands and you may accept my assurance that no hands could be safer or more responsible." [42]

What was happening to the loan bill, meanwhile, in the legislature? Immediately after the arrival of Armstrong, Gibson did an about-face. He said in the legislature on August 11 that he was not in favor of borrowing "except in the ordinary way from the moneyed men of the country." Representative Castle was glad to hear that the minister was not now in favor of borrowing. But how was he going to raise money from domestic sources without a loan act? Thurston said that at that time he did not know whether he was a government man or not. For once, he and Gibson were seeing eye-to-eye. Thurston was pleased that no loan bill was going to be brought in.[43]

Why did Gibson change his mind about a loan? Now there was someone else in the field (Armstong) besides the person who had previously had everything his own way (Spreckels). When the loan was to come from the person who pulled the cabinet strings, it was a good thing. But when it looked as if it might be placed elsewhere, Gibson had some second thoughts about borrowing,[44] even though he had had a hand in the preliminary overtures to London.

Gibson vacillated on the question of a loan and where it was to come from. He was pushed in different directions by the wishes of Kalakaua and Spreckels, and by his own designs for power. He had given assurances to Spreckels before his departure that no loan would be made.

As Wodehouse wrote to the British Foreign Office: "[Gibson] does not on the one hand wish to encourage it [a loan in London] on account of his promise to Mr. Spreckels, and on the other hand he dare not oppose it because to do so would be to incur the King's displeasure, and the loss of his present position." Wodehouse added that Spreckels' followers were furious at the idea of a loan from anyone except him. But Kalakaua was determined to rid himself of American control, whatever the consequences.[45]

Now a person was on the scene with proposals that might free the kingdom from debts owed to Spreckels. On Saturday, August 7, Armstrong had arrived in Honolulu on the "Alameda"[46] and no time was lost in introducing him to King Kalakaua. George Macfarlane, a prominent businessman in Hawaii, presented him on Monday morning.[47] Spreckels was not around to prevent the king from listening attentively to Armstrong's proposals.

During his stay, Armstrong was greatly entertained by Kalakaua, and in turn entertained him. The Saturday after his arrival a *luau* was given in Armstrong's honor at the king's boathouse. "A number of speeches were made in which the future of

Hawaii was somewhat foreshadowed." [48] The king also gave a lavish breakfast for Armstrong at the palace. A few days later he was honored with a band concert at the Hawaiian Hotel. Afterwards, he was host at a supper for the king and twenty guests. [49]

Upon Armstrong's arrival in Honolulu, the *Gazette* had reported that the purpose of his visit was "to extend commercial and financial relations with this Kingdom." [50] He proposed to estimate the borrowing capacity of the islands and work up preliminary matters on a London loan. He would then go back to England to complete organization of an underwriting syndicate. He hoped the syndicate would pay him for his trouble and also give him a share of the profits. Because Armstrong felt he needed assistance in getting the loan bill through the legislature, he joined forces with George Macfarlane who was a natural choice. [51] He was of English descent, a member of the Hawaiian House of Nobles, and a close friend and adviser of King Kalakaua.

Armstrong's presence in Honolulu disturbed Gibson, in spite of earlier friendly correspondence about the London loan. [52] After all, promises had been made to Spreckels. Gibson, a master of equivocation, failed to give Armstrong satisfactory answers to his proposals. The premier would have much to say about the form and substance of the loan bill in the legislature. Armstrong became disgusted with Gibson's methods. When the time came for Armstrong to depart for London he was doubtful about the idea of floating a loan there. He left Honolulu on August 28, but before he left Macfarlane persuaded him to remain in San Francisco for a while and await developments instead of going directly to London. [53]

With Macfarlane working behind the scenes on behalf of Armstrong and Kalakaua, and with Gibson still hopeful that a loan, if any, would be placed only with Spreckels, there was another change of direction on the bill.

The special committee for the bill, with Thurston as chairman, returned it on August 26 without recommendation. "The intro-

ducer of said bill [Gibson] has, on behalf of the Government . . .
stated to the Assembly that the Government no longer considered
a loan necessary, and . . . no change of such policy has since been
announced by the Government." [54] The next day Thurston said
it would be a waste of time to consider a loan bill until Gibson
made clear the policy of the government. At first there had been
a lot of talk about loans. Then the talk had died down. The
reason for this, said Thurston, was that "Mr. Spreckels had de-
clared . . . a loan was unnecessary." [55]

Gibson said this was just "street talk." To be sure, the legislature had been for a time in the mood for retrenchment, after
the king's economy message. Now the mood had changed. Gibson denied the government's course was being dictated by the
gentleman from San Francisco. "Mr. Spreckels had told him,
about the time he introduced this bill, that he thought it advisable
for the Government to borrow money, and he believed the whole
amount could be obtained in San Francisco." [56]

In an attempt to get a statement of government policy, Dole
asked Gibson if he now favored the loan bill. Gibson answered
that he did, with some amendments. He favored it more now than
he had two months before. He also said that $1,000,000 of the
loan would be to pay debts, and the government might not want
to borrow more than $750,000. Presumably this was a net figure
and Gibson had in mind a loan of $1,750,000. Thurston said:
"They could depend on it that this Government would borrow
every dollar it could get anybody to lend it." He believed what
Gibson had said several days earlier—that no loan was needed.[57]
Despite such opposition of the Independents led by Thurston and
Dole, the Gibson ministry with a majority in the legislature was
able to keep the loan bill alive.

On August 31, in the final debate on the original loan bill, it
became clear that the government intended to float at least part
of the amount in London. The assembly argued over provision
for a 5 per cent commission, or $100,000 on the $2,000,000 to be
borrowed. Both Thurston and Cleghorn argued against this provision. Cleghorn moved that it be stricken. Macfarlane said a

loan could not be floated in London except through a syndicate. The syndicate would require a 5 per cent commission. If the commission were left in the bill, said Cleghorn, "some one would get it." There was no need to go abroad. The loan could be raised locally. Did not Honolulu have two banks whose credit was good? Cleghorn thought it looked as if Macfarlane had some connection with the gentlemen who were interested in this bill.[58]

Macfarlane denied that he had any personal interest in the loan or that any money had been promised to him. If the loan could be floated locally he had no objection. But "he understood it was the intention of the Government to place a portion . . . on the London market." That could not be done, said Macfarlane, without the 5 per cent commission. Thurston moved the commission be allowed only on portions of the loan placed abroad, and not on bonds sold within the Hawaiian kingdom or to its residents. This motion passed.[59]

Gibson moved that Section 4 of the bill be amended by substituting a new schedule of 12 items for which the $2,000,000 was to be used.[60] Both Thurston and Dole objected to hurried consideration of the uses of the loan. Nevertheless, Gibson's amendment passed. The entire bill then passed on second reading, and the next morning on third reading.[61] By two o'clock that afternoon, September 1, the act had been approved and signed by King Kalakaua.

CHAPTER XVIII

Amended Loan
Act: Downfall

Why did King Kalakaua sign the Loan Act so quickly, in fact less than four hours after passage? There were good reasons for haste. The steamer "Australia" was clearing for San Francisco on the afternoon of September 1 and Macfarlane wanted to be on that ship with a copy of the act in his pocket, so he could reach Armstrong in San Francisco before he returned to London. Moreover, the "Australia" was the first ship that could bring news of the Loan Act to the coast. Macfarlane wanted to get to Spreckels and "explain" to him what had happened before that short-tempered gentleman got the news from other sources. The steamer was held up for a half hour to permit Macfarlane to hurry aboard.[1] Kalakaua and his chamberlain came down to see the ship off. They were closeted with Macfarlane for some time on board, presumably to give him last-minute instructions.[2]

Clearly, there was quite a bit of dissension within the government about the desirability of a loan in London. Just a few days after Macfarlane left for San Francisco, a columnist of the *Hawaiian Gazette* who signed himself "Zip" wrote: " 'Times are out of joint,' and if you don't hear of a political earthquake before this day month, then I can't tell when payday comes." [3] The earthquake came—and the author missed it by only a week.

On the surface nevertheless, Macfarlane's mission to the Coast was successful. He conferred with Armstrong and also with Spreckels. Spreckels was to put in with the London syndicate and take part of the loan. He was evidently friendly, but wanted some amendments to the act, particularly with respect to uses to which the funds were to be put.[4] The original act provided $300,000 for redemption of 7 and 9 per cent bonds, and $1,700,000 for public improvements. Spreckels wanted an amended act, to provide $1,235,000 for redemption of all outstanding bonds and only $765,000 for public improvements.[5]

From Spreckels' viewpoint the amendment had advantages both financial and political. He would get his $500,000 worth of outstanding 6 per cent bonds paid off at par. Then he would put in with the London syndicate and subscribe for $500,000 worth of new 6 per cent bonds. These would cost only $475,000 under the proposed arrangement to issue the bonds at a commission of 5 per cent. Here was a neat, quick profit of $25,000 for Spreckels. He would also share in any other syndicate profits. The reduction in amount for public improvements from $1,700,000 to $765,000 would mean less "pork-barreling" and would force the government to economize, as Spreckels wanted.

The amended bill was drawn up in San Francisco to the apparent satisfaction of Spreckels, Macfarlane, and Armstrong,[6] and was sent to Honolulu some time after the middle of September. According to Gibson, Spreckels wrote that he had agreed to share the loan with the London syndicate. He had no objection to plans for borrowing part of the money in England.[7]

Before long, Spreckels had some misgivings about the Loan Act, even with the contemplated amendment. No doubt he began to feel that the London loan was a move by Kalakaua to rid the kingdom of the Spreckels influence. As will be seen, Spreckels was also worried that the loan would take priority over existing debts to him if the government should fail to pay these off immediately from the proceeds of the new loan. In the last week of September Spreckels sailed for Honolulu. He intended to freeze out the syndicate and take the whole loan for himself.[8]

He arrived on October 2. The *Gazette* columnist "Zip" reported: "He had blood in his eye. I am told that he spent two hours and a half in the palace Sunday [October 3]." [9] It is likely that Spreckels used every item of cajolery and every threat he could muster to dissuade the king from borrowing in London.

Spreckels' arrival in Honolulu was unexpected. Several days earlier Gibson had received the letter containing the amended loan bill as drawn up on the Coast. Heeding the apparent wishes of Spreckels, Macfarlane, and Armstrong, Gibson notified the legislature on September 29 that he would introduce the amendment.[10] He must have felt relieved that a compromise had been reached. It would remove him from the cross fire between Kalakaua and Spreckels over the proposed loan.

Again, there was much evidence of haste. The bill was introduced the very next day, though it had been agreed that no new business would be introduced. Representative Kalua objected to introduction of the amendment only one month after passage of the original Loan Act. No good reason had been given. Gibson said the proposed amendment was more in line with the ability of the kingdom to pay. The borrowing would be solely on the good name of the country, with no need to give security. A larger part of the old debt would now be refunded from proceeds of the new one, and the kingdom would have only one creditor.[11]

Representative Dole quickly noted that there was little point in redeeming outstanding 6 per cent bonds (in addition to 7 and 9 per cent bonds as provided in the original act) when the new bonds were also to be at 6 per cent. "We are asked to pass the bill so that the capitalists can pocket 5 percent on $2,000,000," said Dole. "Our Government is controlled by an alien capitalist."[12] He thought that the "member for Molokai," Thurston, had been right when he asked the question about who was king—Kalakaua or Spreckels.

C. R. Bishop said that the loss in borrowing money to pay off a debt that was not at all pressing would be $50,000 or more. He also noted that the original Loan Act had prohibited payment of a 5 per cent commission on bonds issued within the Hawaiian kingdom or to its residents. In the amended act this restriction had been deleted.[13] Bishop thought that Gibson's remark about the advisability of the whole debt being held by one strong person was a new idea of public debt.[14]

Despite these objections the legislature swiftly passed the amended loan bill on second reading and ordered it to be engrossed. It was to come up for the third reading the next day, October 1. For lack of a quorum, the bill did not come up for the third (and final) reading on that day.

As already noted, Spreckels arrived on October 2. He soon made it known that he wanted another amendment to the loan bill besides the one pending in the legislature. Though under severe pressure from Spreckels, Kalakaua was still anxious for a loan in London. No doubt the king was disturbed by the tone of the debate in the legislature, particularly by the references to Spreckels as the second king and as the capitalist in control of the kingdom. Under pressure from both Kalakaua and Spreckels, Gibson now found himself once more in a quandary since he had made it all too clear in the debate on September 30 that he favored a loan from Spreckels.

Nothing more was heard of the loan bill in the legislature for several days. Kalakaua tried to gain time pending the return of his adviser Macfarlane, who arrived in Honolulu on October 9. Macfarlane had stayed on in San Francisco for a few days, probably to be in cable communication with potential members of the London syndicate and was unaware until his return to Honolulu that Spreckels had become hostile and was trying to take the whole loan for himself.

There came a last day of ostensible good fellowship between Kalakaua and Spreckels. On October 7 Kalakaua held a reception at the palace, and awarded several decorations. He made Spreckels a Grand Officer of the Royal Order of Kapiolani, and W. G. Irwin, his partner, a Knight Commander of the same order. Afterward they had lunch with the king. Several toasts were drunk. When a toast was offered to Spreckels he looked back over the fruitful years in the islands, and he looked to the future. He was full of plans. He said that there was plenty of room in the islands for a million people. Indeed, he hoped to see more than a quarter of that number living there during his own lifetime. He identified himself with the kingdom and said he would always try to promote its interests. Many new industries could be started and he hoped, for example, to make the wine industry as prosperous as that of sugar.[15]

When the amended loan bill came up for the third reading on October 12, Spreckels supported a further change in it. He sat watchfully in the visitors' gallery as Attorney General Dare moved the bill be further amended as follows: "Provided, that hereafter no bonded debt shall be incurred nor any bonds issued prior to the maturity of the bonds issued hereunder, unless provision be first made for the payment of bonds issued under and in accordance with the provisions of this Act." [16]

Thurston remarked that what they did not know about this loan bill would fill a book. The ministers had not explained things. Some persons said that Spreckels was going to take the loan; others that a London syndicate was going to take it. Were we a lot of sheep to be led around? What was the policy of the ministers? It seemed they had no policy at all.

Gibson said that if they wanted to borrow there were two sources: first, the creditor they already had in San Francisco (Spreckels), which might be considered a domestic market; second, the syndicate in London, a foreign market. Spreckels was willing to lend without security; the London syndicate wanted a pledge of the "consolidated revenues" of the kingdom.

They [the Hawaiian government] were in the position of an individual who had borrowed money on the strength of his good name, and then went somewhere else and borrowed on his property as security. That would certainly damage his first creditor and would not be fair. The first creditor would naturally say, give me an assurance that you will not borrow from someone else on the pledge of all your resources. As far as he [Gibson] could see there was only one source—that from which they had already borrowed [Spreckels]—from whence they could be sure of being able to borrow money.[17]

Upon a motion for postponing action on Dare's amendment, Gibson said he had no objection provided nothing else was added to the bill. Spreckels should have assurance that if he lent the money nothing would be done to hurt his interest. After an unsecured loan from him, the kingdom should not borrow elsewhere and give the new creditor a pledge of security. A motion to postpone action on the amendment to the following day was then carried.[18]

Next day, Representative Aholo said he could not support Dare's amendment. Aholo moved for a different one. The principal feature of Aholo's amendment was that interest on the bonds should be a charge on the consolidated revenue of the kingdom.[19] This provision was intended to "secure" any lenders under the act. It was obnoxious to Spreckels because his bonds were unsecured. The "charge upon the consolidated revenue" later raised some questions, also, in the United States about impairment of the sovereignty and independence of Hawaii.[20]

In support of his measure, Aholo attacked a statement by Gibson that the only security needed was the good name of the government. On the contrary, Aholo thought it better to give security as implied in his amendment. This would force the government to economize. If Dare's measure passed they would not be able to borrow without first paying what they already owed. The hands of the government would be tied. Dare's amendment was solely in the interest of one man, though Section 13 of the Constitution prohibited any such action in the interest of one man. Aholo said his amendment was not contrary to the Constitution. His amendment was for the benefit of all; Dare's was for the benefit of Spreckels.

After mentioning rumors of a meeting the day before between Gibson and Spreckels, Aholo said he was not accusing the ministry of dishonesty. But he himself was not under the influence of any one man. "Now is the day and this is the hour, let [us] all stand together and oppose the amendment of the Attorney General." [21]

Representative Kaulukou did not think it wise to follow Aholo's advice blindly, though Kaulukou too deplored outside meddling. It was bad to have talk of two kings, but he did not want any borrowing in England. Soon England would control Hawaii as she controlled Egypt. In event of default on a loan British officers would take over the customs house.

"Who was Mr. Armstrong?" asked Kaulukou. He did not know, nor did anyone else. All he knew was that Armstrong was a newcomer, a comparative stranger. On the other hand, who was this person Spreckels, supposed to be standing behind the ministry?

They all knew who he was. He was a man having a large interest in the island of Maui. He [Kaulukou] understood the Government owed Mr. Spreckels $600,000 or $700,000. He had lent them money in the past, and were they prepared to go and say to him we have found new friends in England—to give him a slap in the face? He did not see much wisdom in action of that kind. This amendment of the Attorney-General provides that if they want to borrow money they must pay Mr. Spreckels first. He considered it a good amendment; that is what they ought to do.[22]

Attorney General Dare denied that his amendment was in the interest of one man. It was, rather, in the interest of the whole kingdom. "A loan act had been passed without providing for repayment of loans already outstanding. Then an amended loan act had been brought in providing for such repayment. This injured no one, unless it be political adventurers" (those supporting a loan in London).[23] Now, his latest amendment merely provided that if they wanted to borrow, they could not do so in addition to what was provided under the latest act without repaying what was already owing.

Macfarlane then remarked: "The amended schedule read by the Minister of the Interior [Gibson] when this bill was introduced was drawn up in San Francisco by Mr. Armstrong, Mr. Spreckels, and [myself]."

Dare hurried to smooth things over. He claimed his amendment originated with Gibson. Dare added:

What does the opposition to this amendment want—indiscriminate borrowing and still more indiscriminate squandering? Do they want the financial affairs of this Government administered with wisdom and integrity, or by political adventurers who had not money enough to pay for the whiskey with which they attempted to debauch those who backed them?[24]

Noble J. E. Bush wanted to know which political adventurers were meant—those recently arrived (the London crowd), or those who had been here for some time (the Gibson-Spreckels crowd). Dare said heatedly he was not Mr. Spreckels' slave, and added that he thought "the House was being led astray. If they killed this amendment it would be like killing the goose with the golden egg."

The debate was almost over. Representative Kaunamano clearly summarized the points at issue:

The great trouble seemed to be with Mr. Spreckels, who had lent money and, it was said, had gone back to San Francisco boasting that he held the government of this country in his fist. He understood that was what had given rise to a great deal of the opposition. If honorable members objected to Mr. Spreckels being in the position towards the Government in which he was they had better raise some money, pay him off, and let him go. The Government owed him a great deal of money and how were they going to pay him? They would be prevented by the amendment from borrowing money until they had made provision for what they already owe. If they wanted to keep their good name they must pay their debts—pay their first creditors first. A great many people complained about Mr. Spreckels having the Government in his power. They put the ring in the nose themselves, tied a cord to it, and gave him the end, and when he pulls they have to go. It was wrong to blame him for it.[25]

The official account of the legislative proceedings for October 13, contains only the following about the Loan Act:

"At 12 M., the House took a recess to 1:30 P.M.

"On reassembling, the Loan Bill was then taken up for consideration, amended and passed." [26]

These two sentences mark the virtual end of Spreckels' political influence in Hawaii. As finally passed, the amended Loan Act did not include the Dare amendment on which Spreckels had staked his political future. The assembly defeated the amendment, 23 to 14. In this vote the Independents formed a coalition with

one wing of the government party which had been split into pro-
and anti-Spreckels factions.

Representative Baker said he had seen a great many newspaper
references to "a certain gentleman as a second King." The Hawaiians did not want any foreigner to be called king. Therefore
he had voted against the Dare amendment. Representative
Aholo's amendment was then passed, together with another by
him providing that bonds could be issued at a discount of 2 per
cent besides the commission of 5 per cent.[27]

Perhaps the best firsthand account of what happened to the
amendment supported by Spreckels is that of Gibson in a letter
to Carter, the Hawaiian minister at Washington:

> You will . . . have in mind that the Legislature passed a Loan Act, and
> subsequently an Amended Loan Act. The latter was actually framed by
> Mr. Spreckels and by parties representing London capitalists, and was
> sent here for the approval of His Majesty and the Ministry. Being accepted
> it was submitted to the Legislature and would undoubtedly have been
> passed in the form in which it was presented. It had been passed to
> engrossment when Mr. Spreckels unexpectedly arrived in Honolulu. He
> then brought forward an additional amendment in the shape of a restric-
> tive clause [the Dare Amendment]. . . . This new amendment was after
> deliberation accepted by the Ministry, yet with a reluctance which was
> fully shared by Mr. Spreckels' own particular friends in the Cabinet
> [Creighton and Dare]. His Majesty also fully concurred, and I have no
> doubt that this restrictive clause would have passed the Assembly. But
> Mr. Spreckels on one or two occasions, and especially at my residence
> on October 13th, ventured to express himself in such a dictatorial manner
> to His Majesty in the presence of several members of the Assembly—
> saying that his views must be carried out or he would "fight," and ex-
> claiming that this meant a withholding of financial accommodation and
> an immediate demand for what was owing to him—that he aroused then
> and there a determination on the part of the native members present to
> resist the dictation of "ona miliona" [multimillionaire] (Mr. Spreckels),
> and as they themselves avowed, to see whether their chief Kalakaua or
> Mr. Spreckels were king. This occurred during the noon recess of the
> Legislature and at 2 P.M. of the same day the opposition to the proposed
> amendment was open and manifest. This amendment devised and insisted
> upon by Mr. Spreckels was voted down by a large majority. It will be
> claimed there were other influences at work, especially that of parties
> representing London Capitalists. The influence existed and had been
> brought to bear to some extent on the Government, yet I can say positively
> that this influence had ceased to command attention, that His Majesty
> and His Ministers had distinctly decided to accept Mr. Spreckels' amended

Loan Act as transmitted from San Francisco by him, and that they had agreed to permit the loan to be floated by his agency. . . . It was through Mr. Spreckels' offensive dictatorial manner arousing the sensitive native members to indignation, that these arrangements were thrown aside at the last moment.[28]

After defeat of the Dare amendment, the cabinet fell—Gibson, Creighton, Dare, and Kanoa resigned that night. Never again was Spreckels, the "cabinetmaker," to pull the strings. Gibson, it is said, went on his knees to Kalakaua and begged to be reappointed.[29] The next day he was again premier, with three native Hawaiians as colleagues. But he no longer had his former influence.

Spreckels prepared to cut loose from the political wreckage. He went in person to the office of the king's chamberlain to return all his royal decorations, and "declined on persuasion to retain them." [30] "It is reported [said the *Gazette*] that a few second-hand decorations may be had at a low figure by those who desire to decorate their persons with these gorgeous baubles." [31]

Spreckels showed his anger in other ways too. He expressed his contempt for the future credit of the Hawaiian kingdom by offering his own outstanding bonds of $500,000 at a discount of 10 per cent on the streets of Honolulu. He found no takers, either in the government or elsewhere. As to the loan to be floated in London, he was offered any part of it that he wanted at 93 (100 less 2 per cent discount and 5 per cent commission). He refused.[32] He filed a lawsuit against Macfarlane, on a business matter unrelated to the Loan Act, in a vain attempt to stop him from leaving Honolulu as agent of the kingdom for the London loan.[33]

On October 23 Spreckels sailed for San Francisco. Usually when he left Hawaii, Kalakaua came down to the wharf to bid him *aloha*. Almost always the Royal Hawaiian band played. This time the king did not appear and the band did not play. The "Mariposa," scheduled to sail at 5 P.M., was delayed for about half an hour. Then Mr. and Mrs. Spreckels hurried aboard.[34]

CHAPTER XIX

Aftermath of Loan

W*hen* Spreckels reached San Francisco, he gave his version of recent events in Hawaii to a *San Francisco Call* reporter. The *Hawaiian Gazette* characterized the sugar king's remarks as those of a "very angry man." What he said had created a sensation in California, and would injure the credit of the Hawaiian kingdom.[1]

The *Call* reporter asked Spreckels if he had broken with the king and returned his royal decorations. Spreckels said emphatically that this was true. He went on:

> The King has for a long time been led by gin-drinking adventurers, men who have nothing to lose and everything to gain by leading His Majesty into escapades, and upon a course of wildest dissipation. He is easily approached when sought at the drinking or gaming table. The two leading courtiers are Colonels Macfarlane and Armstrong, both Englishmen, the latter an agent for Portuguese immigrants. These men have got to the ear of the King and persuaded him that they could float a loan in England for him at remarkably low rates.[2]

Spreckels said he was the principal creditor of the kingdom. The government owed him about $720,000, including 6 per cent bonds of $500,000 and loans of $220,000 on open account at 9 per cent. When the question of the $2,000,000 loan came up, he had agreed to lend $1,280,000 more. But he wanted a provision in the bill to prevent any further loans by the kingdom until his had been paid.

My reason for demanding the insertion of this clause was because I knew the King was crazy upon the subject of loans. In June last he sent Sam Parker and Kaulukou, two of his Ministers, to me to advise with him and them upon the best means of floating a loan of $10,000,000, to organize and equip an army and establish a navy for the Hawaiian Government. I asked them where the $600,000 per annum was coming from to pay the interest on the loan; they did not know and I told them to tell the King from me that I would rather see him going barefoot as an independent King, than to see him rolling in luxury for a few years and then to find his Kingdom slipping from under his feet. The King, at this time, had become dazed with a scheme to visit Australia and meet the Prince of Wales there, and in order to make the journey in regal style he wanted an Hawaiian navy to carry him in state to the southern world. Kalakaua is a man that cannot be reached by calm reason, but can be ruled by the gin-bottle; that is his divinity, and whoever worships at the shrine of Bacchus will find an open-armed welcome from him.[3]

Spreckels claimed he had stopped the $10,000,000 loan. Thereafter, the "courtiers" had been making proposals to King Kalakaua for a loan in England. Spreckels said he had the best interests of the Hawaiian government at heart because he had a heavy financial interest in the country. In a brief review of his connection with the Hawaiian Islands since 1876, he pointed out that exports of sugar had increased from 16,000 to 105,000 tons, and the total value of all exports from $2,000,000 to $9,000,000. He left the implication (no doubt valid) that his investments and his efforts had been largely responsible for this increase.

But the King is not satisfied; he wants more money, and he has men continually around him who fill his head with chimerical schemes of expenditure.... I have tried to hold him in check, and have on all occasions pointed out the importance of reducing rather than increasing the expenses of the Kingdom. The finances of the Government, as managed at present, must lead to ultimate bankruptcy.

. . . .

I think the move to secure the $2,000,000 loan in England was a positive indignity to me, for I have the greatest interest in the islands, and being a citizen of the United States, the country with the closest commercial relations and the most natural geographical situation for inter-commerce, I think that after offering the Government all the money it was judicious for them to spend, at a rate more advantageous than the loan they have accepted, the whole proceeding was a studied insult, and I returned the decorations to the King, which I had never sought, and the possession of which has always been irksome.[4]

Of particular interest in the above is Spreckels' assumption that because of his large interests in Hawaii it was up to him to decide how much the government should spend and where it should get the money. Now he was the complaining creditor whose debtor had escaped from him.

Spreckels' remarks were soon disputed. An article signed "Old resident of Hawaii," appeared in the *San Francisco Examiner* several days later reviewing Spreckels' relations with the kingdom and the events leading to the Loan Act. The author thought it was unfair of Spreckels to denounce Kalakaua in such harsh terms. The king had conferred many royal favors on Spreckels. Kalakaua was a gracious gentleman who had deferred to Spreckels' views by placing his California friends (Creighton and Dare) in the cabinet. There was no good reason why Spreckels should assail his majesty. But "after Colonel Spreckels found he could no longer rule the finances of the Hawaiian Government nor dictate to a new Ministry, he became violently abusive toward all who opposed him, and, after denouncing the King and His Ministry, he returns the decorations."[5]

The Loan Act had not been intended as an insult to any creditor of the government, said "Old resident." It was simply a plan to consolidate debt and pay a reasonable rate of interest. Spreckels had at first agreed to be a member of the syndicate that would float the loan: "But as it afterward appeared to him in doing this he would no longer be able to wholly control the finances of the Kingdom or dictate to its Ministers, he withdrew and then sought to defeat the Loan Act, and failing in this, has consequently lost his political and financial influence with the Government."[6]

The later events may now be told, with special attention to the cost of the loan, payment of debt to Spreckels, and certain international complications. These last arose from what was essentially an attempt to get rid of him. The loan also reflected, however, the Hawaiian kingdom's pressing desire for funds, no matter from what source.

Under the amended Loan Act $500,000 in bonds were floated in Honolulu in late 1886. Macfarlane and Armstrong received identical appointments from the Hawaiian kingdom as agents to negotiate the loan in London. Under the appointments they had wide discretion. They got no other formal instructions. Armstrong went to London to take care of preliminary details, including talks with the syndicate. Macfarlane remained for the time being in San Francisco. There he could communicate with London by cable and telegraph and with Honolulu by ship's mail.[7]

Macfarlane received a cable from London, dated December 17, 1886: the loan was a huge success. An offer of $1,000,000 in bonds was oversubscribed more than tenfold. Soon the bonds went to a premium of 5 on the London Stock Exchange. The cable was published in San Francisco newspapers together with a statement by Macfarlane as the "King's Version of the Loan." No doubt the statement was intended to counteract many previous newspaper reports that were feared to be damaging to the credit of the Hawaiian kingdom.

Macfarlane denied Spreckels' charges of personal extravagance by the king and of ambitions by him to have a large army and navy. He also denied a report that the loan had given the British government a mortgage on Hawaiian revenues. One purpose of the loan, he claimed, was to "relieve the government of what was regarded as a mild form of commercial tyranny."[8] This was an allusion to control exercised by Spreckels through previous loans.

Macfarlane said the loan had no political significance. It could not properly be called an English loan. In support of this he said that $500,000 had been subscribed by residents of the Hawaiian kingdom, apart from the $1,000,000 in London. He also denied there was any intent to hurt the Spreckels interests. "On the contrary, everything will be done to assist Mr. Spreckels in his commercial enterprises as much as any other capitalist."[9]

One part of the Macfarlane statement requires special attention. He claimed the loan had been negotiated in London rather than in New York, Boston, or San Francisco because money could be obtained cheaper there.[10]

Any joy in the Hawaiian kingdom over the "success" of the London loan did not last long. As the months went by it became evident that expenses went beyond anything that had been expected. There had also been many technical violations of the Loan Act. Issue of the definitive bonds was delayed because the first set printed was not in accordance with the law.

Concern over technical violations was probably subordinate to concern over cost. Two legislative committees tried to obtain a proper accounting of expenses. But the kingdom got only vague and unsatisfactory statements from Macfarlane in person and from Armstrong by mail. Proper vouchers were not available. There was an "absolute dearth of evidence." The most damaging item was an unitemized and unsupported charge of $75,000 beyond the 5 per cent commission and 2 per cent discount allowed by the act. Moreover, it was reported (and not denied) that Macfarlane had received a $10,000 commission from the syndicate, though as agent of the kingdom he had been reimbursed by the government for travel and incidental expenses.[11]

The 1888 legislature voted $5,000 for a suit to recover the $75,000 which was unaccounted for. The Hawaiian government retained a Colonel James T. Griffin as its London agent to make an investigation. Probably not more than $5,000 could be recovered from Armstrong, reported Griffin. Because of the expense involved, he suggested that no further action be taken. The kingdom accepted this advice and wrote the $75,000 off as a loss.[12]

The total cost of the London loan is significant because one of the arguments in favor of it had been that it would be cheap—presumably cheaper than borrowing from Spreckels. It can be shown that the kingdom bought its freedom from Spreckels at a heavy price. (Of course, money was not the only consideration in getting free of him.) According to the *Intermediate Report of the Minister of Finance, 1887,* the admitted cost of the $1,000,000 loan was $169,000, not counting interest. In a letter to the editor of the *Bulletin* (Honolulu), November 22, 1887, P. C. Jones, a prominent Honolulu businessman and financier, made estimates of future cost. These included "commissions" of $70,000 on future payments of interest and on eventual payment of principal. This $70,000 plus admitted costs of $169,000 already incurred totals $239,000, not counting interest!

A special committee of the 1887 legislature reported that a Mr. Wildy, a London stockbroker visiting in Honolulu, had testified: "They don't do nothing for nothing in London!" The committee commented: "This seems to have been our experience. . . . We are buying our experience pretty dearly." [13]

Of the $1,300,000 Hawaiian public debt, $700,000 was due Spreckels: $200,000 on open account at 9 per cent,[14] "special loan" through Irwin and Company, and $500,000 in 6 per cent bonds. The bonds had been issued in 1884 in connection with the Kalakaua silver coinage.

The open account of $200,000 was paid from proceeds of $500,000 in bonds floated in Honolulu in 1886 under the new Loan Act.[15] This left $500,000 in Spreckels' 6 per cent bonds outstanding. There were good reasons for redeeming these as quickly as possible: (1) Spreckels' grip on the Hawaiian kingdom would not be completely shaken off until he was paid.[16] (2) His statements in San Francisco were damaging to the credit of the kingdom; disturbing to the London syndicate, because the price of the bonds might be depressed or further issues impeded; and damaging to American-Hawaiian relations. (3) When the London loan of $1,000,000 was fully subscribed, it was costing the Hawaiian government 6 per cent interest, but the government could not get the use of the money until the definitive bonds were printed and issued. In the meantime, the deposit money received from purchasers of the bonds and held by Matheson and Company in London, was put out in call loans to the credit of the Hawaiian government at 3½ per cent or less. The Spreckels bonds were also drawing 6 per cent. Macfarlane therefore felt there would be a saving of interest if these bonds were redeemed.[17]

In accordance with usual practice in bond matters, Matheson and Company did not want to release any of the deposit money until the definitive bonds were issued. But Macfarlane persuaded Matheson to permit the withdrawal of $500,000. This was placed to the credit of the Hawaiian government with the Bank of California, San Francisco, in March, 1887. With this money the Spreckels bonds were redeemed.[18]

The cost of the transaction to the Hawaiian kingdom is worth looking at. Before Spreckels left Honolulu in October he offered his bonds at 90; that is, the government could have bought them for $450,000. The cost of the $1,000,000 loan in London was approximately $200,000. Allocating this cost to half the issue gives a cost of $100,000 for the $500,000 used to redeem the Spreckels bonds. In other words, the Hawaiian government redeemed these bonds at a total cost of $600,000, or $150,000 more than the amount for which it could have obtained them earlier.

The London loan threatened international complications.[19] These were, however, quickly resolved. There was a long history of rivalry between British and American interests in Hawaii, with the Americans usually having the upper hand. Consular officials of both countries watched sharply for signs of relative change in influence. In July, 1886, Commissioner Wodehouse wrote the British Foreign Office: "The King feels . . . very keenly the humiliating position in which he is placed, obliged to obey the behests of Colonel Claus Spreckels. . . . The King is always being swayed in different directions, he is now, whatever Mr. Gibson may be, in favor of closer relations with Great Britain, and does not wish for any increase in American influence, but all this might change again." [20]

Thus, Kalakaua's idea of a loan in London was not only directed against Spreckels—it was directed against American influence in general. The king chafed somewhat at what seemed to him the morally restrictive climate that had been created by American missionary influence. Further, the Reciprocity Treaty with the United States, in spite of the great benefits it had conferred, was not uniformly popular with Hawaiians. To some extent they saw in it a loss of independence and sovereignty. This feeling was increased by the proposed amendment in mid-1886 ceding the use of Pearl Harbor to the United States.

There was concern in both Hawaii and the United States about the effect of the loan, and of statements about it by Spreckels and others, on Hawaiian-American relations.[21] Many persons in both countries feared possible failure of the Reciprocity Treaty. Its renewal was pending in the Congress of the United States. Americans in both Hawaii and the United States feared that the loan: (1) would cause a resurgence of British influence in Hawaii; (2) would involve a mortgage on Hawaiian revenues, with possible compromise of sovereignty and loss of independence in case of default.

The United States might "punish" Hawaii for going to London for funds, by failing to renew the Reciprocity Treaty. Or, the United States might try to bind Hawaii more closely in spite of the loan, by renewing the treaty. The *Bulletin* said that the loan was not likely to lead the United States to abrogate the treaty. It would have the opposite effect. Just a few weeks before (early December, 1886), President Cleveland had urged, in his message to Congress, continuance of the treaty, and at the time, he knew about the proposed London loan. When the United States first entered into the Reciprocity Treaty, the reasons were mainly political rather than commercial. Political reasons would lead to its renewal. It was in the interest of the United States to maintain the paramount influence that she had acquired in Hawaii.[22]

The prospectus issued by the London syndicate placed emphasis on the loan as a mortgage on Hawaiian revenues. On page one the prospectus indicated: "The *principal and interest* [italics added] are . . . secured upon the consolidated revenue of the Hawaiian Kingdom." There was another statement to the same effect at the bottom of the page.[23] This, even though the Loan Act itself made only *interest* a charge on consolidated revenue.[24] There was also concern in the United States about the proposed wording of a preliminary bond to be deposited as security for the subscribers to the bond issue. This was said to give the subscribers "a first mortgage on the Kingdom."

The seriousness with which United States Secretary of State T. F. Bayard viewed the loan was shown in many representations made to H. A. P. Carter, and also in a letter the secretary wrote to the United States minister in Hawaii.[25] Carter wrote to Gibson explaining Bayard's concern. Gibson answered:

> Your Excellency knows the strongly vindictive character of Mr. Spreckels. Since the rupture with him he has outspokenly threatened to have revenge against His Majesty & their Government, more especially at Washington. He is a man well known to spend money freely in politics and in lobbying. He has boasted on our streets of spending $40,000 to influence California Republican politics and of spending $50,000 in Washington to influence action favorable to his personal enterprises. It is hardly perhaps too much to assume that he is the source from which the erroneous information which disquieted Mr. Bayard's mind has originally come.[26]

Carter finally satisfied Bayard that the London loan would not compromise Hawaiian sovereignty. This he did by showing him a copy of the preliminary bond to be deposited in London. He also discussed with Bayard the relations of Spreckels with the Hawaiian government. Carter then conveyed to Gibson his impression that any protests by Spreckels in Washington would carry no more weight than those of any American citizen with interests in Hawaii.[27]

Fears over renewal of the Reciprocity Treaty proved unjustified. One argument against the treaty, Spreckels' hold on the Hawaiian government, had in fact been swept away. In 1887 the United States agreed to renew the treaty.

Overthrow of Spreckels' political influence in Hawaii was one of the chief results of the London loan. The Kalakaua-Gibson-Spreckels triumvirate had been shattered. Spreckels still had large economic interests in the kingdom, but could no longer extend them by government favor. His interests gradually declined from 1886 to his death.

CHAPTER XX

Fall of
the Monarchy

There was by no means complete rejoicing in the islands at Spreckels' departure in 1886—not even by those businessmen who had often opposed him and complained of his influence in government. At the annual meeting of the Planters' Labor and Supply Company in late October, J. M. Horner, chairman of the legislative committee, said:

> While former Cabinets were piloting and steering the ship of State, with Mr. Spreckels behind the curtain as prompter, we felt safe, although things were not quite to our liking; but now I feel that we are drifting— drifting upon an unknown sea, with neither compass, chart nor rudder, and where we will fetch up no one knows. We felt safe under the pilotage of former Cabinets, because we knew them to be intelligent and sprung from the ruling race. I have an exalted idea of the high destiny of the white man and of his power to control and govern both men and elements.[1]

This indicated some feeling that Spreckels had, usually at least, maneuvered able men into office. The statement also represented a complaint against growing Hawaiian nationalism and against the trend toward putting Hawaiians in high office.

The year after Spreckels' exit turned out to be one of the stormiest of King Kalakaua's unsettled reign. The 1886 legislature had provided for licensing the sale of opium because it felt the traffic could not be suppressed. Understandably, this law did not sit well with supporters of the missionary tradition in Hawaii. But later events shocked them even more. Kalakaua accepted a "fee" of $60,000 from one Tong Aki for a supposedly exclusive license to sell opium. Then the king gently hinted that another person (Chung Lung) was offering a higher price for the license. Tong Aki paid $15,000 more. The license went nevertheless to Chung Lung for $80,000. Aki got neither the privilege to sell opium nor the return of his money.[2] His anger reverberated throughout Honolulu.

The opium scandal sent off a reaction by those opposed to the Kalakaua regime. Under the leadership of Lorrin A. Thurston, opponents of the "palace party" had formed the Hawaiian League early in 1887. Two factions developed within the league. One of them aimed at reform by constitutional means. The other aimed to overthrow the monarchy and set up an independent republic. The second faction also considered the possibility of annexation to the United States. Z. S. Spalding, a member of the league (and probably of its conservative faction, since he had extensive sugar interests), interpreted "reform" to mean that "the rights of the white people would be more respected and observed."[3]

On June 30, 1887, the league sponsored a mass meeting in Honolulu. Those present charged the government with failure to protect personal and property rights. They demanded a new cabinet, amendment of the Constitution to reduce the king's control of the cabinet, and guarantees by him against interference with legislative process.

Kalakaua could hardly misunderstand the revolutionary temper of the meeting. He knew that failure to meet the demands of the reformers might mean the end of the monarchy. Therefore he yielded on practically all counts. He proclaimed a new Constitution which limited the power of the native government, made the ministry responsible to the legislature, required cabinet approval for official acts of the king, enlarged the suffrage of non-Hawaiian residents, and provided for election, rather than for appointment, to the House of Nobles. Since voting was limited by property and income qualifications, this last provision brought the House of Nobles largely under non-Hawaiian control.

As the opium scandal was related to Kalakaua's ever-pressing need for money, one may speculate whether Spreckels' presence in Honolulu might have changed the course of the Revolution of 1887. This seems doubtful, for the causes of that revolution were deep-seated. Among other things, non-Hawaiian property owners had long feared the political and economic threats posed by a rising nationalism among the Hawaiian people.

At any rate, Spreckels was not in the islands in 1887 or 1888. His verbal attack on the king in 1886 would indeed seem to have shut the door on any reconciliation between the two men. Spreckels nevertheless returned to Honolulu on February 18, 1889, after an absence of more than two years. By March 1 the *Bulletin* (Honolulu) reported rumors that Kalakaua and Spreckels had exchanged visits. Kalakaua gave a breakfast several days later for Elisha H. Allen, Hawaiian consul general in New York.[4] Also among those present were Mr. and Mrs. Claus Spreckels, Queen Kapiolani, Princess Liliuokalani (heir apparent), J. O. Dominis (her husband, governor of Oahu), Mr. and Mrs. W. G. Irwin, and Col. G. W. Macfarlane (then the king's chamberlain).[5]

Whether this apparent reconciliation between the king of Hawaii and the sugar king was anything other than coolly official is not clear. Kalakaua was not one to bear grudges. He may well have forgiven Spreckels for his harsh words in San Francisco. Or, it may be that the king did not think it wise to remain angry with a rich man whose purse might once again be opened.

Spreckels left Honolulu for San Francisco on March 14, 1889. He returned the next year at the end of June and stayed in the islands to the end of August. One reason for the visit was the incorporation of William G. Irwin and Company, the former partnership of Spreckels and Irwin. On this visit Spreckels again saw Kalakaua several times. The king gave a formal dinner on August 6 at Iolani Palace for Rear Admiral George Brown, U.S.N., the largest state dinner since the coronation. The Royal Hawaiian Band played for the entertainment of about fifty guests,

among them Claus Spreckels.⁶ A few days later he in turn entertained the king and queen at his Punahou mansion.⁷

The king and queen honored the Spreckels family and Mr.
and Mrs. Abraham Hoffnung at a party on August 26. Hoffnung
had been an important figure in the 1886 London loan, and
Spreckels had once been the chief creditor of the Hawaiian kingdom. The newspapers therefore speculated that money matters
were discussed at the party but Spreckels denied this.

Kalakaua was by now an ailing man. In November, 1890, he
left for a visit to the United States in search of health. He was
entertained in San Francisco by John and Adolph Spreckels, and
one night received Spreckels and his son Adolph in the royal suite
at the Palace Hotel. A few days later, on January 20, 1891, Kalakaua died. Claus Spreckels was one of the few persons present
at the bedside.

Nine days later the U.S.S. "Charleston," bearing the body of
the king, entered Honolulu harbor. The ship was draped in black,
her yards aslant, and both the Hawaiian and American flags at
half-mast. A crowd had been preparing to give the king a joyous
welcome at the wharf. Nearby stood an arch of triumph trimmed
in gilt and stripes of red and black. The king's coach, drawn by
four white horses, was to have passed under the arch.

Now, instead of joyous shouts, loud wailing was heard on all
sides. A launch bore the casket to the dock. The casket was placed
on a gun carriage and then passed under the big arch that had
been hurriedly draped in black. The procession marched slowly
to the palace where the body was to lie in state.

On the same day that the "Charleston" arrived, Chief Justice
Judd swore in Kalakaua's sister, Liliuokalani, as queen. Before
the cabinet ministers, supreme court judges, and the Privy Council,
the queen swore to support the Constitution of 1887.⁸

Liliuokalani was a woman of culture and ability, strong-willed,
and critical of foreign interference in Hawaii. She quickly made
it clear that she intended to "rule" in the tradition of the great

217

Hawaiian *ali'i* ("chiefs"), rather than merely to reign as a passive constitutional monarch. When the "bayonet" Constitution of 1887 was wrested from Kalakaua she had been away in England. She now wanted to throw off the limitations on the monarchy under that Constitution and return to one more like that of 1864. With great skill and determination she also resisted attempts of the reformers to force upon her a cabinet not of her own choosing.

Liliuokalani's accession took place at a time of much economic distress from the McKinley Tariff of 1890. That law removed the duty on sugar brought into the United States and gave domestic growers a bounty of two cents a pound. Though the United States–Hawaiian Reciprocity Treaty remained in force, the McKinley Tariff nullified its effectiveness. The result was economic and consequent political unrest in Hawaii, leading to some increase in annexationist sentiment.

Only a little more than a month after the new queen came to the throne an article by Claus Spreckels appeared in the March, 1891, *North American Review*. It dealt with the "Future of the Sandwich Islands." The Revolution of 1887, an abortive rebellion of 1889,[9] the restlessness pervading the islands, and the obvious weakness of the monarchy had evidently caused Spreckels to become concerned about his remaining investments in Hawaii.

He said that Kalakaua's death had stimulated interest in Hawaiian affairs. It was generally assumed that at the time of his death the king had been trying to foster closer relations with the United States. The islands were thoroughly American in "sentiment and sympathy." Indeed, the islanders celebrated the Fourth of July as a national holiday.

Spreckels pointed out that Americans controlled about $23 million of some $33 million invested in sugar. They also controlled the banks of the kingdom and about 72 per cent of the shipping used in foreign trade. The foreign trade of the islands totaled about $20 million (1889). Of this, about $14 million was with the United States.

"It is only natural from a consideration of these facts [Spreckels went on] that American citizens should take a deep interest in

Hawaiian affairs. . . . The late revolutionary movement, which resulted in the proclamation of an amended constitution [1887], might, under favoring circumstances be successfully imitated by the reactionary party, although Wilcox failed in his attempt [1889]: in that case how would American investments be affected? and would the United States government retain its interest in Hawaiian affairs?"

Spreckels thought the chances were against any organized attempt to change the political status quo. Nevertheless the United States should build up rather than impair its influence in Hawaiian affairs. The islands were the key to the Pacific. How could American influence be strengthened? Spreckels mentioned United States control of Pearl Harbor under the amended Reciprocity Treaty. Why not negotiate for perpetual control of the harbor and improve it?

The overshadowing influence of the United States in the industries and trade of the Hawaiian Islands renders it eminently proper that it should protect its commerce and the investments of its citizens against any possible combination or attack from without. This should not, and, indeed, need not, involve any attack upon the independence of the islands. *No one could be more opposed to their annexation to the United States than I am* [italics added]. It could do no possible good, and might do a great deal of injury, but only good could result from the plan I have suggested. It would restore confidence in the stability of Hawaiian institutions, and stimulate industrial enterprise on the islands. This would necessarily react favorably upon American trade, and help to build up the shipping interests of this country, which are now at so low an ebb.[10]

Early in the reign of Queen Liliuokalani about seventeen persons led by Lorrin A. Thurston formed an Annexation Club. Thurston was not really a representative of the weathy or planter interests. He was rather a "radical" representing non-Hawaiians who were not especially men of property. Many of his followers were struggling young business and professional men with a keen interest in politics. They felt the monarchy was incompetent and therefore a danger to their future.

The planter interests, on the other hand, were by no means

favorable to annexation. They feared that Chinese immigration and contract labor would then be outlawed, with consequent damage to the sugar industry. In a showdown, however, between Hawaiian nationalists and the revolutionists led by Thurston, there was little question that the planters would side with the Thurston group.

One purpose of the Annexation Club was to steer affairs in Hawaii toward annexation. Another purpose was to sound out sentiment in the United States on the question of taking over the islands, and to promote such sentiment. In 1892, Thurston made a trip to the United States for this purpose. He found expansionist feelings in various quarters there, which encouraged him to perfect his plans for overthrow of the monarchy so that he might be ready to strike at the proper time.

Solid evidence of Thurston's intentions can be found in a memorandum of May 27, 1892, to U. S. Secretary of States James G. Blaine. An enclosure covered the subject of "Annexation of Hawaii to the United States." At the end of the introductory memorandum Thurston wrote: "I have today had an interview with Claus Spreckles [sic] upon this subject. He expressed himself in favor of the proposition. He stated that he would undertake to see you in regard to the matter. I did not tell him that I had seen you, and leave it to your discretion to tell him so or not as you think best." [11]

The enclosure began with the statement that "within the past year or two [annexation] has developed from a theoretical proposition to one of practical discussion and importance at the Islands." Thurston said that three groups in Hawaii favored annexation:

1. Nonpermanent settlers having financial interests in the islands. (Thurston would no doubt have put Spreckels in this class.)

2. Permanent settlers having financial interests.

3. Hawaiian leaders of the so-called Liberal Party.

Opposed to annexation were:

1. The queen and her immediate personal following.

2. The common Hawaiians.

3. An English faction led by Commissioner Wodehouse.

4. A faction surrounding A. S. Cleghorn, a Scotsman who was father of Princess Kaiulani, the heir presumptive to the throne.

Further, Thurston wrote:

> The reasons why annexation is favored by the foreign investors of capital, are mainly because of the changed conditions brought about by the McKinley tariff bill.
>
> Under the conditions existing prior to that time, $33,000,000 of foreign capital invested in the sugar business at the Islands was yielding a handsome profit under the protection of the United States sugar tariff, and the reciprocity treaty. By the abolition of the duty on sugar, the price of sugar has been reduced from approximately $100 a ton, to approximately $60 a ton. This sudden and great change has reduced the receipts of many of the plantations to such an extent that they are now selling sugar at less than the cost of production. . . .
>
> Under these circumstances, a continuance under existing conditions is impossible. Any change promising even a chance of preservation will be accepted as preferable to inevitable destruction.
>
> Annexation has heretofore been opposed by most of the planters, for the reason that under the terms of the United States constitution the Hawaiian system of labor contracts could no longer be enforced, whereby an entire revolution in the labor conditions would take place. This objection still exists; but it is offset by the fact that annexation to the United States would give the planters the immediate benefit of the bounty now paid for sugar. It is not believed by the planters that the bounty system will last long; but they do believe that when it is abolished, that a reasonable duty on sugar will be imposed, sufficient to compensate American sugar producers, for the extra cost of labor, which will be sufficient to more than compensate for the loss which would ensue at the islands by reason of the high wages necessarily paid there.[12]

Another reason why annexation was favored, according to Thurston, was that

> the country does not possess the elements necessary to maintain a continuous strong government. Four-fifths of the property of the country is owned by foreigners, while out of an electorate of 15,000, but four thousand voters are foreigners; thus placing the natives in an overwhelming majority.

. . . .

> So long as any common danger, or matter of great public interest involving all classes exists, there is concerted action; but as soon as the crisis is past, the community is divided into factions, principally on race

lines; the principal divisions being American, English, German and Portuguese. Japanese and Chinese are not allowed to participate in the franchise. The result of this situation is a dissatisfied native element, and an irresponsible foreign element which has everything to gain, and nothing to lose by a disturbance of the peace, who are constantly, more or less openly, threatening revolution and disturbance. The Government in and of itself does not possess and has not the means to possess sufficient strength to protect itself against a violent overturning. It is extremely probable that but for the presence of a United States Man-of-War in the harbor of Honolulu, the existing Government would be overturned in a month.[13]

Thurston said that the instability of the government caused capitalists to lack confidence in Hawaii. The country's development was therefore delayed. He said the permanent residents having financial interests thought the only road to stable government was by way of union with the United States or England. "Every interest, political, commercial, financial and previous friendship points in the direction of the United States; but they feel that if they cannot secure the desired union with the United States, a union with England would be preferable to a continuance under existing circumstances." [14]

As to the form of government in case of union with the United States: "The territorial form ... would secure all legitimate desires for a local self government, while retaining in the general government a veto power over any unwise action which might be taken by the legislature. This form of union would probably find a much more general support among the natives than would the proposition to treat the Islands as a government reservation."

The document went on with a discussion of the difficulties to be overcome. These were what to do about the queen and royal family, and how to overcome the opposition of the common Hawaiians. Thurston said the queen would no doubt be allowed to retire peaceably on a liberal pension. If she refused, she would be removed by force. The Hawaiians, through their leaders, would be "educated." A provisional government would be set up pending union with the United States.

The last section of Thurston's enclosure to Blaine, "Proposed

Line of Action," contains a remarkable blueprint for revolution:

> Pending the Presidential election, it is proposed to hold the public developement [*sic*] of the subject in check; reorganize the Cabinet, and securing the appointment of a Cabinet at the Islands, committed to annexation; proceed with the education of the Island people in favor of annexation, and secure the adhesion of as many native leaders as possible; have the Legislature adjourn when it gets through business next August or September, instead of being prorogued as usual. This will allow the Legislature to assemble again upon their own volition without the necessity of being called together for extra session by the Queen; if the sentiment in Washington is found to be favorable to the proposition next December when Congress meets, assemble the Legislature and, according as circumstances at the time seem to dictate, either submit a general proposition to the people, allowing them to vote upon the one question of annexation or not without going into detail, and thereopon [*sic*] appoint a commission with full powers to go to Washington and negotiate the terms of the annexation; or in case this does not seem advisable, to take such action by the Legislature directly without submitting the question to the people.[15]

The annexationists were a small but aggressive minority. As one writer puts it: "A relatively ruthless and unscrupulous conspiracy existed in 1892 against the autonomy of the kingdom." [16] The Thurston group had every reason to believe it would have the support of J. L. Stevens, U. S. minister to Hawaii, a rabid annexationist who wrote in a well-known dispatch of November 20, 1892, to the State Department: "I cannot refrain from expressing the opinion with emphasis that the golden hour [for annexation] is near at hand." [17]

During the long and bitter legislative session of 1892 there were many battles between the queen and the reform elements over cabinet appointments. Passage of an opium bill and a lottery bill, both of which the queen signed, led to further disharmony.

On Saturday, January 14, 1893, after the legislative session had ended, Queen Liliuokalani tried to proclaim a new constitution modeled after that of 1864. Knowing that the manner of its promulgation was not in keeping with the Constitution of 1887, her ministers refused to approve and sign the new document.

The queen then told her people that the promulgation would be postponed.

The Annexation Club formed a small Committee of Safety, and immediately took advantage of the queen's "revolutionary" act. The committee sounded out Minister Stevens about the possibility of landing United States troops from the warship "Boston." Plans were also made to test the sentiment of the Honolulu community.

At the urging of her advisers, the queen signed a proclamation on Monday, January 16, that she would not seek a new constitution except by legal means. But Thurston and his followers dismissed the document as a meaningless gesture. They pushed ahead with their plans for a mass meeting. The Committee of Safety did not reveal how far it was prepared to go, but assumed from the sentiment of the meeting that plans for overthrow of the monarchy could be carried out.

Late in the afternoon of Monday, January 16, troops from the U.S.S. "Boston" went ashore, presumably to protect American citizens and property. Just what the role of the troops was, and to what extent they indirectly gave aid and comfort to the revolutionists, has been a subject of much controversy. There can be little doubt that the royalist forces were intimidated and *felt* that the United States forces were on the side of the revolutionists.

The Committee of Safety persuaded Sanford B. Dole to head a provisional government. Through the night they perfected their plans. With the firing of hardly a shot, the revolutionists took control of a few government buildings on the afternoon of the 17th. They announced the overthrow of the monarchy and the formation of the Provisional Government.

Queen Liliuokalani stated that she yielded to the superior force of the United States until such time as that country should investigate and restore her. Minister Stevens quickly recognized the Provisional Government and soon proclaimed a United States protectorate over it. He wrote the State Department on February 1, 1893. "The Hawaiian pear is now fully ripe and this is the golden hour for the United States to pluck it." [18]

An annexation commission of the Provisional Government, consisting of Lorrin A. Thurston, William C. Wilder, William R. Castle, Charles L. Carter, and Joseph Marsden, left Honolulu on January 19 by the "Claudine." Steps had been taken to prevent the deposed queen from sending a representative to Washington by the same steamer. The ship did, however, carry her written appeal to President Harrison.[19] The "Claudine" arrived in San Francisco on January 27. According to Thurston, Spreckels called on the commission and offered his support. He also offered his private railroad car for the trip to Washington but the commissioners declined this last offer.[20] Spreckels later claimed that Thurston had called him and made an appointment to see him.

Under the new constitution proposed by the queen just before her overthrow, said Thurston, she would appoint justices of the supreme court, appoint half the members of the House of Nobles, and confiscate all the property of the white people and take away their right to vote. The whites would have no power; the Hawaiians would have full control. In that case, said Spreckels, it was only proper that a provisional government had been formed.[21]

Persons interested in Hawaiian affairs held a meeting the next day, January 28, in Parlor A of the Palace Hotel. Among those present were commissioners Castle and Marsden (the other commissioners were reported to be "under the weather"); Claus Spreckels, J. D. Spreckels, and C. R. Bishop; and representatives of Williams, Dimond and Company, Welch and Company, M. S. Grinbaum and Company, and other sugar agencies. The participants considered what effect the revolution and possible annexation to the United States might have on American interests in Hawaii. "The only safety to property interests," said the commissioners, "lay in a protectorate by some strong power."[22]

Claus Spreckels wanted to know if the new government would respect property rights. Were taxes likely to rise? The commissioners told him that the only vested interest which might be attacked was that in the crown lands. Every effort would be made to economize in government, and thus keep taxes down. After some further discussion, those present indicated their support for annexation of the islands by the United States. Spreckels in particular would "bring great pressure to bear in that direction." [23]

There was, however, an important qualification. Spreckels said later that those present at the meeting "were not for annexation unless some provision were made for imported labor, something we must have in Hawaii." [24] Whether or not this was the general sentiment of the meeting, Spreckels himself was much concerned with the question of contract labor and continuing immigration from Asia.

As a result of this meeting and, no doubt, of private talks with the commissioners, Spreckels came out with a statement that the United States should at once proclaim a protectorate over the islands. Queen Liliuokalani, like her brother Kalakaua, had tried to establish absolutism and failed. Most foreign residents of the islands were American, and the American residents had the chief financial interests. Annexation would be the "most direct and effective method of intervention. From what I have said [continued Spreckels] you may reasonably conclude that I favor annexation of the Hawaiian Islands by the United States and the establishment of a territorial government." [25]

He warned that the United States could not afford to let any other country take over the islands. They were a natural stopping point and coaling station for ships of the Pacific, and a possible link in a Pacific cable. Americans had the largest investment in Hawaii. Annexation, said Spreckels, would be to the benefit of all. If the United States would not annex Hawaii an independent republic would be formed. Meanwhile the Provisional Government would stand. [26]

When the commissioners reached Washington they ran into trouble on some of their proposals. [27] Secretary of State Foster's refusal to yield on these points in drawing up the annexation treaty, probably had much to do with a change of attitude by Spreckels. Of special concern to him as a sugar planter in the islands were proposals eight, nine, and ten.

Number eight provided that Hawaiian products or manufactures be treated in all respects like those of the United States.

Refusal of this provision meant there was no guarantee that island sugar producers would receive the domestic bounty of two cents a pound under the McKinley Act.[28]

Number nine provided that United States exclusion laws should not apply in Hawaii. This was intended to permit continued immigration of Orientals for "agricultural labor and domestic service, and who by appropriate legislation shall be confined to such employment and to the Hawaiian Islands." [29] Without this there was no assurance that Chinese contract laborers could still be brought to Hawaii.

Number ten provided that existing labor contracts should not be abrogated, though future contracts would not be penally enforceable. Without this provision, island planters had no guarantee that the contract labor system would last for any time at all after annexation.[30]

As will be seen, there is ample evidence that number eight was the least important, and nine and ten the most important to Spreckels. To him cheap labor was the main factor in the success of Hawaiian sugar. The industry could survive without a bounty under the McKinley Act, he thought, but not without cheap labor. He later claimed that Thurston had misrepresented the Hawaiian situation to him: "When he and the other commissioners got to Washington, they did not carry out their intention in regard to labor. They let everything go in the interest of annexation." [31]

The annexation commissioners took pains in Washington, D.C., and elsewhere to counter the charge that Spreckels and the sugar trust were back of the revolution. Castle tells of an interview in the *Baltimore American* office on February 15, 1893, "refuting the assertion that the movement is a Spreckels one. The enemies of annexation are full of 'Spreckels and Sugar' as the secret springs of this movement." [32]

Prompt action was needed if annexation were to be approved before the end of the Harrison administration. Although many of their demands were not met the Hawaiian commissioners quickly yielded. Secretary of State Foster signed an annexation treaty on February 14, and it came before the Senate the next day. President Harrison was somewhat troubled by failure of the proposed treaty to provide for a plebiscite in Hawaii on the question of annexation. Such a provision would of course have been anathema to the Thurston group. In the Senate, Democrats blocked passage of the treaty pending the inauguration of Grover Cleveland on March 4.[33]

At the urging of the new Secretary of State, Walter Q. Gresham, Cleveland withdrew the treaty from the Senate amid a growing clamor in the nation's press. Loud voices were raised both for and against annexation. Clearly the outcry showed the need for more thought and further investigation. On March 11 Cleveland accordingly appointed James H. Blount (who had served for 18 years in the House of Representatives, from Georgia) as his special commissioner to make a firsthand report on the overthrow of the monarchy. He was to enlighten the president fully.

Blount's commission made it clear that in matters pertinent to the investigation his authority was "paramount," exceeding even that of Minister Resident Stevens. Soon the commissioner became known as Paramount Blount. He reached Honolulu on March 29 and politely rejected the proffered hospitality of U. S. Minister Resident Stevens and members of the Provisional Government. He took the same attitude toward the royalists. Outwardly at least, he gave the appearance of getting ready for a completely impartial investigation.[34]

Meanwhile, by late March, 1893, a change in attitude of the Spreckels interests toward annexation had become quite clear. C. A. (Gus) Spreckels, no doubt reflecting the views of his father, said he did not believe the sugar bounty under the McKinley Act was going to last much longer. "Nothing could be gained by annexation," he said. "We can do a more profitable business with our contract labor than we could under the laws of the United States, and for that reason we are opposed to a change. We would much prefer that Hawaii remain a kingdom and then we would know that our business would not be interfered with."[35]

Gus Spreckels also denied that the Spreckels interests had anything to do with the overthrow of the queen. A short time before the revolution, he pointed out, the Spreckels bank had made a loan to the monarchy. It was not likely that it would lend money to the government and then help overthrow it.[36]

These were the views of son Gus. Spreckels himself became more and more disturbed by reports from the islands. He suddenly made up his mind to go to Hawaii and see for himself what was going on. Perhaps he could straighten things out.

CHAPTER XXI

The Sugar
King Returns

O*n* April 18, 1893, the "Australia" steamed into Honolulu harbor from San Francisco. This surprised the residents because the ship was docking a full day ahead of schedule. It was a rainy morning. Nevertheless a large crowd gathered expectantly at the wharf. Was Claus Spreckels aboard? Was there any startling political news? Had the steamer left San Francisco ahead of time?

These questions were soon answered. Claus Spreckels was aboard with his wife Anna, his daughter Emma, and his son Rudolph. There was no startling political news to report. The steamer had left on time, and had made a record run of 5 days, 19 hours, and 33 minutes, breaking the record of 5 days, 21 hours set by the "Mariposa" on her maiden voyage in 1883. One can easily imagine Spreckels standing next to Captain Houdlette on the bridge of the "Australia," and telling him to "Pour on the coal!" [1]

According to Spreckels, on the day of his arrival, U. S. Minister John L. Stevens sent a message asking to see him. Spreckels saw him at four o'clock that afternoon. Stevens told him that Paul Neumann could control the queen, and that Spreckels could control Neumann. Stevens wanted Neumann to have the queen come out in favor of annexation. She in turn would presumably persuade her followers to do the same.[2]

Within a few days after his arrival Spreckels also conferred with Queen Liliuokalani and with President Sanford B. Dole. The *Hawaiian Star* reported that the queen got little comfort from Spreckels on the question of getting back her throne. In a half-hour interview at her Washington Place home he told her that "royal institutions here had come to a decisive end."[3] According to the *Star,* he assured President Dole that he would support the Provisional Government.[4]

But Spreckels wanted to leave the question of the final form of government open. He was not opposed to annexation but wanted to consider the idea of a republic. "Let me say [Spreckels told a reporter of the *Star*] I have not yet made up my mind about the thing; I am not here to tear down the Provisional Government, but I am here to see justice done to all parties, and when I have determined what I regard as justice I will be heard fast enough."[5]

These statements evaded the question of contract labor, which certainly was much on Spreckels' mind. Perhaps a better statement of his views at this time is contained in an interview of April 26 with an Associated Press correspondent. Spreckels said to him:

I have come down to investigate. . . . The labor question is the all important one and constitutes my only objection to annexation. . . . The contract labor system will not be tolerated by the United States, but that system is essential. The monarchy cannot be restored. . . . When Kalakaua was King I practically ran the country.

.   .   .   .

If I could find a man of ability whom I could trust I would favor a republic—the thing to do is to find the man.[6] These people [the Provisional Government] can't remain in power always.

.   .   .   .

I can lead the Kanakas ["native Hawaiians"],[7] for I know them, and they come to consult me about their affairs. If I could find a man I would favor a republic; give the United States a place at Pearl Harbor in fee simple—that's all they want.[8] They would keep their ships there and protect us if we couldn't take care of ourselves. . . . Uncle Sam wouldn't allow any power to take these islands. . . . The Kanakas, though, are easily influenced, and I can't be here all the time. Some smooth talker from the States, Australia or the South Seas could come here and lead them astray.[9]

Spreckels determined to enlist the support of the sugar planters for his views. Accordingly, several planters and sugar agents met on April 25 at the office of W. O. Smith, an attorney. They discussed the political outlook, the needs and prospects of the sugar industry, and the contract labor question. A letter from Spreckels was read and referred to a committee of three, which was to report on it in a few days. It was expected also that the planters would prepare a statement for Commissioner Blount. They were reported to be generally favorable to annexation.[10]

Two days later they held another meeting to consider the committee report on the Spreckels letter. They decided not to make any formal statement to Blount on the effects of annexation on the sugar industry.[11] Several different versions of what took place at this meeting and at the previous one appeared in the newspapers. There was much speculation about the precise contents of the Spreckels letter.

To offset many contradictory reports and rumors, W. G. Irwin wrote a letter to the *Bulletin* (Honolulu) on June 6, explaining what had taken place. Soon after Spreckels arrived in Honolulu he had invited Irwin and H. P. Baldwin, a prominent Maui planter, to his home to discuss how annexation might affect the planters. Irwin drew up a letter which he claimed Baldwin also endorsed to a great extent. The letter was then presented to the planters over Spreckels' signature. Irwin said that a majority of the planters at the meeting approved the letter but they thought it best not to present it to Blount because the endorsement was not unanimous. In essence the letter was as follows.

As for annexation, one of the main points was the effect on the sugar industry, the most important industry in the islands. The laws of the United States would stop contract labor and also curtail Oriental immigration. But contract labor had been a subject of much experiment and expense by the planters. Laborers other than Oriental (e.g., Scandinavian) had not proved satisfactory.

The Hawaiian legislature amended its laws to induce Chinese immigration. Since not enough Chinese had come in, Hawaii entered into a convention with Japan to encourage Japanese immigration under three-year contracts.

The contract system assured repayment of advances by the planters for the laborers' transportation. It also protected the planters against strikes and labor combinations, which would be especially serious at harvest time. Not only did the contract protect the planter, it also assured the laborer regular employment. The Japanese government therefore regarded the contract as a protection for its subjects.

The contract labor system (concluded the Spreckels letter) was the only one that the planters could rely on. Disturbance of the system by annexation would cripple the sugar industry and the United States would only get a bankrupt group of islands.[12]

Irwin said he agreed completely with Spreckels that "annexation pure and simple, without regard to our present labor system, on which the existence of our sugar industry depends, or [without] protection of the civil rights of Hawaiians against the host of political intriguers who would no doubt invade our shores as soon as the treaty was passed, would prove a disaster instead of a boon to these islands." [13]

Possibly because the planters had failed to endorse his letter, Spreckels stated his views in an interview with Charles Nordhoff of the *New York Herald* on May 2, 1893. This interview and one with Commissioner Blount on June 5 further illustrate Spreckels' attitude at this time on Hawaiian questions.

In the first part of the Nordhoff interview Spreckels repeated and enlarged on much of what he had said in the letter to the planters. Nordhoff then asked whether the other planters agreed with him on the need for the contract labor system. Spreckels said that they did. But some planters thought, he added, that on annexation the United States would permit Hawaii to have its own immigration laws and to keep the contract labor system. Spreckels himself did not believe this would be done.

To Nordhoff's question, "Is sugar the only possible important crop of the islands?" Spreckels answered: "Yes, I say that confidently, other things have been tried.... If the sugar were destroyed the islands would relapse into a big cow pasture which they were before sugar was begun."

Nordhoff remarked that some annexationists thought political stability was not possible without annexation.

"I can't see why we should not have stable independent government," Spreckels answered. "I am sure that stable, orderly, and economical government is possible here, and as I am the largest taxpayer on the islands, and have more property at stake and pay more taxes than the whole Provisional Government, you will admit that my interests make me conservative. I need a stable and economical government more than any man on the islands."

"Has the government not been wasteful in the past?" Nordhoff asked.

"Of course it has," said Spreckels. "Under the [reciprocity] treaty and your [U.S.] sugar duties everybody got rapidly rich here.... There was naturally no disposition to economy and the government became extravagant because everybody was extravagant. Now at last the wheel has turned, and we must economize on the plantations, in our daily lives, and of course in the government."

The reporter asked what he thought about the future of the islands. Spreckels said that when President Cleveland and the United States Congress knew the truth, they would understand that annexation "would be an act of great injustice, whilst it would also ruin the sugar industry, on which depends the prosperity of all the people of the islands."

Spreckels had not at first opposed annexation, he explained. The revolution occurred suddenly, and he did not have full knowledge of what was going on.

It was a complete surprise to me. I was in San Francisco and my resident partner, Mr. Irwin, was in New York...when the revolution broke out. . . . Many planters were brought to acquiesce in it by delusive promises that they would get the sugar bounty if annexation came, and that the labor system would not be disturbed; that the United States was so eager to possess the islands, that any terms demanded here would be at once granted, and other nonsense of that kind.[14]

Newspapers that favored the Provisional Government (*Hawaiian Star, Hawaiian Gazette, Pacific Commercial Advertiser*) politely insinuated that Spreckels had been misquoted. He attacked these insinuations with his usual bluntness: "In my interview with Mr. Chas. Nordhoff, recently published in the local papers, I said just what I wanted to say and what I believe to be true." [15]

Of this endorsement the *Gazette* said: "While it is not so wide as a church door, viewed politically, nor so deep as a well, viewed logically, it will suffice." [16] The editor also denied Spreckels' statement in the Nordhoff interview that the planters agreed with his views. Had they not refused to endorse the Spreckels-Irwin letter for presentation to Blount? "The fact is they [the planters] disagree with Mr. Spreckels almost to a man." [17]

As of May 17 Spreckels was still trying to promote the idea of an independent republic.[18] On that same date Blount formally replaced Stevens as United States Minister. Blount interviewed Spreckels on June 5, about a month after the Nordhoff interview and Spreckels said again that most of the planters did not want annexation if they could not get contract labor. President Dole had asked him to discuss the labor question with the cabinet of the Provisional Government. "I went there [said Spreckels] and I asked President Dole whether he had studied the [U.S.] immigration laws and whether he found that I was correct. He answered that he found I was correct in that way. 'But [Dole said] I have [the] belief that the United States will give us a separate law [so] that we can get laborers here.' " [19]

The following part of the Blount-Spreckels interview makes clear the sugar king's attitude toward the Provisional Government:

Q. Would they [the Provisional Government] be in favor of any form of government that would leave the natives a majority of the voters?
A. No sir; they would not.
Q. Would they consider any such government a stable government?

A. They think it would be stable with the United States cutting out the Kanakas ["native Hawaiians"] so that they could not vote.

Q. This is, then, largely a struggle to take political power from the natives and put it in the hands of the whites?

A. Exactly.

Q. And that is what they hope to get in the event of annexation?

A. Exactly.

Q. What is the feeling of the natives on the subject of annexation?

A. I think that seven-eighths at least would be opposed to it.[20]

. . . .

Q. Suppose the Government of the United States were to decline to annex the islands, would the Provisional Government be able to maintain itself without outside aid?

A. If the money would hold out and the people were willing to pay what they pay for soldiers, they could hold it.

Q. You think, with an army maintained here, that the natives would stay quiet for all time?

A. They cannot help themselves. They have nothing. All ammunition taken away from them. Everything like weapons forbidden....

Q. Suppose they had arms?

A. Then the Government could not stand. They would bring the Queen back to the throne. That is my idea. The Provisional Government would never be there if the United States troops were not landed, and they knew that long before they landed.[21]

Between the Nordhoff and Blount interviews discussed above Spreckels' first act of open hostility toward the Provisional Government occurred. This concerned a loan of $95,000 made to the monarchy during Liliuokalani's reign by the Spreckels bank. Notes covering the loan had been signed by officials of the Hawaiian postal savings bank.[22] After the revolution the Provisional Government became responsible for the notes.

As to the financial strength of that government, Liliuokalani had said to Commissioner Blount that much depended on Spreckels. He and also C. R. Bishop, of Bishop and Company bank, had been lenders to the government. She thought that "if Mr. Spreckels did not advance [money] to the Government ... it would go to pieces." [23] In her diary dated May 29 the queen had written that Sam Parker had told her that Spreckels was going to call the loan and thereby put her back on the throne. Spreckels came to see her about noon, according to the queen, and confirmed what Parker had said. She asked him to help her form a cabinet.

He said he would help and would stay until everything was settled. He also said that when he called the loan the government would fall. Cashier Spaulding of the Spreckels bank demanded payment of the $95,000 in notes from Postmaster General J. Mort Oat that same afternoon.[24] The call for payment was unexpected. It had been understood that the Spreckels bank was satisfied to earn interest on the loan and was in no hurry to collect the principal.[25]

The government did not have the money to pay immediately, and Minister of Finance S. M. Damon therefore faced a minor crisis. Failure to pay would probably cause a loss of confidence in the Provisional Government. No doubt this was what Spreckels intended, though he later denied any such intent.[26]

The government went out on the streets of Honolulu, and obtained pledges from Honolulu businessmen for the entire amount due in two hours,[27] and on June 1, $45,000 plus $1,400 in interest was paid to the Spreckels bank. The balance of $50,000 plus $1,808 in interest was paid on June 3.[28] These payments and the prompt payment of $30,000 semiannual interest on the London loan bolstered the confidence of supporters of the Provisional Government. The newspapers favorable to them now increased their attacks on Spreckels and the royalists.

"The prophets of the royalist cause [said the *Gazette*] are experiencing the nausea produced by hope deferred. Since the days of Shakespeare, the calling in of gold has been a typical method of taking revenge on the unsuspicious debtor." [29] The same newspaper later said that Hawaii had "refused to be reduced to bankruptcy at the nod of the chief Hawaiian boodler and politician." [30]

Spreckels began freely voicing his opinion that the Provisional Government could not last. The queen would be put back on the throne. In reply, the *Star* on June 9, 1893, published an article entitled "Herr Rothschild von Katzenjammer" (Spreckels) containing an obvious threat about what might happen to him if he did not stop his seditious talk. The scene was laid in "Germany":

"When the contest between the crown and the people of Germany came to an end, Herr Rothschild von Katzenjammer, who had large holdings in the land but had been living abroad, returned to Prussia, and espoused the cause of the ex-Emperor. The government of Germany, then in a transition state and controlled by a committee of the Reichstag, was disposed on many accounts to be lenient with Herr von Katzenjammer, a fact which he mistook for an exhibition of weakness." [31]

The article went on to say that the extravagance of imperial Germany had resulted in indebtedness to Herr von Katzenjammer which was assumed by the transitional state. "His next move was to attack his debtors—who were the dominant party— through the courts, and by a quiet word here and useful thaler there, influence the Royalist faction and induce it, in spite of its great respect for its own neck, to commit some overt act." [32]

The state, being under martial law, brought Herr von Katzenjammer before a military court. "It appeared that the inculpated millionaire had carried his sedition on his sleeve. He had run at the mouth about his plans and had entrusted grave secrets to men who could not retain them. It was easy therefore to prove that he was a conspirator against the peace and dignity of the Provisional Government of Germany. The sentence of the court was that his estates and credits should be confiscated and his person banished from the country." [33]

Spreckels of course was furious. He immediately brought suit for libel. "It was the *Star*'s prayerful hope [said the newspaper] that some of the ambitious Royalists . . . might find, in this innocent and sweet-tempered allegory a suggestion as to the pitfalls in politics which warn them in time. . . . Katzenjammer! Little did he imagine, poor old thing of vagrant shreds and patches, that his elusive personality would be mistaken for the corporeal substance of Claus Spreckels. Who could have thought it?" [34]

Three days after this comment appeared, the libel charge by Spreckels resulted in the arrest of Walter G. Smith, editor of the *Star*. After six months of litigation the case was thrown out of court in mid-December, 1893, because of a technical defect in the complaint. Judge Cooper of the circuit court refused to allow an amended complaint.[35]

The Katzenjammer story implied that action might be taken against Spreckels' property in Hawaii. Going beyond this, the next important incident involved a threat against his life. As he was about to step into his carriage on the morning of June 22, 1893, he noticed a sign on the gatepost of his Punahou home: "Gold and silver will not stop lead!" Pictures of a skull and crossbones and of a coffin embellished the sign, which was in blood-red color.[36]

Whether or not the threat was serious, there is little question that Spreckels thought so. He at once applied to Minister Blount [37] for protection. Blount sent Spreckels' request to Dole, and added: "Mr. Spreckels is an American citizen and it becomes my duty to call your attention to this matter." [38] Dole acknowledged Blount's letter and referred it to Attorney General W. O. Smith, who in turn instructed Marshal E. G. Hitchcock to give Spreckels protection.[39] Soon a Hawaiian policeman was pacing back and forth in front of the Punahou home.[40]

All the newspapers condemned the posting of the placard on Spreckels' gate. But the *Gazette* sneered at his request for police protection.[41] That newspaper also denied there was any evidence "to show that the coward who committed the indecency on Mr. Spreckels was an annexationist." [42] The *Star* said it begged "to assure the Sugar King that its objections to him as a politician, which are more then ever pronounced, do not preclude it from the hope that the person who put up the offensive placard may be caught and made an example of." [43] The *Advertiser* called the sign on the gate "an idiotic trick." [44] The *Bulletin* said: "Such men as Col. Spreckels cannot be met by these annexation jackals in the open, and be opposed by the legitimate weapons of political warfare. No, such a course would end in the prompt discomfiture of the Colonel's . . . opponents, who, too craven to face him in fair controversy, resort to the tactics of the ruffian and the blackguard." [45]

From time to time there were rumors that the person who

posted the sign was known and would be arrested. Deputy Marshal Brown denied these rumors. He had no clue to the identity of the culprit, he said.[46] But there is some excellent later evidence on this point. During an investigation of royalist attempts to restore the queen, Harry A. Juen in December, 1893, made the following sworn statement:

I . . . was [in May 1893] a police officer serving as a Captain of the Honolulu Police under E. G. Hitchcock the Marshal. At this time I was approached by Klemme, an officer in the mounted police who made a proposition to me to join him in a plot, the object of which should be to blow up with dynamite the residences and persons of the Queen, Colonel Claus Spreckels and Charles Nordhoff. Klemme made me understand that he belonged to a secret organization which had the aforesaid purpose for its object.

. . . .

The plot against Spreckels' and Nordhoff's lives was abandoned on my refusing to join Klemme, but after the dynamite episode Klemme told me that he intended to put a placard of a threatening nature on the gate of Claus Spreckels, so as to scare him out of the Islands. This I did in company with him.[47]

About ten years after the incident of the sign on the gate, Thurston ran into Spreckels in San Francisco. The sugar king did not at first recognize him.

"Good morning, Mr. Spreckels. This is Mr. Thurston of Honolulu."

Spreckels glared. "Oh, yes! You fellows down there wanted to shoot me, eh?"

"Oh, no!" said Thurston. "Nobody in Honolulu wanted to shoot you; that placard was simply a bluff."

"Yes, you did!" Spreckels insisted. "Yes, you did! Yes, you did!" [48]

Thwarted, ridiculed, threatened, Spreckels prepared to leave for San Francisco in July, 1893. He would carry on his war against the Provisional Government there and in Washington, D. C. An unnamed friend of Spreckels said that the sugar king "meant to do up the Provisional people, the *Star,* and all concerned in a very small package when he got to California." [49] Shortly before he left, the police returned the threatening sign to him. He would take it back with him to be reproduced in the San Francisco newspapers. He would also "parade it before the horror-stricken eyes of the President and Secretary of State," [50] and begin lobbying in Washington against annexation.

Spreckels called on Liliuokalani on July 15 to tell her that he was leaving. He said he would tell President Cleveland that the monarchy should be restored with her as queen. He made some statements about the types of nobles and ministers who should be appointed. The queen suspected that he was grinding his own axe: "To watch for Mr. Spreckles [*sic*] interest if it is within the pale of the law is all that he ought to expect and not more than the law provides for. I said nothing. I never like to make promises and I do not think he ought say who I should appoint for ministers. I will appoint such men who would act with me and not study the interest of any private individual or firm." [51]

Spreckels' departure on July 19 on the "Australia" occasioned somewhat more than the usual fanfare at the wharf. The Hawaiian National Band (the old Royal Hawaiian Band under the monarchy) got permission from Captain King, minister of the interior, to play farewell music. Why did they need permission? A few days earlier the Hawaiian National Band had gotten into a fight at the wharf with the Provisional Government Band. Several musicians ended up in the ocean.[52]

With the "Australia" scheduled to sail at noon, a crowd began to assemble at the wharf. By eleven o'clock it was swarming with people, mostly royalists. Soon after eleven, Spreckels, his wife Anna, and his daughter Emma reached the gangplank. A throng of Hawaiian women surrounded them and bedecked them with flower garlands. Spreckels was the center of attention. He "paraded the deck absolutely embowered in *leis* . . . his head rising amid the expanse of roses and posies, like a pumpkin in a big flower patch. Not a sign of his clothing could be seen, so harnessed, sashed, and surcingled was he with flower offerings." [53] Spreckels went to Captain Houdlette's cabin about eleven-thirty.

There he was soon joined by a number of royalists led by Charles Creighton (son of R. J. Creighton) and J. E. Bush.

Creighton presented Spreckels with a gold-headed cane, inscribed in passable English, poor German, and worse Latin:

Ave! Claus! Morituri te Salutans.
In Memoriam
From your Fellow Citizens
Doomed to Die
At the Hands of the Murder Society
of the Annexation Club
"Threatened men live long."
Leben Sie hundert Jahre und niemals sterben.
[May you live a hundred years and never die.]

Below this salute were engraved the following names: Liliuokalani, R.; James Blount; Claus Spreckels; Samuel Parker; V. V. Ashford; C. W. Ashford; John Cummins; J. E. Bush; Chas. Creighton; Antone Rosa; A. P. Peterson; Dr. Foote; C. B. Wilson; J. W. Robertson; John Bowler; C. O. Berger; E. B. Thomas; G. C. Kenyon; E. Norrie; W. H. Rickard; J. F. Colburn; W. H. Cornwell; James Campbell.[54]

Spreckels gave thanks for the cane. He also said that he hoped the donors would be decorating his grave rather than he theirs; but before he fell by the hands of the assassins he felt sure that he would see right and justice done to the Hawaiians.[55]

John E. Bush then made a speech for the Hawaiian Patriotic League, which he claimed represented 99 per cent of the Hawaiian people:

On their behalf [I] offer to you their heartfelt appreciation of your conduct toward them ... in the bold and fearless stand you have taken in opposing the high handed measures to rob them of their birthright, and as human beings to leave them without a voice in the disposition of its autonomy as an independent state.

In our intercourse with you as a merchant, a planter, and a capitalist, the Hawaiians have yet to find your peer for just dealing, for enterprise and energy, and for liberality.... Many in this country can stand up today and point to you as the initiator of their present prosperity and success in life. In the development of the sugar industry in this country under the impetus which it received from the reciprocity treaty, you landed here with your own capital, and with a dash and vigor stimulated it.... Your advent in the community was viewed with fear and envy among our usurers and snail-like business men. When accepting your liberal offers and large advances of money, which saved many who are wealthy today, that would have been bankrupts, they feared and detested you in their hearts. . . . These are the very men who threaten and if they dared would take your life and whose bitterness leads them to placard your residence with their threats. . . .

In your contention against the unjust usurpations of their rights by others, the Hawaiian people feel thankful that your powerful influence has been exercised and will be continued in their favor after you have gone away from us. . . . Let me close with wishing you and your family "aloha nui" ["much affection"] and "bon voyage," and the prayer that we shall meet again here under different auspices than at present exist.[56]

Spreckels said that when he came to the islands in 1876 he had found a peaceful and intelligent race. Then he could walk the streets without fear. Now all this was changed. But "Old Spreckels will see that justice is done, . . . the natives can depend on that." He would go straight to Washington, talk with President Cleveland, and expose the schemes of the Provisional Government. The crowd in the cabin then drank Spreckels' health in wine and champagne—at his expense.

Royalists on the wharf, meanwhile, repeatedly called out, "Where's Spreckels?" He went out on deck to wave and smile at the crowd. Calling on Bush to translate into Hawaiian for him, he started to make a speech. The ship's gong muffled his opening words, but at the end he said that he and his entire family had the warmest *aloha* for the Hawaiians.[57]

While Spreckels was still speaking, Professor J. Q. Wood of Oahu College called for the college yell by some students on the wharf, to drown out the sugar king's remarks. Bush retaliated at the end of the speech by waving his hat with gusto to lead a "hip, hip, hurrah!" for Spreckels. President Hosmer of Oahu College, who was on the deck above Spreckels, then called for three cheers for the Provisional Government. These were given while the band played *Aloha Oe* (Farewell to Thee). The bitterness of the Hawaiians at this interruption of *Aloha Oe* can be readily imagined. Queen Liliuokalani herself wrote the words and it is still one of Hawaii's best loved songs.

Spreckels retreated to his cabin in displeasure. The ship's whistle blew, warning friends and relatives of departing passengers to go ashore. When the deck hands had cast off the lines, the passengers threw leis to persons on the wharf. The band played *Hawaii Ponoi* (the Hawaiian national anthem, composed by King Kalakaua) as the "Australia" began her run to the coast.[58] It is not recorded that Spreckels shed any tears. But no one who has witnessed a Hawaiian steamer departure could blame him if he did—and for him this was no ordinary departure.

Said the *Star:*

The visit of the Sugar King...involved his final discomfiture on this soil. He has often been beaten in his political efforts before, but these were "affairs of outposts." This was a last desperate struggle for individual primacy.

Mr. Spreckels sought first to deprive the Government of the loyal support of the planters.... He then tried to embarrass the Government by demanding payment of the money he had loaned its royal predecessor. Promptly his bill was settled and he could do no more than Giant Pagan did in Bunyan's tale—sit at the mouth of his cave and gnash his crumbling teeth and shake his withered fist at the passers by. He has now been carried out of the country *hors du combate* [*sic*], and his last look at the receding shores of Oahu doubtless caught the glint of the stars and stripes over the housetops and of the emblem of Provisional authority waving unchallenged from the towers of the deroyalized house of government. What were his feelings then? Surely no man will envy him their possession.[59]

CHAPTER XXII

The Struggle
for Restoration

T*he* cane presented to Spreckels upon his July, 1893, departure from Honolulu soon became a symbol to make him look ridiculous. The affair was widely reported in American newspapers, and was blown up out of all proportion to its importance. It even threatened to become an international incident.

After the noon sailing of the "Australia" a *Hawaiian Star* reporter asked Blount if he had given permission to use his name on the cane.

"What cane?" he snorted. "What are you talking about?"

The reporter then told him of the inscription and said the royalists were boasting that Blount was one of the signers.

"Please say for me that there is not a word of truth in the report," he answered. "It is an outrage. I did not think there was any one mean enough in Honolulu to perpetrate such an outrage." [1]

Blount at once wrote Dole, asking him to investigate: "I had no knowledge . . . of a purpose on the part of any person to present Mr. Spreckels with a cane or any other article. I can but feel aggrieved at the liberty taken with my name." [2]

Dole read Blount's complaint the next day (July 20) to the

executive council of the Provisional Government.[3] On the same day the *Bulletin* (Honolulu) published a letter by Charles Creighton. In it he claimed that editor Arthur Johnstone of the *Pacific Commercial Advertiser* was author of a list of persons to be murdered by the Annexation Club. This list was published in the San Francisco newspapers on July 6. Creighton wrote that the named victims decided to treat the list as a joke.

"In order to perpetuate the joke and immortalize the stupidity of the editor of the Advertiser . . . [they thought] it would be a good idea to present a cane to Colonel Spreckels," with the names engraved thereon. Creighton said there was no general subscription for the cane, and that some of the persons whose names were on it, including Blount and Spreckels, knew nothing in advance about the gift.[4]

Dole wrote Creighton on July 24 asking further explanation and an apology: "The inscription and the circumstances of the presentation of the cane characterize the affair as one of political significance, which fact makes the unauthorized use of the Minister's name not only an act of discourtesy to him, but one that might be distinctly injurious to his reputation as a diplomatic officer." [5]

Creighton replied in a letter of July 26, denying that the inscription on the cane was intended to indicate Blount was one of the donors. Creighton also said no insult to Blount was intended.[6] Dole rejected this reply as unsatisfactory. He said he considered the correspondence ended unless Creighton would reply "in a form which will permit it to be publicly used for the protection of Mr. Blount, from any possible injurious implications and impressions which might be caused by the liberty taken with his name." [7] There is no record of a further reply by Creighton. Officially, the matter was evidently dropped.[8]

On his arrival in San Francisco, Spreckels told what the *San Francisco Chronicle* called a "strange story." He claimed it was true that the persons named on the cane were to be assassinated by members of the Annexation Club. "But they had another murderous plan on hand, and that was to deport, if not murder the Queen." Spreckels said this was to have been done while Blount was away on Maui for a few days. He continued:

> However, one of about fourteen conspirators whipped his wife, and she, being highly indignant at it, and knowing the murderous conspiracy, told it to another woman, and it was repeated to another till eventually one came to the Queen and told her. Sam Parker at once came to me and told me of it, and said they would do it over his dead body. He felt sure he would be killed....
>
> Two men, Wagner and Clunis, that night took a position where they could see the conspirators, and they did see them too, but they were unable to carry out this conspiracy.[9]

Spreckels also told a reporter of the *San Francisco Bulletin* that he did not consider the assassination program a joke: "I don't say things I don't know. People who know me know that. I know there was a man appointed to kill me. I know he watched for me. I know he is a member of the Annexation Club. My informant is a member of the same club. He kept me posted constantly." [10]

The monarchy had been overthrown by conspiracy, said Spreckels. The Provisional Government did not have the approval of the people, and the queen ought to be restored to the throne. The masses would put her there even if blood had to flow. "Annexation under the conditions would be wrong.... I state this as an American citizen who is paying more than one-fourth of the entire taxes of Hawaii." [11] He repeated his by now well-known views: With annexation the Hawaiian Islands would become nothing but a cow pasture. Without contract labor the sugar industry would be ruined. If Queen Liliuokalani were put back on the throne this would not cost the United States anything, and it would still control the islands.

Dole had said, according to Spreckels, that there were 7,000 members in the Annexation Club. In view of this Spreckels suggested to him: "As there are but 11,000 voters in Hawaii, why not submit the matter of what kind of a Government there should be to the voters?"

Dole answered (Spreckels' version): "We would be beaten."

"Yes you would," said Spreckels, "you would be beaten so bad that you would not know what was the matter with you." [12]

Spreckels was on his way to Washington by early September, 1893, to do all he could against annexation. Before leaving San Francisco, he said to a reporter of the *San Francisco Bulletin:* "Suppose I had a house, and I said to you that you could go ahead and live in it rent free. I would see that everything was taken care of, and that no one should make you go away or take the house away from you. That's the position I'm in favor of leaving the islands. We'll have a protectorate or a careful watch over them to see that everything goes right. By and by, some time, they may be annexed, but not now. I'll guarantee to deliver them at any time." [13]

One of the less charitable, yet incisive, comments on Spreckels' attitude toward annexation, including his claims that it would ruin the sugar industry, was the following, in a letter to the *New York Sun* of October 9, 1893. The letter was signed "One who knows."

Mr. Spreckels has but one interest: the interest of Mr. Spreckels....
If Mr. Planter Spreckels were getting ruined, we know that Mr. Refiner Spreckels would not be starving.
But then there are yet other Mr. Spreckelses. There is Mr. Beet Sugar Grower Spreckels. This gentleman grows sugar beets in California, which he sells to Mr. Beet Sugar Maker Spreckels, and we suppose there is money, both in the growing and the making.... Then Mr. Beet Sugar Maker Spreckels receives a bounty of 2 cents per pound from a paternal Government....
Suppose we take as gospel the statement that Mr. Hawaiian Cane Sugar Grower Spreckels would be ruined by ... annexation.... Mr. Refiner Spreckels would be making money in his business of refining and selling what he buys from Mr. Cane Planter Spreckels. Then again, we know that Mr. Beet Sugar Grower Spreckels and Mr. Raw Beet Sugar Maker Spreckels are making money with the aid of a bounty; also that Mr. Refiner Spreckels comes in again to make his share of profit out of what he buys from Mr. Beet Sugar Maker Spreckels, and in the selling thereof....
Thus we have a handsome family tree of sweet Spreckels, and all of the name of Claus Spreckels, only one of whom is afraid of being ruined. ...We need not feel uneasy. The President, Mr. Paramount Blount, and the people of the United States need have no alarm that Mr. Cane Sugar Planter Spreckels will ever be in need or go hungry.

On hearing that Spreckels was on his way to Washington, the *Hawaiian Star* said:

It is evident that Claus Spreckels is himself again. With that curious mixture of conceit, ignorance, and bombast which enters into the man, he comes out and says he is going to Washington to defeat annexation; that if annexation ever becomes necessary he can "deliver the Islands at any time." . . . Spreckels would live in the pages of Bierce as a sort of Brummagen [*sic*] Falstaff, boastful as the knight of the buckram nine, "unlettered as the backside of a tombstone," bombastic and impracticable as Don Quixote or Colonel Sellers, and as little feared by the enemies before whom he brandishes his hacked and rusty sword as a scarecrow in a corn field would be by a flock of eagles overhead.

. . . .

As the head and front of the royalist movement; as the intriguing agent of the sugar trust; as the blatant and egotistical old demagogue his praise would be a bane to any cause and his curses a reward of merit. By all means give him way and room at Washington. We need him there.[14]

Spreckels' actions in Washington and his numerous statements do not make clear exactly what he wanted. But it is clear that he did not want annexation—except possibly he might favor making Hawaii a part of California. In mid-September he attended a dinner given by the Oxnard brothers, who were sugar people. Several United States senators were present, including Perkins of California. Perkins suggested that Hawaii be annexed as part of California. The *Hawaiian Star* speculated that Spreckels was behind the idea, because Perkins was his good friend.[15] The *Tacoma Ledger* thought the Spreckels crowd believed they could more easily control Hawaiian affairs through the California legislature than through the United States Congress.[16]

Another proposal made by Spreckels in Washington was for a protectorate over the Hawaiian Islands. If the United States established a protectorate he would use his influence to get that country a naval coaling station near the entrance to Honolulu harbor. He claimed that this location was superior to all others including Pearl Harbor and said that the land needed would cost no more than $75,000. He would see that the United States received it, even if he had to buy and present the land himself. "Ridiculous," said the *Star*, claiming American naval engineers had already recommended against the Honolulu harbor location.[17]

On September 19, Spreckels published in the *Washington Post* an open letter to Lorrin A. Thurston, who was in Washington to press the cause of annexation. Spreckels made certain charges against the Provisional Government and asked certain questions. Thurston replied with a letter in the *Post* two days later.

Spreckels asked why, if the people had confidence in the Provisional Government as claimed by Thurston, the government found it necessary to station many soldiers and guns about the palace. Thurston said that Spreckels exaggerated the military precautions, but these were for the purpose of preventing "you [Spreckels] and other royalist supporters from carrying out your constantly reiterated threats of deposing the government and restoring the queen by force."

"You have constantly denounced the leaders of the Provisional Government," Thurston went on, "as 'thieves,' 'liars,' and 'murderers'; you have thrown all the influence of your name and money, and devoted all your energies to injure and discredit the Provisional Government and to stirring up the dregs of the population in Honolulu, both native and white, principally the latter, to insurrection." [18]

No plantation in Hawaii, said Spreckels, could exist without contract labor. Some planters sided with the Provisional Government and favored annexation only because they hoped to get the bounty of two cents a pound under the McKinley Act. Thurston countered that most of the planters were basically for annexation. He recalled that they had rebuffed Spreckels' efforts to have them come out with a statement against it. Thurston said the planters preferred to take their chances without contract labor. They preferred "annexation, peace, quiet, and stability with less money to an increased income and a continuance of the strife and uncertainty of independent government."

Of the bounty Thurston said: "The Hawaiian planters know . . . that there is as much probability of receiving two cents a pound bounty on their sugar as there is of the traditional rich man entering the kingdom of heaven." He said the issue between

Spreckels and the Provisional Government was "one of dollars and cents against flesh and blood. The flesh and blood is from the same stock that successfully established liberty in America, and it will establish it in Hawaii." [19]

Spreckels sought a personal interview with President Cleveland to urge a protectorate for Hawaii rather than annexation.[20] The *Star* reported that a member of the Provisional Government had a private letter from Washington about this. The President gave Spreckels a "curt but polite refusal" in answer to his request for an audience. "In other words," said the *Star*, "the aged coolie driver got about the worst snub he ever got in his life, and it is no wonder he soon shook the dust of Washington from his feet." [21] The *Star* regretted that Cleveland's snub of Spreckels caused him to leave Washington so quickly. By his presence there and by his attacks on the Provisional Government, he was "doing the cause of annexation a vast amount of good." [22]

Some supporters of the Provisional Government remained fearful of what Spreckels might do. For example, W. N. Armstrong wrote Thurston on November 1:

[H. P.] Baldwin gives facts and reasons to show that in the event of your establishing a permanent government in Hawaii, that Spreckles [*sic*] can largely control Maui, and can have great influence in other parts of the islands. If this is true it is a very serious matter. Spreckles at the head of affairs will be "cussed," but no more so than the average cussedness of American politicians. . . . If he has such power, would it not be the "wisdom of the hour" to take him and prevent any split in the white element? . . . He is no statesman, and takes no "large" views, and I have a strong belief that you could use him instead of being used by him. . . . I believe he is strongly in favor of good government, but he has had no faith that it could be established. . . . He is a strong factor in your affairs, and it is important to use him and not quarrel with him. I have often seen the most bitter political enemies join in a common cause. . . . If he wishes to insert a feather in his behind and be called a "bird of paradise," then call him so, humor his conceit and bring his power in line.[23]

Meanwhile, "Paramount" Blount had completed his investigation of Hawaiian affairs. In October, 1893, he made his report, which was published the next month. He felt that the revolution could not have succeeded except for the aid and comfort given by Minister Stevens to the annexationists. Denouncing Stevens' collusion with the leaders of the revolution, Blount made it clear that he thought Hawaiian sentiment against annexation was overwhelming. News of the Blount report reached Honolulu in November. Royalist hopes surged. Supporters of the Provisional Government, somewhat taken aback, denounced Blount's views as flagrantly biased.

After studying the Blount report, Secretary of State Gresham wrote Cleveland suggesting restoration of the queen. Cleveland sent Minister Albert S. Willis to Honolulu in November, 1893. Many newspapers reported that Willis was to try to put Liliuokalani back on the throne. It was a difficult task, made hopeless by the queen's intransigeance and her understandably vengeful attitude toward those who had taken part in the revolution. Nor was restoration in accord with the political realities. The Provisional Government rightly guessed that Minister Willis' demands would not be backed up by U. S. guns turned against Americans— even though they were expatriate Americans. Thurston seems to have had inside knowledge that force would not be used. Indeed, newspapers in the United States were saying openly that force would not be used to restore the queen.[24]

President Cleveland, in his message of December 18, 1893, dropped the Hawaiian problem into the lap of Congress. He strongly indicated that he generally agreed with the Blount report, and that he did not favor annexation. Both houses of Congress adopted a hands-off policy toward Hawaii.

At the end of 1893, Liliuokalani wrote in her diary: "Washington Place. . . . 12 Midnight—Woke up by the sound of bell[s] and bombs—the Hawaiian National Band playing Hawaii Ponoi —and firecrackers. Bells ringing the old year out and the New Year in—all that transpired in 1893 is of the past, we commence anew with the New Year. Thankful to our Creator for all we have enjoyed during the past and hoping for all that is good for the future. That our Nation may be restored by President Cleveland and Congress is my earnest prayer and of my people, to our just rights." [25]

Spreckels was in San Francisco in November, 1893, when the Gresham letter to Cleveland, implying that the queen should be restored, was made public. The sugar king expressed his satisfaction with the letter and said: "The men who represent the so-called Provisional Government had no more right to depose the Queen of Hawaii . . . than I would to demand of President Cleveland his seat in Washington." A reporter asked him whether he expected trouble when attempts should be made to restore the queen. "No, I do not," Spreckels said. "There have been threats made that the Queen would never live to rule Hawaii again, but I have regarded them as foolish utterances. . . . The natives are peaceable as a rule, and love their Queen. Should, however, an attempt at violence ever occur, they would certainly be aroused, and wreak a terrible vengeance."

The reporter asked him if he contemplated a trip to the islands in view of the queen's expected return to the throne. "No," said Spreckels, "my interests are well taken care of there, and I am needed here in other matters." [26]

It may well be that he did not feel it prudent to return until the queen should again be securely on the throne. Then he could proceed in triumph to Honolulu and claim credit for restoring her. But the chance for such a triumphal visit never came. Toward the close of 1893 the *Star* said that Spreckels' political influence in Hawaii and on the national policy of the United States had been broken down and could not be repaired.[27]

Spreckels nevertheless continued to fight annexation during the Cleveland and McKinley regimes. He also tried to avenge himself on those island planters who had failed to support him. In these struggles he acted both individually and as a member of the sugar trust. For example, the sugar trust unsuccessfully fought to defeat the Wilson-Gorman Act (1894) which ended the bonus to United States sugar producers and restored the tariff on sugar. In effect this law restored the benefits of reciprocity to Hawaiian planters.

Spreckels then began to fight for abrogation of the Reciprocity Treaty, using mainly the home-industry argument, for his interests in U. S. beet sugar had been increasing. "I cannot blind myself," he said, "to the fact that reciprocal advantages to the United States are almost nil, while an enormous and constantly growing bonus is paid to the islands to the detriment of our new [beet] sugar industry on the coast." [28]

"My opposition to the Hawaiian reciprocity treaty," he also said, "is inspired by the desire to encourage investment of American capital in this State [California] instead of paying millions each year to foreigners—not Hawaiians—who largely control the sugar product of the islands." He denied that he had always been strongly in favor of the treaty. "No one was more bitterly opposed to it when it was under consideration than I, and I spent at one time about $2,800 in sending a petition with a long list of signatures to Washington in 1876 in opposition to it." [29]

On November 1, 1897, a contract between the Hawaiian planters and the Western Sugar Refinery (this refinery was jointly controlled by Spreckels and the sugar trust) came up for renewal. Western Sugar Refinery had exercised almost complete control over Hawaiian sugar under the contract. The planters, except Spreckels and Davies who controlled about 20 plantations, refused to renew. Instead, they planned to send 80,000 tons of sugar to New York by way of Cape Horn. The balance was to be refined in a California refinery to be bought or erected by the Hawaiian planters. They thought that they would save about $100,000 in commissions. It did not work out because the long trip around the Horn meant a long lapse before the proceeds were received, higher freight rates, and more expensive insurance. But the action of the planters gave the trust another reason to oppose annexation.[30]

Henry Oxnard, a national representative of the sugar trust, and Claus Spreckels collaborated in the fight against annexation. In the summer of 1897, Spreckels' son John, ex-Senator Felton of California, and Oxnard spent two months in Washington lobbying against it. Claus bought the *San Francisco Call* in the name of his son John for the purpose of fighting annexation. Beginning with the December 1, 1897 issue, copies of the *Call* were mailed free to each member of Congress.

Claus Spreckels and Henry Oxnard also conducted a campaign in California, primarily at Sacramento, the state capitol. In addition, Spreckels sent agents up and down the coast to get petitions and resolutions against annexation. Oxnard tried to create confusion and dissension among the beet sugar growers. He offered California growers 50 cents a ton more for their beets if annexation were defeated. In Nebraska he told the beet growers they would get 50 cents a ton less for their beets if annexation were accomplished.[31]

In the islands, annexationists bided their time after founding the Republic of Hawaii in 1894 to replace the Provisional Government. Fruitless efforts were made in the United States Senate in early 1898 to get an annexation treaty ratified. But the forces of anti-imperialism and opposition of the United States sugar interests could not be overcome. The Spanish-American War, however, focused attention on Hawaii as a way station to the Philippines. Moreover, newspapers in the United States expressed concern about the tenuous legal rights of the United States to Pearl Harbor. There was therefore much talk about annexing Hawaii as a war measure. In Hawaii, President Dole encouraged such talk. He even offered help in making Hawaii a base against Spain.

The war thus turned the balance in favor of renewed annexation efforts that were already under way. Because a treaty could probably not get the required two-thirds vote in the United States Senate, it was decided to turn to the method of joint resolution. This method, used earlier in the case of Texas, needed only a simple majority in both houses of Congress. Both houses passed the resolution, and President McKinley signed it on July 7, 1898. In ceremonies at Iolani Palace on August 12 the Hawaiian flag was struck and the islands became a territory of the United States.

Spreckels returned to Honolulu in 1905, after an absence of 12 years. There was a stirring in commercial circles. The Hawaiian Hotel was up for sale. Was Spreckels going to buy the hotel? No, he soon made it clear that this was not a business trip; he was only in search of health and relaxation. He was seventy-seven years old. A few years earlier he had suffered a stroke.

William G. Irwin's carriage was waiting at the dock. Spreckels stepped into the carriage, and the two men drove to Irwin's home at Waikiki. Spreckels soon went into Honolulu again to look over the city he once knew well. He walked up and down the streets saying hello to old friends. The sugar king could contemplate his vanished Hawaiian empire without bitterness, for his success in California beet sugar had surpassed that of his greatest days in Hawaii. The years had also mellowed the old animosity toward Spreckels in the islands. Newspaper accounts of his visit were full of praise.

After walking for a while, Spreckels decided to return to Irwin's home at Waikiki Beach. While he sat in Chambers' drugstore waiting for the electric streetcar, a reporter asked him what he thought of the changes in the city. In the bitterness of his 1893 departure, Spreckels had vowed he would live to see grass growing in the streets of Honolulu.

"Honolulu is greatly improved since I left," he said. "There have been buildings erected which would do credit to a large city on the mainland. Oh, the city has been tremendously improved."

As Spreckels left on the streetcar, Manuel Reis, a veteran hackman who had driven him scores of times in bygone days, said: "I wish Mr. Spreckels would have let me drive him home. I would do it for nothing just for old-times' sake."

After staying a few weeks with Irwin at Waikiki, Spreckels unshuttered his Punahou home and brought his family down from San Francisco. There was talk that he would spend the rest of his days in Honolulu. But in a few months he became restless to get back to California, back to work. He left Honolulu for the last time. Three years later, in 1908, he died.

Of Spreckels' Hawaiian career, what evidence remains? In the Punahou district of Honolulu a street named after Spreckels extends for only a few hundred feet. Here his three-story mansion once stood. In 1913 it was dismantled and rebuilt in another part of town with one story cut off—a stunted relic of days past, until 1954 when it accidentally burned to the ground. In downtown Honolulu, the valuable Spreckels Block has long since been sold off and the block no longer bears the family name.

On Maui, some of the residents of Spreckelsville have only vague notions about how the small plantation town got its name. From the rise of Puunene, near Spreckelsville, one can see for miles around the fields of waving cane where once lay only wasteland. Today the green fields on the central plains of Maui stand as the most striking monument to the sugar king's Hawaiian career.

A
Spreckels
Album

Farmhouse in Lamstedt, Germany, shows the type of house where Claus Spreckels was born. Photo by Willie Klenck, former teacher in Lamstedt

Claus Spreckels seems a Lincolnesque figure in this picture, about 1863. He was 35 and son John 10. Source: H. Austin Adams, "The Man, John D. Spreckels"

Claus Spreckels,
1828–1908. Portrait at
California Historical
Society, San Francisco.
Painted by Toby E.
Rosenthal, 1879.
Source: W. W. Cordray

Anna C. M. Spreckels,
1830–1910. Childhood
sweetheart of Claus,
and his wife for 56
years. Rosenthal por-
trait, California His-
torical Society. Source:
W. W. Cordray

*Walter Murray Gibson,
1823?–1888, King Kala-
kaua's "Minister of Everything," 1822–1887. With
Kalakaua and Spreckels,
he controlled the kingdom.
Source: Archives of Hawaii*

*King David Kala-
kaua reigned 1874–
1891. He dreamed of
reviving Hawaii's
past glory. He leaned
on Gibson for polit-
ical and on Spreckels
for financial sup-
port. Source:
Archives of Hawaii*

At his boathouse on the Honolulu waterfront, Kalakaua gave many luaus and often played cards with Spreckels. Source: Bishop Museum

Here one night in July, 1878, champagne flowed. Then Kalakaua turned his cabinet out of office and granted Spreckels valuable water rights.

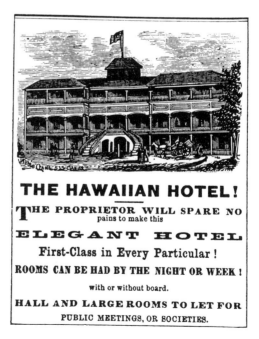

THE HAWAIIAN HOTEL!

THE PROPRIETOR WILL SPARE NO
pains to make this

ELEGANT HOTEL

First-Class in Every Particular!

ROOMS CAN BE HAD BY THE NIGHT OR WEEK!

with or without board.

HALL AND LARGE ROOMS TO LET FOR
PUBLIC MEETINGS, OR SOCIETIES.

Entrance to Spreckels Building, San Francisco.
The building withstood the earthquake of 1906.

*Insignia from
1881 invitation
to laying of
cornerstone of
California
Sugar Refinery.*

*Bronze doorknobs of Spreckels Building still show
his ornate initials.*

California Sugar Refinery, 1885. Claus Spreckels is third figure from left. Source: W. W. Cordray

Cornerstone, opened 1951, yielded 1881 newspapers, documents, coins, and stamps. Source: W. W. Cordray

Claus Spreckels. Drawing from Gutkunst photo

California Sugar Refinery.

STANDARD SYRUP

— OF THE —

[TRADE MARK.]

This is a superior quality of Syrup, and is put up in barrels expressly for home consumption. The quality is guaranteed in every respect. Our Extra Heavy Syrup, in barrels, is especially designed for a foreign market, a is inferior to the Standard Syrup above mentioned.

CALIFORNIA SUGAR REFINERY,

Office 215 Front Street

Honolulu July. 1878

Cash   Sundries 41,730.37 41730 37

Amt following rents
    Land Rents
        Milton & Co   700.-
        T. Spencer   30.-
        F. Spencer   163.87
        E. Sinclair   262.50
        Lands on Maui   71.50
        Keanae   125.-
        Waialua   100.-
        J. McColgan   50.-
        M. J. Rose   227.50   1730.37

Bills Payable
Amt 4 Notes dated July 8th 1878 given
by His Majesty favor of Claus Spreckles
for 10,000 each at 2, 3, 4, & 5 years with
int. at 7 per cent per annum payable
semiannually and secured by net receipts
of Crown lands   40,000

Kalakaua's cash book shows Spreckels'
loan. Source: Archives of Hawaii

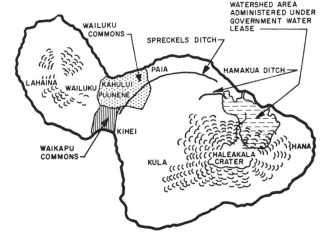

Island of Maui,
showing Spreckels'
land. (Wailuku
and Waikapu
commons) and
ditch about 1885.

Part of central plain, Wailuku, Island of Maui.

Main head gate of Spreckels ditch intake dam, Waihee Valley, Maui. Taken at a dedication ceremony about 1882. Source: Archives of Hawaii

Samuel Parker (left) and
John Cummins (right) hold
kahilis over Princess Ruth.
Spreckels bought her claim to
Hawaiian Crown Lands.
Source: Bishop Museum

Rep. George Washington
Pilipo, the "Lion of North
Kona," vainly fought
Spreckels' land claim.
Source: Archives of Hawaii

No. 3343

ROYAL PATENT.
GRANT.

Kalakaua, **By the Grace of God, King of the Hawaiian Islands:**

By this His Royal Patent, makes known to all men, that he hath for himself, his heirs and successors, this day granted and given unto Claus Spreckels under and by virtue of the provisions of an Act of the Legislature Assembly of the Hawaiian Islands approved on the 21st. day of July 1882 entitled an Act to authorize the Commissioners of Crown Lands to convey certain portions of such lands to Claus Spreckels in satisfaction of all claims he may have on such lands

Containing   24,000   Acres more or less; excepting and reserving to the Hawaiian Government all mineral or metalic mines of every description.

To Have and to Hold the above granted Land in Fee Simple, unto the said CLAUS SPRECKELS   his Heirs and Assigns forever.

Witness Ourself at Honolulu, this   30th day of September   1882, in the   Ninth year of Our Reign.

BY THE KING: (Sgnd)   KALAKAUA REX

The Minister of the Interior,

(SGND)   JNO E BUSH

Joseph Moore (top) and son Andrew (below) built the Spreckelsville mills on Maui in 1882. These were the first five-roller mills in Hawaii, and among the finest in the world. Sources: Joseph, Society of California Pioneers; Andrew, Dina Moore Bowden

Royal grant of Wailuku crown lands to Spreckels.

Spreckelsville mills about 1885. The mills set an example for the Hawaiian sugar industry.

Spreckels was the first to use railroads for intra-plantation cane hauling, 1881.

Steam plow, first used in Hawaii at Sprecklesville, 1880. Source: Archives of Hawaii

William G. Irwin, 1843–1914,
Spreckels' most trusted associate
in Hawaii. The two men
were partners in the Irwin and
Co. sugar agency and
the Spreckels bank. Source:
Archives of Hawaii

Wm. G. Irwin and Co. office,
1879–1884, Queen and
Fort streets, Honolulu. Source:
Archives of Hawaii

Brig "Wm. G. Irwin"
of the Spreckels and
Bros. fleet. Source:
San Francisco
Maritime Museum

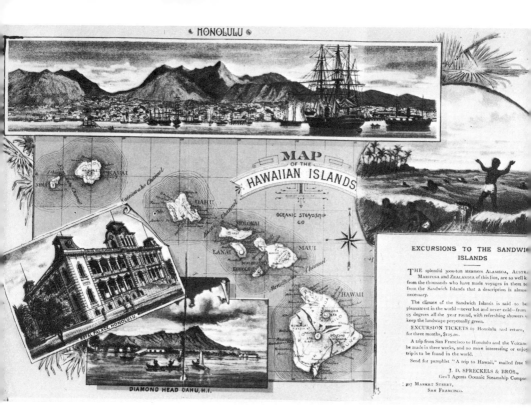

MAP
OF THE
HAWAIIAN ISLANDS

OCEANIC STEAMSHIP CO.

ROYAL PALACE HONOLULU.

DIAMOND HEAD OAHU, H.I.

EXCURSIONS TO THE SANDWICH ISLANDS

THE splendid 3000-ton steamers ALAMEDA, AUSTRALIA, MARIPOSA and ZEALANDIA of this line, are so well known from the thousands who have made voyages in them to and from the Sandwich Islands that a description is almost unnecessary.

The climate of the Sandwich Islands is said to be the pleasantest in the world—never hot and never cold—from 55 degrees all the year round, with refreshing showers to keep the landscape perpetually green.

EXCURSION TICKETS to Honolulu and return, for three months, $125.00.

A trip from San Francisco to Honolulu and the Volcano can be made in three weeks, and no more interesting or enjoyable trip is to be found in the world.

Send for pamphlet "A trip to Hawaii," mailed free to

J. D. SPRECKELS & BROS.,
Gen'l Agents Oceanic Steamship Company
327 MARKET STREET,
SAN FRANCISCO

Spreckels and Bros. promise passengers a delightful trip to Hawaii by the Oceanic Steamship Co. Oceanic also controlled the transport of Hawaiian sugar. Source: Bishop Museum

Oceanic line took over the "John D. Spreckels" in 1882. Source: San Francisco Maritime Museum

The Oceanic Steamship Company's "Alameda" reached Honolulu in October, 1883, on her first voyage.

The "Mariposa" in July, 1883, inaugurated semimonthly steamer service between San Francisco and Honolulu. Source: San Francisco Maritime Museum

King Kalakaua and Premier Gibson
made Spreckels Hawaii's agent to
mint $1,000,000 in silver in the U. S,
In Hawaii, the coinage caused
outcries of "too much silver." Dies
(below) show slashes across the
face of Kalakaua to prevent re-use.
Source: Archives of Hawaii

The Spreckels bank, a partnership of Spreckels and Irwin,
brought banking competition to Hawaii in the post-reciprocity
boom. In 1884 the bank circulated the controversial
Kalakaua silver. Source: Archives of Hawaii

Site of Spreckels
bank on
Merchant Street,
Honolulu.
Source: Archives of
Hawaii

Captain Berger's Royal Hawaiian Band often played at Spreckels' arrivals and departures.

"Gold and Silver will not stop Lead." Sign placed on Spreckels' Honolulu mansion on June 21, 1893, because he wanted to put the queen back on the throne. Source: Archives of Hawaii

Despite the leis this is Spreckels' saddest departure
from Honolulu. Queen Liliuokalani had not been restored.
Spreckels leans on gold-headed cane, a Royalist gift.

The Oceanic
steamer
"Australia"
carried
Spreckels from
Honolulu
after he failed
to unscramble
the Hawaiian
Revolution
of 1893.
Source:
Archives of
Hawaii

Spreckels' Honolulu home in the Punahou district.
In 1921 Jonah Kumalae, a ukulele maker, cut off one story
and moved the home to the Moiliili district.

In 1954 the stunted remains of the Spreckels home
burned to the ground. Source: Archives of Hawaii

Spreckels' San Francisco mansion, Van Ness and
Sacramento streets. The interior (below) seems
surprisingly ornate for a person who even after he
had become rich went to work as a laborer in a
German beet sugar factory. Source:
California Historical Society

Spreckels Building, Third and Market streets, San Francisco, before it was remodeled. Source: California Society of Pioneers

Spreckels at his beet sugar factory, Watsonville, California in early 1887. He looks more like a rugged craftsman than an industrialist. Source: Austin Armer

*Spreckels Building,
San Francisco, after
being remodeled.
It is now known as
the Central Tower.
Source:
W. W. Cordray*

*Western Sugar Refinery, San Francisco, in 1951. It grew out of
the California Sugar Refinery, shown as of 1867 and 1881
in inserts. Source: W. W. Cordray*

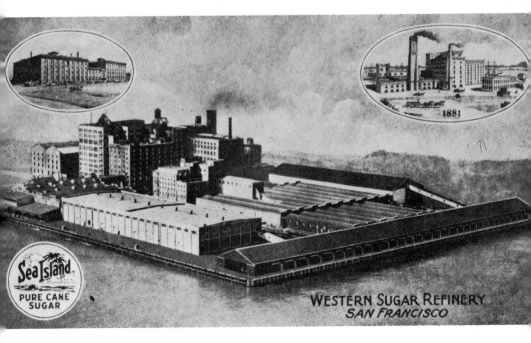

CLAUS SPRECKELS' TRIPS TO HAWAII

Arrivals at Honolulu from San Francisco
Departures from Honolulu for San Francisco

YEAR	ARRIVAL	DEPARTURE	INCLUSIVE DAYS IN HAWAII
1876	August 24	September 12	20
1877	*Not in Hawaii*		
1878	May 21	July 9	50
1879	April 22	May 13	22
1880	March 27	July 6	102
	September 5	September 27	23
1881	June 12	July 5	24
1882	April 18	September 26	162
1883	July 31	October 15	77
1884	January 9	February 15	38
	July 8	August 1	25
1885	January 22	January 31	10
	March 22	May 15	55
1886	March 21	July 31	133
	October 2	October 23	22
1887	*Not in Hawaii*		
1888	*Not in Hawaii*		
1889	February 18	March 14	25
1890	June 27	August 29	64
1891	*Not in Hawaii*		
1892	July 13	August 17	36
1893	April 18	July 19	93
1894	*Not in Hawaii*		
. .	. . . .	. . . .	.
1905	April 21	May 23	33
	June 23	August 30	69

TOTAL DAYS IN HAWAII 1,083

285

NOTES

Abbreviations:

AH: Public Archives of Hawaii
HMCS: Hawaiian Mission Children's Society
LC: Library of Congress
NA: National Archives

I: Spreckels and Reciprocity

1. *Pacific Commercial Advertiser,* August 26, 1876.

2. Recalling that Spreckels had been on the same ship that brought to Hawaii news about ratification of reciprocity, the *San Francisco Bulletin* a few years later called him an "early bird," and said: "That he had wit as well as a pleasant song for the Islanders—the results have shown. The early bird not only catches the worm, but feathers his nest as well—a most proper and justifiable outcome of early habits." As to jealousy of Spreckels in the islands, the article continued: "Lots of late birds and slow birds find fault with the early bird—will insist that his plumage is black, that his song is that of a siren, that he belongs to the carnivorous species, in short, that he has no business to get up so early!" (*San Francisco Bulletin,* April 14, 1881, as quoted in *Hawaiian Gazette,* May 11, 1881.)

3. *Hawaiian Gazette,* September 13, 1876. See also *Pacific Commercial Advertiser,* September 16, 1876.

4. *Pacific Commercial Advertiser,* October 14, 1876.

5. Whaling ship arrivals numbered 549 in 1859 and only 37 in 1876 (*Thrum's Hawaiian Annual,* 1890, p. 25). Exports of sugar increased from 900 tons in 1859 to 13,000 tons in 1876, a 14-fold increase (Theodore Morgan, *Hawaii: A Century of Economic Change, 1778–1876* [Cambridge: Harvard University Press, 1948], pp. 227–228).

6. Morgan, *Hawaii,* p. 206. Morgan's work is a systematic attempt to cover the economic history of Hawaii for the century before reciprocity. The first two volumes of Ralph S. Kuykendall's monumental study, *The Hawaiian Kingdom,* are the standard source for the general history of the kingdom. The third volume, which will cover the reigns of Kalakaua and Liliuokalani, is now in preparation. While Dr. Kuykendall was a historian rather than an economist, even on economic matters his work is often more complete than that of Morgan, particularly with respect to the development of institutions.

7. Ralph S. Kuykendall, *The Hawaiian Kingdom, 1778–1854: Foundation and Transformation* (Honolulu: University of Hawaii, 1938; reprinted, University of Hawaii Press, 1947), pp. 172–173; Ralph S. Kuykendall and A. Grove Day, *Hawaii: A History* (New York: Prentice-Hall, 1948), p. 92; Morgan, *Hawaii*, p. 174.

8. Kuykendall, *Hawaiian Kingdom, 1778–1854*, pp. 175–176, 181–182, 314, 325.

9. *Ibid.*, p. 315; *Story of Sugar in Hawaii* (Honolulu: Hawaiian Sugar Planters' Association, 1926), p. 94.

10. Morgan, *Hawaii*, p. 177.

11. Kuykendall, *Hawaiian Kingdom, 1778–1854*, p. 141.

12. Morgan, *Hawaii*, pp. 214–215.

13. *Ibid.*, p. 188.

14. Kuykendall, *Hawaiian Kingdom, 1778–1854*, pp. 172, 176, 181.

15. *Ibid.*, pp. 328–329; Morgan, *Hawaii*, p. 189.

16. Kuykendall, *Hawaiian Kingdom, 1778–1854*, p. 329.

17. Morgan, *Hawaii*, p. 189.

18. Kuykendall and Day, *Hawaii: A History*, p. 156.

19. Morgan, *Hawaii*, p. 188. On his plantations Spreckels used both free and contract labor, as did other planters. Following the overthrow of the monarchy in 1893, one of Spreckels' main reasons for opposing annexation was that this would mean the end of the contract labor system and curtailment of Chinese immigration (U. S. Congress, Senate, *Hawaiian Islands: Report of the Committee on Foreign Relations* [2 vols., Washington: GPO, 1894], II, p. 1784).

20. Morgan, *Hawaii*, p. 181.

21. Ralph S. Kuykendall, *The Hawaiian Kingdom, 1854–1874: Twenty Critical Years* (Honolulu: University of Hawaii Press, 1953), pp. 145, 326.

22. *Ibid.*, pp. 144–145.

23. Morgan, *Hawaii*, p. 184.

24. This project was to be exceeded by the Spreckels and Hamakua ditches. See chapters 3 and 4.

25. Kuykendall, *Hawaiian Kingdom, 1854–1874*, pp. 145–146; Morgan, *Hawaii*, p. 185.

26. Kuykendall, *Hawaiian Kingdom, 1854–1874*, p. 331.

27. Cecil G. Tilton, *History of Banking in Hawaii* (Honolulu: University of Hawaii, 1927), pp. 43, 49–58.

28. Kuykendall, *Hawaiian Kingdom, 1778–1854*, p. 331.

29. See p. 97.

30. Just about the time Spreckels started his plantation in Hawaii, the following appeared in the *Hawaiian Gazette* (September 4, 1878): "At present the growing of sugar is the leading industry, which requires a large expenditure of capital before realizing a return, and it is a fact that cannot be denied that some are engaged in the culture of cane, who have not the means to carry . . . through from the time they put in their first plant till the crop matures. . . . To the man with ample capital at his command, there is no place in the world where a fortune is surer than on these Islands, in the sugar culture, if advantageously located; because no where else can such large results be obtained in the way of a crop."

31. Kuykendall, *Hawaiian Kingdom, 1778–1854*, p. 315.

32. Morgan, *Hawaii*, p. 175.

33. Kuykendall, *Hawaiian Kingdom, 1778–1854*, pp. 323–324; Morgan, *Hawaii*, p. 178; Kuykendall and Day, *Hawaii: A History*, p. 93.

34. Kuykendall, *Hawaiian Kingdom, 1778–1854*, p. 331.
35. *Ibid.*, p. 140.
36. Morgan, *Hawaii*, pp. 179–180.
37. Kuykendall, *Hawaiian Kingdom, 1854–1874*, pp. 143–148.
38. *Pacific Commercial Advertiser*, August 26, 1876.
39. *Hawaiian Gazette*, October 11, 1876.
40. The San Francisco refiners got the benefit of a small fraction of the tariff remission (F. W. Taussig, *Some Aspects of the Tariff Question* [Cambridge: Harvard University Press, 1931], p. 108).
41. The United States made no use of Pearl Harbor, despite the treaty provision, until after annexation.
42. Kuykendall and Day, *Hawaii: A History*, pp. 175, 186.
43. *Bulletin* (Honolulu), April 19, 1884.
44. *Story of Sugar in Hawaii*, p. 94.
45. Morgan, *Hawaii*, pp. 214–215.
46. *Ibid.*, p. 213.
47. The agency system has been a subject of much controversy. There can be little doubt that the agencies have played a large role in the economy of Hawaii for over a hundred years. The extent of their control at various times, the extent to which such control promoted or retarded economic development, and the political and social aspects of the system have yet to be the subject of a definitive study.
48. *Hawaiian Gazette*, July 31, 1878. On the agency system, see Kuykendall, *Hawaiian Kingdom, 1854–1874*, and references cited by him. See also: *Sugar in Hawaii*, pp. 32–41; A. L. Dean, *Cooperation in the Sugar Industry of Hawaii* (New York: Institute of Pacific Relations, 1933), pp. 11–17; *The First 100 Years: A Report on the Operations of Castle & Cooke* (Honolulu: privately printed, 1951), pp. 57–59; Josephine Sullivan, *A History of C. Brewer & Co., Ltd.* (Boston: Walton Advertising and Printing Co., 1926), pp. 171–173.
49. *Pacific Commercial Advertiser*, supplement, June 15, 1885, reporting testimony of Claus Spreckels in the trial of his son, A. B. Spreckels, for the shooting of M. H. De Young, owner of the *San Francisco Chronicle*. Around 1876 more than half of the sugar shipped from Hawaii was over 12 Dutch standard. The Dutch standard was one for grading sugar by color, and was superseded around 1880 by polarization tests. See Taussig, *Some Aspects of the Tariff Question*, pp. 100–101.
50. *Hawaiian Gazette*, March 24, 1875, citing Washington dispatch to *San Francisco Bulletin*, date line February 16, 1875.
51. In recent years the islands have produced about one million tons of sugar a year.
52. *Pacific Commercial Advertiser*, March 13, 1875.
53. Kuykendall, *Hawaiian Kingdom, 1874–1893* (in press), chapter II.

II: *King Kalakaua and King Claus*

1. See W. D. Alexander, *History of Later Years of the Hawaiian Monarchy and Revolution of 1893* (Honolulu: 1896), pp. 1–25; Kuykendall and Day, *Hawaii: A History*, pp. 162–173; Leo L. Partlow, "Merry Monarch of Hawaii," *Asia*, XXXII (February, March, 1932), 73–79, 156–161. This last article

presents Kalakaua as a fascinating study in cultural conflict. A definitive study of the Kalakaua regime is much needed. Dr. Kuykendall's forthcoming *Hawaiian Kingdom, 1874–1893,* will doubtless fill this need.

2. The avowed basis of opposition to the Kalakaua regime was a moral one, and the opponents claimed to be interested in good government. No doubt they were, but a probing of their less altruistic motives would make a worth-while study.

3. A highly readable sketch of Gibson, with some suggestions that his character is not as black as it has often been painted, is contained in James A. Michener and A. Grove Day, *Rascals in Paradise* (New York: Random House, 1957), pp. 112–146. See also Esther L. F. Sousa, "Walter Murray Gibson's Rise to Power in Hawaii" (unpublished master's thesis, No. 195, University of Hawaii, 1942).

4. Alexander, *History of Later Years of the Hawaiian Monarchy,* p. 7.

5. *Ibid.,* p. 18.

6. This section relies mainly on the only comprehensive account of Spreckels' life thus far written: W. W. Cordray, "Claus Spreckels of California" (unpublished doctoral dissertation, University of Southern California, 1955). See also: George F. Nellist, ed., *Builders of Hawaii* (Honolulu: Star-Bulletin, 1925), pp. 179–180; Lorrin A. Thurston, *Memoirs of the Hawaiian Revolution* (Honolulu: Advertiser Pub. Co., 1936), pp. 81–90; Dumas Malone, ed., *Dictionary of American Biography* (New York: Scribners, 1935), XVII, pp. 478–479; *Hawaiian Gazette,* April 25, August 22, 1905; *New York Times,* December 27, 1908; *Hawaiian Star,* December 26, 1908; *Evening Bulletin* (Honolulu), December 26, 1908; *Honolulu Star-Bulletin,* August 17, 1935, "Claus Spreckels, the Sugar King," by D. Billam-Walker; *Honolulu Star-Bulletin,* December 22, 1938; *Pacific Commercial Advertiser,* January 25, 1902, December 27, 1908.

7. W. Klenck (retired teacher, Lamstedt, Germany) to Jacob Adler, May 6, June 5, 1958.

8. W. Klenck, *Heimatkunde des ehemaligen Kreises Neuhaus an der Oste* (Stade: 1957), p. 237.

9. In later years Spreckels helped several persons to emigrate from Lamstedt, but once they reached the United States he offered them no more help. He had "made it" on his own and he expected them to do the same. (W. Klenck to Jacob Adler, June 5, 1958.)

10. Cordray, "Claus Spreckels of California," p. 81, quoting *San Francisco Morning Call,* May 6, 1888.

11. *Ibid.,* p. 105, quoting *Pajaronian* (Pajaro Valley, California), November 10, 1887.

12. *Ibid.,* p. 115, quoting *San Francisco Call,* August 2, 1896.

13. Besides his connection with the San Francisco and San Joaquin Valley Railroad, Spreckels founded the Pajaro Valley Railroad in 1889 to serve the Western Beet Sugar Refinery at Watsonville. This road was later extended to Salinas and to Spreckels to serve the beet sugar plant there. By 1900 the road had 33 miles of track. Although primarily used by the Spreckels interests, the road also gave general service to the residents of Pajaro Valley.

On Spreckels' intraplantation railroad in the Hawaiian Islands, see Chapter 7.

14. Cordray, "Claus Spreckels of California," p. 199, quoting Charles M. Coleman, *Pacific Gas and Electric of California* (New York: McGraw-Hill, 1952), p. 90.

15. See Chapter 17.

16. *Pacific Commercial Advertiser,* December 27, 1908.

III: *Water Rights and Cabinet Shuffles*

1. *Sugar in Hawaii*, p. 17.

2. In recent years the Hawaiian sugar industry has needed about 1,600 million gallons of water a day. Much of this has been provided by investments of about $50,000,000 in irrigation. (*Thrum's Hawaiian Annual*, 1954, p. 42; *Honolulu Advertiser*, July 1, 1956, "Big Gamble Paid Off for Maui Sugar Men.")

3. *Pacific Commercial Advertiser*, May 22, 1875.

4. *Pacific Commercial Advertiser*, June 5, 1875. The editor's opinion that private enterprise would not build the needed irrigation works was soon proved wrong.

5. *Ibid.*

6. *Ibid.* On the importance of irrigation and calls for government action, see also *Pacific Commercial Advertiser*, June 24, 1876, and *Hawaiian Gazette*, July 11, 1877.

7. *Pacific Commercial Advertiser*, August 26, 1876. Mention of the Reciprocity Treaty with the United States deserves further emphasis. In 1893, when Spreckels was being interviewed by Commissioner J. H. Blount, who had been sent by President Cleveland to investigate the overthrow of the monarchy, the sugar king indicated that the treaty had furnished the chief stimulus to irrigation projects (*Report of the Committee on Foreign Relations*, II, pp. 1782–1783).

8. Alexander, *History of Later Years of the Hawaiian Monarchy*, p. 3; *Directory of the Hawaiian Kingdom*, 1880–1881 (San Francisco: 1881), p. 506. Spreckels left Honolulu for Lahaina, Maui, on August 28, 1876, and returned to Honolulu on September 8. He left for San Francisco a few days later. (*Pacific Commercial Advertiser*, September 2, 9, 1876.)

9. *Pacific Commercial Advertiser*, October 12, 1878.

10. *Pacific Commercial Advertiser*, April 7, 1877. This quotation would lead one to suspect that Spreckels corresponded with the Hawaiian government between September, 1876, when he left the islands, and May, 1878, when he returned. No such correspondence has been uncovered by the present writer.

11. *Hawaiian Gazette*, March 27, 1878.

12. *Pacific Commercial Advertiser*, May 4, 1878; *Hawaiian Gazette*, May 8, 1878.

13. *Pacific Commercial Advertiser*, May 4, 1878. The Wailuku Commons was at a greater distance from Mount Haleakala than the area to be irrigated by the Hamakua ditch of Baldwin and Alexander.

14. *Pacific Commercial Advertiser*, October 12, 1878.

15. Lease of Wailuku crown lands to Claus Spreckels by Commissioners of Crown Lands, effective July 1, 1878, Bureau of Conveyances, Honolulu, book 55, pp. 196–200; book 57, pp. 299–304.

16. Copy of petition in Water-Maui-Molokai-Sundries, 1866–1885, file, AH.

17. Spreckels' attempt to get the water rights may have been a factor in the motion of lack of confidence. However, there had been much friction on other matters between ministry and legislature, and ministry and king.

18. Alexander, *History of Later Years of the Hawaiian Monarchy*, p. 4.

19. *Hawaiian Gazette*, July 10, 1878.

20. *Hawaiian Gazette*, July 3, 1878. "By Authority Notice."

James M. Comly, United States minister resident, described the members of the new cabinet as follows:

"Wilder is of American birth, a noble of the Kingdom, of fine business ability in conducting his large shipping and other interests. . . .

"Kapena was with the King in America. A native of good ability . . . but timid and somewhat vacillating.

"Kaai, a native of above average ability. . . . He was the native leader of Mr. Gibson's agitators. . . .

"Preston is an Englishman. . . . He is a lawyer of considerable practice. He is represented to be a hard drinker. . . ." (Comly to Secretary of State, No. 44, July 8, 1878, Despatches from U. S. Ministers in Hawaii, NA; on microfilm, University of Hawaii Library, Honolulu.)

21. Wodehouse to "My Lord," July 8, 1878, British Public Records Office, FO 58/162, pp. 78–79 (on microfilm, University of Hawaii Library, Honolulu).

22. Comly to Secretary of State, No. 43, July 8, 1878, Despatches from U. S. Ministers in Hawaii, NA.

23. *Hawaiian Gazette,* July 17, 1878, letter signed "Hawaii." For a firsthand report of the meeting at Kaumakapili Church, see *Ko Hawaii Pae Aina* (Hawaiian language newspaper), July 13, 1878, report signed by C. P. Iaukea who was secretary of the meeting.

For an interesting sidelight on why the Hawaiians seem to have been receptive to Spreckels from the start, see editorial in *Ka Nupepa Kuokoa,* July 13, 1878, entitled "Hooulu Lahui." This means "increase and preservation of the race," said to have been one of the principal slogans of the Kalakaua regime. The gist of the editorial, freely translated and paraphrased, is as follows:

Ka Haole Dala nui o Kaleponi ("the white foreign capitalist from California"), Claus Spreckels, has bought extensive lands on Maui. He will bring the waters from the mountains and plant the lands to sugar. Within the next few years he will invest one and a half million dollars in the islands.

One of his ideas concerns the increase and preservation of the Hawaiian race. He will divide these lands into small districts, and settle whole families on them. They will plant sugar on shares and get paid for their labors. The country will become prosperous and the people will multiply. Thus the idea of *ho'oulu lahui* will become a reality.

24. *Pacific Commercial Advertiser,* October 5, 1878, citing portions of an article in the *Alta California,* September 5, 1878. An undated clipping of what was probably the original of the *Alta California* article is contained in the letter of C. C. Harris to E. H. Allen, October 4, 1878.

25. Kalakaua Cash Book, July 1878, p. 51, AH.

26. C. C. Harris to E. H. Allen, October 4, 1878, Elisha H. Allen Papers, LC (on microfilm, University of Hawaii Library, Honolulu).

27. Parker was a Honolulu businessman and landowner who inherited a large cattle ranch on the island of Hawaii. He was friendly to Spreckels throughout the latter's Hawaiian career. Parker was a poker-playing crony of Spreckels and Kalakaua, and when the furnishings of Spreckels' Punahou home were sold in 1913, he bought the massive poker table for "old times' sake."

28. C. C. Harris to E. H. Allen, October 4, 1878.

29. Harris to Allen, undated, but probably written in July, 1878, Allen Papers.

30. Journal of the Legislative Assembly, 1880, proceedings of August 5, 1880, p. 264, AH.

31. *Pacific Commercial Advertiser,* August 7, 1880.

32. *Ibid.*

33. *Ibid.*

34. *Hawaiian Gazette,* August 11, 1880.

35. *Ibid.*

36. Journal of the Legislative Assembly, 1880, proceedings of August 12, 1880, pp. 285–286, AH.

37. *Pacific Commercial Advertiser,* August 14, 1880.

38. *Ibid.*

39. *Hawaiian Gazette,* August 18, 1880. The $30,000 advanced to the Commissioners of Crown Lands was eventually returned to the treasury in full (*Pacific Commercial Advertiser,* June 14, 1884).

IV: *The Spreckels Ditch*

1. Copy of lease in Miscellaneous Interior file, AH.

2. *Pacific Commercial Advertiser,* July 12, 1878. The Risdon Iron Works was later to design and construct sugar mills for the Spreckelsville plantation. See Chapter 7.

3. *Hawaiian Gazette,* October 16, 1878.

4. *Pacific Commercial Advertiser,* July 12, 1878.

5. See Chapter 7. The Hawaiian Commercial Company (later, 1882, the Hawaiian Commercial and Sugar Company) was the instrument through which Spreckels controlled the Spreckelsville plantation on Maui.

6. *Directory of Hawaiian Kingdom,* 1880–1881, pp. 506, 507.

7. *Ibid.* See also *Hawaiian Gazette,* November 6, 1878; *Pacific Commercial Advertiser,* November 9, 1878.

8. *Hawaiian Gazette,* December 4, 1878; *Pacific Commercial Advertiser,* December 7, 1878. Mention of William G. Irwin and Company in this notice furnishes one of the early links between Spreckels and Irwin. Irwin was later to become the sugar king's most important business associate in the islands. See Chapter 9.

9. *Pacific Commercial Advertiser,* December 7, 1878.

10. *Directory of Hawaiian Kingdom,* 1880–1881, p. 507.

11. *Pacific Commercial Advertiser,* April 12, 1879.

12. *Pacific Commercial Advertiser,* May 10, 1879.

13. *Pacific Commercial Advertiser,* May 24, 1879.

14. *Hawaiian Gazette,* June 25, 1879. Former Mayor McCoppin of San Francisco made a pleasure trip to the islands in 1879, and was attracted by the prospects of sugar on Maui. He planted over 400 acres in 1880, all irrigated by the ditch. With the exception of the Spreckels acreage this was the most extensive planting during the year. (*Saturday Press,* November 20, 1880.)

15. *Pacific Commercial Advertiser,* October 4, 1879.

16. *Pacific Commercial Advertiser,* October 11, 1879.

17. *Hawaiian Gazette,* March 24, 1880.

18. *Hawaiian Gazette,* April 14, 21, 1880.

19. *Hawaiian Gazette,* June 2, 1880.

20. H. M. Whitney, *Tourists' Guide through the Hawaiian Islands* (Honolulu: Hawaiian Gazette Co., 1890), p. 84.

21. *Ibid.*

22. *Hawaiian Gazette,* June 7, 28, July 26, August 16, 23, 30, 1882; *Pacific Commercial Advertiser,* October 14, 1882. Interestingly enough, Spreckels paid $10,000 a year to the Wailuku Sugar Company for water rights involved in the Waihee ditch, whereas his government lease for the Spreckels ditch cost only $500 a year (*Pacific Commercial Advertiser,* August 16, 1892). This, in spite of the fact that the Spreckels ditch delivered more water than the Waihee ditch.

23. John W. Vandercook, *King Cane* (New York: Harper, 1939), pp. 67–70.

24. The first cost estimate for the Hamakua ditch was $25,000. As the costs mounted, Castle and Cooke, a Honolulu sugar agency, helped with financing. Without this help Baldwin and Alexander would have been hard put to complete the work.

25. *Honolulu Advertiser,* August 14, 1942; H. A. Wadsworth, "A Historical Summary of Irrigation in Hawaii," *Planters' Monthly,* XXXVIII (October, 1933), 144; Arthur L. Dean, *Alexander and Baldwin, Ltd.* (Honolulu: Alexander and Baldwin, 1950), pp. 16, 18.

26. *Pacific Commercial Advertiser,* January 4, 1886.

27. See chapters 19, 20, 21.

28. *Bulletin* (Honolulu), May 15, 1893.

29. *Hawaiian Star,* August 3, 1893.

V: Princess Ruth and the Crown Lands

1. On development of the Hawaiian land system and origin of the crown lands, see: Thomas M. Spaulding, *Crown Lands of Hawaii* (Honolulu: University of Hawaii, 1923); Jon J. Chinen, *The Great Mahele* (Honolulu: University of Hawaii Press, 1958); Kuykendall, *The Hawaiian Kingdom, 1778–1854,* pp. 269–298; Sanford B. Dole, *Evolution of Hawaiian Land Tenures* (Hawaiian Historical Society Papers, No. 3, Honolulu: 1892); W. D. Alexander, "A Brief History of Land Titles in the Hawaiian Kingdom," *Thrum's Hawaiian Annual,* 1891, pp. 105–124.

2. Princess Ruth Keelikolani (1826–1883) was the daughter of Governor Kekuanaoa and Pauahi, and a half sister of Kamehameha IV and Kamehameha V. She was thus of high rank and was once talked about as a possible heir to the throne. Among official positions she held were those of Governess of Hawaii and member of the Hawaiian House of Nobles. She was steeped in Hawaiian traditions, cared little for the ways of the foreigner, and spoke little English. Her son by adoption was William Pitt Leleiohoku, heir apparent and brother of Kalakaua. Leleiohoku died in his youth. (Kuykendall, *The Hawaiian Kingdom, 1854–1874,* p. 241; *Bulletin* (Honolulu), May 28, 1883; *Hawaiian Gazette,* May 30, 1883.)

3. John F. G. Stokes, "Kaoleioku: Paternity and Biographical Sketch," *Forty-third Annual Report, Hawaiian Historical Society* (Honolulu: 1935). This article is a remarkable bit of genealogical detective work.

4. Cordray, "Claus Spreckels of California," citing statement made by Claus Spreckels during court fight with son August, reported in *San Francisco Chronicle* November 22, 1895. On Princess Ruth's claim and Spreckels' purchase of it, see also: A. S. Cleghorn to Princess Likelike, September 14, 1880 (note furnished by Ralph S. Kuykendall); *Pacific Commercial Advertiser,* September 18, 24, 1880; *Hawaiian Gazette,* September 15, 22, 1880; *Saturday Press,*

September 18, 1880; *Bulletin* (Honolulu), July 19, 1882; *Hawaiian Star,* August 24, 1893; Spaulding, *Crown Lands,* p. 15; Jean Hobbs, *Hawaii: A Pageant of the Soil* (Palo Alto: Stanford University Press, 1935), pp. 73–74.

5. 6 Hawaiian Reports 447; Interior Department Land File, March, 1893, AH. The deed contains the notation: "Signed, Sealed and Delivered by the above named Ruth Keelikolani, the same having first been interpreted to her in the presence of Simon K. Kaai." This is important in considering the question of possible undue influence by Kaai, because Princess Ruth understood little English.

6. *Pacific Commercial Advertiser,* September 24, 1880.

7. *Ibid.*

8. "Since Princess Ruth never dreamed she had any interest in the property, the offer [of Spreckels] was a pickup, and she promptly accepted" (Thurston, *Memoirs,* p. 83).

9. Kaai must be regarded as a "Spreckels man." It will be recalled that he was a member of the 1878 cabinet that gave Spreckels the Maui water rights, and he also tried to justify this act at a meeting of native Hawaiians.

10. *Saturday Press,* September 18, 1880.

11. "It was thought at the time that Spreckels was purchasing a lawsuit. But the old man knew better; he knew a good thing when he saw it." (*Hawaiian Star,* August 24, 1893.)

12. *Pacific Commercial Advertiser,* May 28, 1885.

13. *Pacific Commercial Advertiser,* June 4, 1885.

14. Victor S. K. Houston Collection, AH. For calling attention to this important document, the present writer is especially indebted to Miss Agnes Conrad, head of the Archives.

W. F. Allen wrote in a letter to his father (after the claim had been settled in the legislature): "Preston and most of the bar have considered this claim good, and we all consider that Spreckels has acted magnanimously in settling it in this way" (W. F. Allen to E. H. Allen, July 22, 1882, Allen Papers, LC).

15. *Hawaiian Gazette,* May 24, 1882, "By Authority" notice.

16. Ernest Andrade, Jr., "The Hawaiian Revolution of 1887" (unpublished master's thesis, University of Hawaii, 1954), p. 24. Andrade does not give his source for this statement, and the present writer has not been able to verify it.

17. W. L. Green to H. A. P. Carter, May 8, 1882, H. A. P. Carter file, AH.

18. *Pacific Commercial Advertiser,* May 27, 1882.

VI: *The Legislature of Many Luaus*

1. "Journal of Legislative Assembly, 1882," proceedings of July 11, 1882, AH.

2. His full name was George Washington Pilipo. "Pilipo is a gentleman of purely native blood; he is advanced in years and has great experience in all native matters: for twelve or fourteen years he has represented the district of North Kona, the constituents of that district having unbounded faith in him.... He is a fearless supporter of native rights pure and simple, with no leanings toward the foreigner: he may be regarded as a typical Hawaiian of the old school." (*Hawaiian Gazette,* December 13, 1882.)

3. *Pacific Commercial Advertiser,* July 19, 1882.

4. *Hawaiian Gazette,* July 26, 1882.

5. *Ibid.*

6. *Pacific Commercial Advertiser,* July 19, 1882.

7. *Ibid.*

8. *Hawaiian Gazette,* July 26, 1882.

9. *Pacific Commercial Advertiser,* July 19, 1882.

10. Preston's version of the background of the claim is somewhat garbled, even with respect to the facts as then understood. In simple terms, Princess Ruth claimed that she was of the Kamehameha line, that she thus had a hereditary interest in the crown lands, and that this interest could not be taken away by the act of January 3, 1865, making the crown lands inalienable.

11. *Pacific Commercial Advertiser,* July 19, 1882.

12. If Kaai thought Princess Ruth had a good claim to a half interest in the crown lands (this half interest being worth about $750,000), one may well ask why he permitted her to sell it to Spreckels for $10,000.

13. *Pacific Commercial Advertiser,* July 19, 1882.

14. *Hawaiian Gazette,* July 26, 1882.

15. *Pacific Commercial Advertiser,* July 19, 1882. It is hard to see how the bill before the legislature could have benefited Princess Ruth in any way.

16. Voting for postponement were: J. Keau, J. W. Kalua, J. Kamakele, J. Gardner, J. Nawahi, J. M. Kauwila, G. W. Pilipo, and S. Aiwohi. Voting against postponement were: W. M. Gibson, S. K. Kaai, J. E. Bush, E. Preston, C. R. Bishop, J. O. Dominis, A. S. Cleghorn, J. P. Parker, P. Isenberg, J. Moanauli, G. Rhodes, J. Mott Smith, E. K. Lilikalani, H. W. Lahilahi, F. Pahia, Frank Brown, S. K. Mahoe, J. Kaluhi, J. L. Kaulukou, L. Aholo, G. E. Richardson, J. Nakookoo, P. Haupu, J. Kauhane, D. H. Nahinu, J. K. Kaunamano, J. Kauai, G. B. Palohau, J. Nakaleka, and J. A. Kaukau. (*Pacific Commercial Advertiser,* July 19, 1882.)

17. A written statement by Preston could hardly have been of much value. He drew up the bill.

18. *Pacific Commercial Advertiser,* July 21, 1882. Oddly enough, on the very day the land bill passed, Princess Ruth and her retinue were being royally entertained at Spreckelsville on Maui (*Hawaiian Gazette,* July 26, 1882).

19. *Session Laws,* 1882, p. 11.

20. *Pacific Commercial Advertiser,* July 22, 1882. The third commissioner was C. H. Judd, who had been chairman of the debate in the legislature.

21. *Bulletin* (Honolulu), August 8, 1882.

22. Copy of quitclaim in Interior Department Land File, August, 1882, AH. Royal Patent 3343, dated September 30, 1882, on file, Office of the Commissioner of Public Lands, Honolulu.

In later years a tradition arose that Spreckels had won the lands in a poker game with Kalakaua. As late as 1934, the head of the Territorial Survey Department, Robert D. King, found it necessary to "explode" this tradition. At a luncheon meeting of the Honolulu Realty Board he gave the facts about the issue of a royal patent to Spreckels after passage of the land bill. (*Honolulu Star-Bulletin,* December 19, 1934.)

23. *Pacific Commercial Advertiser,* May 28, June 4, 1885; *Hawaiian Gazette,* June 3, 10, 1885.

24. "If the Government measure had been defeated," it would have been followed by "a great and costly law suit" (*Pacific Commercial Advertiser,* July 22, 1882). Alexander indicates that the ministry recommended the compromise bill as better than risking a test in the courts (*History of Later Years of the*

Hawaiian Monarchy, p. 8). Hobbs writes: "Spreckels' political power made it expedient that an amicable settlement be reached" (*Hawaii: A Pageant of the Soil,* p. 74).

25. To the foreigner, getting land in Hawaii was a big problem. The crown lands were eyed covetously: "The old and ridiculous notions of primitive times in regard to the effects of alienating territory should have long since been abandoned, and certainly should not be entertained by a government professing to enlightenment, especially at this time, when it is felt as an imperative necessity that everything should be done that will in any way tend to induce an influx of population.... Here alone [in the crown lands] are lands sufficient in area to support a population many times exceeding the number of our entire people, and now hired out to proprietors who might be numbered on a few men's fingers." (*Pacific Commercial Advertiser,* April 1, 1876.)

This, it will be noted, was written in 1876. With the boom following reciprocity there was more pressure on the part of foreigners to get land: "There would be a real advantage to the country if these Crown lands were sold at the present time. Now the crown lands are leased, and the lessees have no desire to make permanent improvements on them; only give the lessee the chance of getting his land in fee simple, and we would find a very different spirit in regard to the land which a man happened to own; who is willing to put expensive buildings on a leased land?

"Another view is worth considering; the moment the Crown lands become private property, they will become taxable and yield a revenue to the country, so that not only from the private view of the royal family, but from that of the nation at large, the scheme appears to be a good one." (*Hawaiian Gazette,* July 4, 1882.)

26. *Ko Hawaii Pae Aina,* July 22, 1882, as cited in *Saturday Press,* July 29, 1882.

27. *Ko Hawaii Pae Aina,* July 29, 1882, as cited in *Saturday Press,* August 5, 1882.

28. So far as can be determined, the constitutionality of the land bill was never tested in court.

29. *Ko Hawaii Pae Aina,* August 5, 1882, as cited in *Hawaiian Gazette,* August 9, 1882.

30. *Ibid.* On loans by Spreckels under the Loan Act of 1882, see chapters 17 and 18.

31. *Ko Hawaii Pae Aina,* November 11, 1882, as cited in *Hawaiian Gazette,* November 15, 1882.

32. *Hawaiian Gazette,* supplement, August 30, 1882. The rate of interest was well below the going rate of interest which was about 9 per cent. The quoted statement, if not true, was probably libelous. Gibson did not sue.

A letter of Queen Emma also mentions this loan by Spreckels to Gibson, and gives the proceeds as $35,000. This was used by Gibson to pay off a mortgage held on his Lanai sheep ranch by James Campbell. (Queen Emma to Mrs. Pierre Jones, August 15, 1882, Flora L. Jones Collection, AH.)

33. *Ko Hawaii Pae Aina,* August 5, 1882, as cited in *Saturday Press,* August 12, 1882. It is not possible to tell from the quotation whether this refers to the $10,000 paid to Princess Ruth, or whether the newspaper was implying that an additional $10,000 was paid to Kaai.

34. Queen Emma to Mrs. Pierre Jones, August 15, 1882.

35. *Hawaiian Gazette,* October 4, 1882.

36. *Hawaiian Gazette,* January 9, 1883.

37. *Hawaiian Gazette,* August 9, 1882.

38. *Bulletin* (Honolulu), October 25, 1882.
39. *Pacific Commercial Advertiser,* November 4, 1882.
40. *Ibid.*
41. Thurston, *Memoirs,* p. 59. Alexander writes: "In order to prevent Pilipo's election, the King proceeded to his district of North Kona, taking with him a number of soldiers and attendants (who voted at the election), besides numerous cases of liquor. He took an active part in the canvass, and succeeded in defeating Pilipo by a small majority. The King's interference nearly provoked a riot, which was averted by Pilipo's strenuous exertions." (*History of Later Years of the Hawaiian Monarchy,* p. 13.)

VII: Spreckelsville Plantation

1. *Honolulu Advertiser,* April 23, 1932.
2. The terms "industrial capitalism" and "financial capitalism" are used here in the same sense that Thorstein Veblen uses them. In highly simplified terms, an industrial capitalist is primarily interested in expanding production of goods and services; a financial capitalist is interested in financial transactions and the papers representing them.
3. *Pacific Commercial Advertiser,* June 22, 1878. Cornwell had bought the Waikapu Commons for $15,000 in 1875 (*Pacific Commercial Advertiser,* November 20, 1875). Thus the half interest sold to Spreckels for $20,000 cost Cornwell about $7,500. This is a good example of what happened to land prices under the stimulus of the Reciprocity Treaty.
4. *Pacific Commercial Advertiser,* June 22, 1878.
5. *Hawaiian Gazette,* June 26, 1878.
6. Certified copy of charter, File HCS, Foreign 13, Office of State Treasurer, Honolulu. Hawaiian Commercial Company did not carry out the fifth of its stated purposes. But see chapters 11 and 12.
7. *Directory of the Hawaiian Kingdom, 1880–1881,* p. 431.
8. *Hawaiian Gazette,* April 12, 1882; *Pacific Commercial Advertiser,* April 22, 1882.
9. Certified copy of charter, File HCS, Foreign 13, Office of State Treasurer, Honolulu.
10. *Hawaiian Gazette,* August 23, 1882.
11. *Honolulu Star-Bulletin,* October 25, 1935.
12. *Hawaiian Gazette,* September 5, 1883.
13. *Directory of the Hawaiian Kingdom, 1880–1881,* p. 431.
14. *Pacific Coast Commercial Record,* May, 1892, p. 21.
15. *Pacific Commercial Advertiser,* August 25, 1883; *Hawaiian Gazette,* May 17, October 4, 1882; August 29, 1883.
16. *Hawaiian Directory and Handbook* (San Francisco: 1888), p. 487.
17. *Hawaiian Directory and Handbook* (San Francisco: 1884), p. 319.
18. *Hawaiian Gazette,* November 13, 1878. There were at least two fairly large ventures at planting on shares with Spreckels: one of about 500 acres by former Mayor McCoppin of San Francisco; another of about 600 acres by W. Y. Horner of Honolulu (*Directory of Hawaiian Kingdom, 1880–1881,* pp. 431, 508).

19. *Pacific Coast Commercial Record,* May, 1892, p. 20.

20. *Ibid.* See also *Directory of Hawaiian Kingdom, 1880–1881,* p. 505; *Hawaiian Gazette,* November 9, 1881; *Maui News,* February 23, 1935; *Hawaiian Directory and Handbook* (1884), p. 318; *Hawaiian Gazette,* September 9, 1885.

21. *Pacific Commercial Advertiser,* December 17, 1881; March 25, 1882.

22. *Honolulu Advertiser,* December 6, 1924.

23. *Pacific Commercial Advertiser,* March 25, 1882.

24. *Bulletin* (Honolulu), January 23, 1893; *Hawaiian Gazette,* November 7, 1883.

25. On the use of electric lights at the palace, see *Hawaiian Gazette,* November 16, 1886.

26. *Saturday Press,* October 1, 1881.

27. *Hawaiian Gazette,* October 5, 1881.

28. Queen Emma to Mrs. Pierre Jones, November 17, 1881, Queen Emma Collection, AH.

29. *Hawaiian Gazette,* August 23, 1882.

30. From the Kahului wharf Spreckels' ships carried the raw sugar to his San Francisco refinery. Many other Maui planters had to transship their raw sugar by way of Honolulu at added cost.

31. *Hawaiian Gazette,* March 16, September 14, 1881; October 24, 1883.

32. *Hawaii's Sugar News,* VII (August, 1957), 3.

33. *Pacific Commercial Advertiser,* December 6, 1879; *Directory of the Hawaiian Kingdom, 1880–1881,* p. 508.

34. Whitney, *Tourists' Guide,* p. 88.

35. *Hawaiian Gazette,* April 28, 1880.

36. *Pacific Commercial Advertiser,* August 26, 1882; *Hawaiian Gazette,* September 6, 1882.

37. *Hawaii's Sugar News,* VII (August, 1957), 3.

38. *Hawaiian Gazette,* October 24, 1883.

39. *Pacific Commercial Advertiser,* October 21, 1884; H. P. Agee, "A Brief History of the Hawaii Sugar Planters' Association," *Thrum's Hawaiian Annual,* 1935, p. 80.

40. Whitney, *Tourists' Guide,* p. 88. Whitney was an important chronicler of the sugar industry.

41. *Hawaiian Gazette,* August 23, 1882.

42. *Hawaiian Gazette,* July 6, 1881.

43. *Ibid.*

44. *Pacific Commercial Advertiser,* April 25, 1882; *Hawaiian Gazette,* April 27, 1886.

45. See Chapter 10.

46. See chapters 11 and 12.

47. *Pacific Commercial Advertiser,* December 6, 1879.

48. *Directory of the Hawaiian Kingdom, 1880–1881,* p. 431.

49. *Thrum's Hawaiian Annual,* 1909, p. 186.

50. *Bulletin* (Honolulu), July 15, 1890; *Honolulu Star-Bulletin,* April 12, 1920; Dean, *Alexander and Baldwin,* p. 30.

51. Hawaiian Commercial and Sugar Company is the seventh largest private landholder in the Hawaiian Islands (*Major Landholdings in Hawaii,* Economic Production and Coordination Authority Staff Report No. 14 [Honolulu: February, 1957], p. 19).

52. *Hawaiian Gazette,* September 22, 1880.

53. *Bulletin* (Honolulu), August 2, 1892.

54. *Hawaiian Star,* August 3, 1893.

VIII: *Hawaiian Commercial and Sugar Company*

1. Dean, *Alexander & Baldwin*, p. 64; *Hawaiian Star,* October 12, 1898; *Pacific Commercial Advertiser,* September 23, 1882, September 9, 1885; *Bulletin* (Honolulu), November 24, 1884.
2. See, for example, *San Francisco Chronicle,* November 24, 1883.
3. *Bulletin* (Honolulu), December 2, 1884.
4. *Pacific Commercial Advertiser,* June 15, 1885.
5. *Pacific Commercial Advertiser,* June 23, 1885.
6. *Pacific Commercial Advertiser,* March 9, 1889.
7. *Bulletin* (Honolulu), December 8, 1884.
8. *Pacific Commercial Advertiser,* December 9, 1884.
9. *Hawaiian Gazette,* September 2, 1885.
10. *Hawaiian Gazette,* January 31, February 14, 1893; Dean, *Alexander & Baldwin,* p. 64.
11. *Hawaiian Gazette,* December 2, 1893.
12. *Hawaiian Gazette,* December 12, 1893.
13. *Hawaiian Gazette,* January 23, 1894.
14. *Ibid.* Battles within the Spreckels family could easily be the subject of a study. It is enough to say here that toward the end of his life Claus became reconciled with Gus and Rudolph, and in fact made them the executors of his will. See "Claus Spreckels and his Family" in Cordray, "Claus Spreckels of California." In sharing control of Hawaiian Commercial and Sugar Company with Gus, Rudolph became a millionaire. At the time of the 1929 crash he was worth about twenty millions. He lost practically everything in the crash and died in 1958, in San Mateo, where he had been living in a small apartment.
15. Dean, *Alexander & Baldwin,* p. 65.
16. *Ibid.,* p. 66.
17. *Hawaiian Star,* October 12, 15, 1898.
18. *Pacific Commercial Advertiser,* October 13, 15, 1898.
19. *Bulletin* (Honolulu), October 12, 1898. In the fight for control of Hawaiian Commercial and Sugar Company, Gus and Rudolph Spreckels surrendered meekly. That Claus Spreckels would have so surrendered is hard to imagine. Everything about the character of the man suggests that he would have battled vigorously to stop the takeover by J. B. Castle and his associates.
20. *Bulletin* (Honolulu), October 27, 1898; *Hawaiian Star,* October 28, 1898.
21. Copy of charter, file HCS, Office of State Treasurer, Honolulu.
22. For information on Hawaiian Commercial and Sugar Company, see annual report of the firm for the year 1957, seventy-fifth anniversary of its founding. This report also contains a sketch of the company's history.

IX: *William G. Irwin: The Man*

1. *Pacific Coast Commercial Record,* May, 1892; George F. Nellist, *Builders of Hawaii* (Honolulu: 1925), p. 123.
2. See Chapter 16.
3. *Pacific Commercial Advertiser,* January 29, 1914.
4. *Pacific Coast Commercial Record,* May, 1892.

5. Irwin and Company was agent for a line of packet ships controlled by J. D. Spreckels and Brothers of San Francisco. The Irwin firm was later agent for the Oceanic Steamship Company, also controlled by the Spreckels interests. See chapters 11 and 12.

6. *Pacific Commercial Advertiser,* July 9, 1881.

7. *Ibid.*

8. *Honolulu Advertiser,* September 13, 1957.

9. *Pacific Commercial Advertiser,* August 21, 1885.

10. *Bulletin* (Honolulu), October 8, 1886.

11. *Hawaiian Gazette,* February 21, 1893, citing *New York Times,* January 29, 1893.

12. *Hawaiian Star,* May 26, 1893.

13. Irwin to Giffard, December 5, 23, 1907; Giffard to Irwin, December 17, 21, 1907, January 3, May 7, 1908 (Irwin-Giffard letters, University of Hawaii Library, Hawaiian and Pacific Section).

14. W. M. Giffard to W. G. Irwin, December 29, 1908 (Irwin-Giffard letters).

15. *Pacific Commercial Advertiser,* January 29, 1914.

X: William G. Irwin: The Company

1. *Pacific Commercial Advertiser,* November 7, 1874.

2. *Ibid.*

3. *Paradise of the Pacific,* XXII (December, 1909), 22.

4. *Hawaiian Gazette,* August 13, 1879.

5. *Pacific Commercial Advertiser,* July 2, 1906.

6. *Hawaiian Gazette,* June 30, 1880.

7. *Ibid.*

8. Alexander, *History of Later Years of the Hawaiian Monarchy,* p. 238.

9. *Pacific Commercial Advertiser,* December 16, 1884; *Bulletin* (Honolulu), December 17, 1884.

10. Copy of charter, W. G. Irwin & Co. file, State Treasurer's Office, Honolulu.

11. *Hawaiian Gazette,* August 12, 1890. As of June, 1893, Spreckels and Irwin each held 2,115 shares of par value $100 each. Their combined holdings had a par value of $423,000. Employees held 770 shares with a par value of $77,000. The number of shares outstanding was 5,000 with a total par value of $500,000. (*Report of the Committee on Foreign Relations,* II, p. 1930.)

12. *Hawaiian Gazette,* August 12, 1890.

13. W. G. Irwin & Co. file, State Treasurer's Office, Honolulu.)

14. *Pacific Coast Commercial Record,* May, 1892.

15. *Pacific Commercial Advertiser,* July 2, 1906.

16. *Pacific Coast Commercial Record,* May, 1892.

17. *Pacific Commercial Advertiser,* October 1, 1886.

18. *Pacific Commercial Advertiser,* August 8, 1885.

19. *Bulletin* (Honolulu), December 31, 1909.

20. *Pacific Commercial Advertiser,* November 6, 1880; *Bulletin* (Honolulu), December 26, 1908.

21. *Pacific Coast Commercial Record,* May, 1892.

22. *Pacific Commercial Advertiser,* July 5, 1886.

23. *Pacific Commercial Advertiser,* August 30, 1886.

24. *Ibid.*

25. See Chapter 18.

26. *Hawaiian Gazette,* February 21, 1893, citing *New York Times,* January 29, 1893. In many accounts of loans by Spreckels and Irwin there seems to be confusion between William G. Irwin and Company and the Claus Spreckels bank. This confusion is of no great moment because both companies were controlled by the two men.

27. *Pacific Commercial Advertiser,* July 22, 1885; August 27, 1885.

28. *Hawaiian Gazette,* June 29, 1886.

29. *Ibid.*

30. See chapters 11 and 12.

31. *Pacific Commercial Advertiser,* May 31, 1886.

32. *Paradise of the Pacific,* XIV (December, 1901), 37.

33. *Paradise of the Pacific,* XV (December, 1902), 57; *Pacific Commercial Advertiser,* July 2, 1906.

34. *Paradise of the Pacific,* XIV (December, 1901), 37; Alexander, *History of Later Years of the Hawaiian Monarchy,* p. 238.

35. *Hawaiian Gazette,* February 18, 1885. On the first and second banks of Claus Spreckels and Company, see Chapter 16.

36. *Hawaiian Gazette,* December 10, 1879; *Honolulu Almanac and Directory,* 1886 (Honolulu: 1886), p. 141.

37. *Pacific Commercial Advertiser,* December 2, 1882.

38. *Ibid.*

39. *Ibid.*

40. *Ibid.*

41. Those in the United States, principally the eastern refiners and southern planters, who hoped that abolition of reciprocity would "break" Spreckels were just whistling in the dark. Spreckels was somewhat indifferent to continuance of the treaty. For this indifference there were good reasons: (1) The treaty did not affect the price at which Spreckels could *buy* sugar for his West Coast refinery, because the price of sugar was largely determined by the world market. (2) On his Hawaiian plantations Spreckels was a low-cost producer, and he felt that he could still produce at a profit even if the two-cent a pound price increase, which was the effect of reciprocity, were taken away. (3) As indicated in the text, even if he broke even or lost on his Hawaiian sugar production, he would still have the profit on his California refining operations. (4) In the declining years of the Reciprocity Treaty, 1894–98, Spreckels had become more interested in beet sugar in the United States than in Hawaiian cane sugar. This last reason was, of course, not applicable at the time of the Irwin interview discussed in the text.

42. *Pacific Coast Commercial Record,* May, 1892.

43. *Report of Committee on Foreign Relations,* II, p. 1783.

44. *Paradise of the Pacific,* XIV (December, 1901), 37; XV (December, 1902), 57; XVIII (December, 1905), 46.

45. *Bulletin* (Honolulu), October 26, 1909.

46. *Ibid.*

47. Sullivan, *C. Brewer & Co.,* p. 170.

48. *Bulletin* (Honolulu), October 26, 1909.

XI: From Sails to Steam

1. J. D. Spreckels and Brothers, a partnership of the sons of Claus Spreckels, was a well-known San Francisco sugar agency and commission house. The firm was agent for buying Hawaiian sugar for Claus Spreckels' California refinery. Spreckels and Brothers became San Francisco agent for Oceanic Steamship Company when the line was founded in 1881. William G. Irwin and Company was Honolulu agent for Spreckels and Brothers, including the Spreckels sailing vessels and, later, the Oceanic line.

2. *Hawaiian Gazette,* June 18, 1879.

3. *Pacific Commercial Advertiser,* July 5, 1879.

4. *Hawaiian Gazette,* July 2, 1879. Twenty-nine years later, on January 21, 1908, the "Claus Spreckels," laden with sugar, went down in a heavy fog off San Francisco (*Thrum's Hawaiian Annual,* 1931, p. 31). Coincidentally, Claus Spreckels himself died in the very year that his namesake was lost.

5. *Pacific Commercial Advertiser,* July 5, 1879.

6. *Pacific Commercial Advertiser,* July 25, 1879.

7. *Pacific Commercial Advertiser,* March 6, 1880. Matthew Turner was a San Francisco shipbuilder.

8. *Hawaiian Gazette,* March 10, 1880.

9. *Hawaiian Gazette,* March 17, 1880.

10. *Pacific Commercial Advertiser,* November 19, 1881.

11. *Pacific Commercial Advertiser,* December 30, 1882. Because of winds, sailing time from Honolulu to San Francisco is longer than that from San Francisco to Honolulu.

12. *Pacific Commercial Advertiser,* March 26, 1880, May 21, 1881; *Saturday Press,* June 11, 1881.

13. *Pacific Commercial Advertiser,* March 26, 1880.

14. *Saturday Press,* June 11, 1881.

15. Why other Hawaiian businessmen and planters did not form a steamship line is not clear. No doubt lack of capital was a principal stumbling block.

16. Oceanic extended its service to Australia and New Zealand in 1885. See Chapter 12.

17. *Pacific Commercial Advertiser,* January 21, 1882. See also *Saturday Press,* January 21, 1882, and *Hawaiian Gazette,* January 18, 1882.

18. *Hawaiian Gazette,* January 25, 1882.

19. *Pacific Commercial Advertiser,* April 22, 1882.

20. *Hawaiian Gazette,* April 12, 1882.

21. *Pacific Commercial Advertiser,* May 6, 1882. On the shortage of shipping space and storage of large quantities of sugar, see also *Hawaiian Gazette,* May 10, 1882.

22. *Bulletin* (Honolulu), June 15, 1882.

23. *Hawaiian Gazette,* July 19, 1882.

24. *Bulletin* (Honolulu), June 23, 1882; *Saturday Press,* July 1, 1882.

25. *Bulletin* (Honolulu), May 23, 1883.

26. *Hawaiian Gazette,* July 4, 1883.

27. *Pacific Commercial Advertiser,* June 17, 1882, quoting letter of May 30, 1882.

28. *Ibid.*

29. *Bulletin* (Honolulu), May 14, 1883.

30. *Pacific Commercial Advertiser,* June 30, 1883.

31. This account of the arrival of the "Mariposa" is based on accounts in *Bulletin* (Honolulu), August 1, 1883; *Hawaiian Gazette,* August 1, 1883; *Pacific Commercial Advertiser,* August 4, 1883.

32. *Pacific Commercial Advertiser,* August 4, 1883.

33. *Ibid.*

34. *Ibid.*

35. *Ibid.*

36. *Pacific Commercial Advertiser,* August 11, 1883.

37. *Hawaiian Gazette,* August 8, 1883; *Pacific Commercial Advertiser,* August 11, 1883.

38. *Bulletin* (Honolulu), August 8, 1883.

39. *Bulletin* (Honolulu), October 23, 1883.

40. *Bulletin* (Honolulu), March 3, 1884.

XII: *Subsidy and Controversy*

1. *Hawaiian Gazette,* October 24, 1883.

2. Gibson to Carter (private), November 10, 1883, Minister and Special Commissioner to Washington, AH.

3. Carter to Gibson, November 1, 1883, Minister and Special Commissioner to Washington, AH. Spreckels was planning to charter temporarily the ships of the Occidental and Oriental line (British) for the Chinese immigration.

4. Carter to Gibson, November 15, 1883, H. A. P. Carter file, AH.

5. Lauterbach to Carter, November 5, 1883, Minister and Special Commissioner to Washington, AH.

6. Gibson to Carter (private), November 10, 1883, Minister and Special Commissioner to Washington, AH.

7. Carter to Gibson, December 12, 1883, H. A. P. Carter file, AH.

8. *Hawaiian Gazette,* January 30, 1884.

9. Gibson to Carter, December 14, 1883, Hawaiian Legation Washington, vol. 1, p. 372, AH.

10. Gibson to Carter, January 2, 1884, Hawaiian Legation Washington, vol. 1, pp. 380–382, AH.

11. *Ibid.*

12. Gibson to Carter, March 14, 1884, Hawaiian Legation, Washington, vol. 1, p. 401, AH.

13. *Bulletin* (Honolulu), December 12, 1883.

14. *Hawaiian Gazette,* April 9, 1884; *Bulletin* (Honolulu), April 10, 1884.

15. *Pacific Commercial Advertiser,* April 12, 1884.

16. F. F. Low to Carter, November 28, 1883, Minister and Special Commissioner to Washington, AH.

17. *Pacific Commercial Advertiser,* April 12, 1884.

18. *Ibid.*

19. *Hawaiian Gazette,* May 24, 1884.

20. *Ibid.* On "depreciated monopoly silver," see chapters 13 and 14 below.

21. *Hawaiian Gazette,* April 29, 1885.

22. *Hawaiian Gazette,* October 7, 1885.

23. *Hawaiian Gazette,* July 19, 1882; *Pacific Commercial Advertiser,* July 29, 1882.

24. *Pacific Commercial Advertiser,* May 31, 1884.
25. *Bulletin* (Honolulu), June 18, 1884. Charles T. Gulick, minister of the interior, presented a report showing that the value of Oceanic privileges for free wharfage, water, special rates for pilotage, etc., came to $27,000 a year (*Bulletin* [Honolulu], July 3, 1884). This was in addition to the direct subsidy of money.
26. *Bulletin* (Honolulu), June 18, 1884.
27. *Ibid.*
28. *Pacific Commercial Advertiser,* July 8, 1884.
29. *Bulletin* (Honolulu), July 10, 1884.
30. *Bulletin* (Honolulu), July 12, 1884.
31. *Pacific Commercial Advertiser,* July 15, 1884.
32. *Ibid.*
33. *Bulletin* (Honolulu), July 14, 1884.
34. *Bulletin* (Honolulu), July 17, 1884.
35. *Session Laws,* 1884, pp. 23–24.
36. *Bulletin* (Honolulu), February 11, 1884.
37. *Pacific Commercial Advertiser,* February 16, 1884; *Bulletin* (Honolulu), March 15, 1884.
38. *Bulletin* (Honolulu), March 15, 1884.
39. *Hawaiian Gazette,* October 7, 1885; *Pacific Commercial Advertiser,* October 20, 27, December 1, 1885.
40. *Pacific Commercial Advertiser,* December 1, 1885.
41. *Pacific Commercial Advertiser,* January 18, 1886.
42. *Hawaiian Gazette,* December 1, 1885.
43. *Pacific Commercial Advertiser,* December 8, 1885.
44. *Pacific Commercial Advertiser,* February 15, 1886.
45. *Bulletin* (Honolulu), January 14, 1886.
46. *Pacific Commercial Advertiser,* March 8, 1886, citing *San Francisco Call,* February 24, 1886; *Hawaiian Gazette,* March 9, 1886; *Pacific Commercial Advertiser,* April 12, 1886.
47. *Bulletin* (Honolulu), March 9, 1886, citing *Alta California,* February 25, 1886.
48. *Hawaiian Gazette,* March 9, 1886.
49. *Pacific Commercial Advertiser,* May 3, 1886.
50. *Ibid.*
51. *Pacific Commercial Advertiser,* June 7, 1886.
52. *Ibid.*
53. *Ibid.*
54. *Pacific Commercial Advertiser,* May 31, 1886.
55. *Pacific Commercial Advertiser,* June 7, 1886.
56. *Hawaiian Gazette,* June 8, 1886.
57. *Ibid.*
58. *Pacific Commercial Advertiser,* July 12, 1886. The last part of the quotation, "because he is an innovator and tramples upon their business traditions," is a perceptive comment on the dislike of Spreckels in the Hawaiian community. He was the "outlander" in the Veblenian sense, a mainland interloper unfettered by the Hawaiian culture or by the (largely missionary) culture that had been superimposed upon it. He just did not fit in with that large segment of Honolulu which had been molded in the missionary tradition.
59. *Pacific Commercial Advertiser,* June 28, 1886. Kaai may have meant that the setting of rates on bananas was not a government matter. His statement might also be interpreted to mean that Spreckels' influence in the government would decide the matter anyhow.

60. *Pacific Commercial Advertiser,* August 23, 1886.
61. *Ibid.*
62. *Bulletin* (Honolulu), August 28, 1886.
63. *Ibid.*
64. *Pacific Commercial Advertiser,* August 30, 1886.
65. Journal of Legislative Assembly, 1886, pp. 388–389, AH. The remarks of the king take on added significance when it is realized that about this time he and Spreckels fell out over the question of a loan in London (see Chapter 18). Under these circumstances the king might have been expected to omit mention of the subsidy and of ocean transport. But these subjects were too important
66. *Matsonews,* V (December, 1943), 16.
67. *Paradise of the Pacific,* XII (December, 1900), 39.
68. *Thrum's Hawaiian Annual,* 1901, p. 179.
69. *Ibid.*
70. *Bulletin* (Honolulu), October 26, 1909.
71. Spreckels had a striking connection with the beginnings of the Matson Navigation Company, successor to Oceanic as the main carrier in the Hawaiian trade. About 1880 William Matson was working as a seaman on a barge, the "William Frederick," which ran coal from Mount Diablo to Spreckels' sugar refinery in San Francisco. In two years Matson made enough money to buy the barge. On his numerous trips to the refinery he became friendly with Spreckels, who advanced $20,000 to Matson to buy the 300-ton schooner "Emma Claudine," named after Spreckels' daughter. Matson sailed the ship to Hilo, Hawaii, in May, 1882, with a cargo of lumber and general manufactures, returning with a cargo of sugar. ("With Matson Down to Melbourne," *Fortune,* XVI [September, 1937], 104; Erna Fergusson, *Our Hawaii* [New York: Knopf, 1942], pp. 6, 7.)
William Matson prospered and acquired more ships. In 1901 he incorporated the Matson Navigation Company in San Francisco. In 1926 the company bought out Oceanic Steamship Company, which had been having numerous unprofitable years in the first quarter of the nineteenth century. Oceanic, a wholly owned subsidiary of Matson, still sails the South Pacific. But the company founded by Spreckels has lost its place in the Hawaiian trade to the company whose first ship he helped to finance.

XIII: King Kalakaua's Coins

1. *Pacific Commercial Advertiser,* August 25, 1883.
2. *Session Laws,* 1876, p. 114.
3. Official notices of such values were often published in the newspapers.
4. Donald Billam-Walker, "Money of Hawaii," *Report, Hawaiian Historical Society,* 1939 (Honolulu: Hawaiian Printing Co., 1940), p. 21.
5. *Session Laws,* 1880, p. 51.
6. *Session Laws,* 1882, pp. 47–49.
7. Without any amendment to the law, the dime was subsequently coined instead of the 12½-cent piece, because of a pending monetary convention between Hawaii and the United States. The convention was not consummated.
8. *Bulletin* (Honolulu), August 15, 1882.
9. *Bulletin* (Honolulu), August 12, 1882.
10. *Bulletin* (Honolulu), December 19, 1882.

11. Gibson to Allen, July 22, 1882, Hawaiian Legation Washington, 1873–1877, vol. 1, p. 255, AH.

12. Cabinet Council Minute Book, 1874–1891, proceedings of September 20, 1882, p. 271, AH.

13. J. Mott Smith to Gibson, September 21, 1882, Minister and Special Commissioner to Washington, 1882, AH.

14. Cabinet Council Minute Book, 1874–1891, p. 281, AH.

15. Authorization in Finance Department, 1883, AH.

16. H. A. P. Carter to J. M. Kapena, June 7, 1883, H. A. P. Carter, 1883, file, AH.

17. For example, in October, 1882, there had been an unsuccessful appeal by the Planters' Labor and Supply Company, numbering many influential businessmen in its membership, for dismissal of the Gibson ministry "in favor of others who have the confidence of the moneyed men, and the great interests of the country" (*Bulletin* [Honolulu], October 20, 1882).

18. *Hawaiian Gazette*, May 16, 1883. Despite certain legitimate complaints about the way the coinage was done, the continuous and violent campaign against it was unfortunate because confidence is important in keeping a monetary system stable.

19. *Saturday Press*, May 26, 1883.

20. *Hawaiian Gazette*, June 6, 1883.

21. *Hawaiian Gazette*, December 19, 1883.

22. *Hawaiian Gazette*, June 13, 1883. It is an interesting question to what extent the attitude of the newspapers promoted and accentuated the feeling of apprehension among businessmen.

23. *Bulletin* (Honolulu), October 6, 1882. The phrase "pander to national vanity" was typical of many slurs cast upon Kalakaua for wanting his image on a national coinage.

24. *Hawaiian Gazette*, May 30, June 13, December 12, 1883.

25. *Bulletin* (Honolulu), August 9, 1883.

26. *Bulletin* (Honolulu), November 9, 1882.

27. *Hawaiian Gazette*, May 30, 1883.

28. *Hawaiian Gazette*, June 6, 1883. The *Gazette* overlooked the point that in order to have a stable subsidiary coinage it was essential that it be of such nature that there could be no incentive to export it.

29. *Hawaiian Gazette*, May 30, June 6, 1883; *Bulletin* (Honolulu), May 23, 1883.

30. *Hawaiian Gazette*, December 12, 1883.

31. *Ibid.*

32. *Bulletin* (Honolulu), December 13, 14, 1883; *Pacific Commercial Advertiser*, December 22, 1883.

33. *Pacific Commercial Advertiser*, December 22, 1883.

34. *Bulletin* (Honolulu), December 15, 1883; *Pacific Commercial Advertiser*, December 22, 1883.

35. *Pacific Commercial Advertiser*, December 22, 1883. Immediately after this preliminary decision on the Castle-Dole-Smith petition, which had the support of many members of the business community, the government retaliated by enforcing the payment of customs duties in gold under the Legal Tender Act. This provision of the act had become more or less a dead letter, duties having been accepted in silver. The howls of the business community (*Hawaiian Gazette*, December 19, 1883) are a telling commentary on the self-righteousness of the Castle-Dole-Smith supporters.

36. *Pacific Commercial Advertiser*, December 15, 1883.

37. Privy Council Records, May 4, 1881 to November 15, 1892, proceedings of December 18, 1883, pp. 114, 116, AH.

38. *Pacific Commercial Advertiser,* December 15, 1883.

39. *Ibid.*

40. *Hawaiian Gazette,* December 19, 1883.

41. *5 Hawaiian Reports* 27.

42. *Pacific Commercial Advertiser,* January 12, 1884.

43. *Ibid.*

44. *Hawaiian Gazette,* January 12, 1884.

45. Gibson to Carter, January 2, 1884, Hawaiian Legation Washington, 1873–1887, I, 380, AH.

46. Just how Spreckels got the bonds and why there was no further court action after he got them is something of a mystery. The following letter to the *Bulletin* (Honolulu; January 9, 1884), signed "Foresight," throws as much light on the subject as do the official records:

"Act 1. Scene—The Government with its bonds, Colonel Spreckels with his silver, and the Bank with gold.

"Act 2. Shuffle No. 1. Scene—The Government still with its bonds, Colonel Spreckels with the gold, and the Bank with the silver, a temporary exchange having been effected between the two latter, which will simplify the issuing of the bonds.

"Act 3. Shuffle No. 2. Scene—The Government with the gold, Colonel Spreckels with the bonds, and the Bank still holding the silver. Thus all legal difficulties have been overcome.

"Act 4. Shuffle No. 3. The Government with the silver, the Bank with its gold again, and Colonel Spreckels still in possession of his bonds. This shuffle having been made between the Government and the Bank, the coin can then be issued and behold!

"Act 5. (The coin paid out.) The Government with nothing, Colonel Spreckels with gold in payment for the bonds, and the Public with the coin and happy at having had to pay for it in gold."

Nevertheless the present writer leans strongly to the view that Spreckels paid $500,000 in Kalakaua silver for the bonds.

47. E. M. Damon, *Sanford Ballard Dole and His Hawaii* (Palo Alto: Pacific Books, 1957), pp. 176–177.

48. Ample means were also available to Spreckels to put the coins into direct circulation without going through the coffers of the government. The silver could be passed through his bank in change or for small loans. It could be used to pay for plantation labor, or for other debts for supplies and services to Spreckels' many interests in Hawaii.

49. See Chapter 14.

50. *Pacific Commercial Advertiser,* December 17, 1884.

51. *Pacific Commercial Advertiser,* January 12, 1884; *Bulletin* (Honolulu), January 12, 1884. Miss Louise Beaudet was appearing in the title role of the play, *Woman of the People, or the Horrors of Drink.* C. R. Buckland, manager of the play, had the coin made into a pendant, and presented it to Miss Beaudet as a memento of her performance. She wore the pendant a few days later while playing in a farce called *Matrimony.*

52. *Bulletin* (Honolulu), January 14, 1884.

53. *Bulletin* (Honolulu), January 15, 1884. On the opening of the Spreckels bank see Chapter 16.

54. *Report of the Minister of Finance,* 1884, p. 12; *Report of the Minister of*

Finance, 1886, p. 3. On the minting of the coins in the United States, and on the switch from the one-eighth dollar to the dime, see correspondence, NA, Record Group 104. This file contains 138 pages of documents, including letters by Spreckels, the Director of the U. S. Bureau of the Mint, and the superintendents of the Philadelphia and San Francisco mints. The coins were designed by Charles E. Barber, engraver of the Philadelphia mint, from suggestions furnished by Spreckels. Spreckels paid $2,750 for the design and preparation of dies. He also furnished bullion for the minting, and paid mint costs of $17,500. The dies were later (May, 1888) defaced and cancelled in the presence of H. A. P. Carter, Hawaiian minister at Washington, and James P. Kimball, Director of the U. S. Bureau of the Mint.

55. *Hawaiian Gazette,* January 23, 1884.

56. *Bulletin* (Honolulu), February 25, 1884.

57. *Pacific Commercial Advertiser,* January 26, 1884.

58. *Ibid.*

59. *Hawaiian Gazette,* January 30, 1884. In popular language, Gresham's law is usually stated as "Bad money drives out good."

60. The term *kimo-ai-luau* does not appear in Hawaiian dictionaries. According to the Hawaiian translator at the Public Archives of Hawaii, Jack Matthews, it means literally "Jimmy eats taro tops." Taro tops (greens) were a common food. Hence *kimo-ai-luau* means "common" or "cheap."

61. *Hawaiian Gazette,* April 16, 1884.

62. *Hawaiian Gazette,* June 17, 1885.

63. *Hawaiian Gazette,* February 18, 1885.

64. *Planters' Monthly,* III (June, 1884), 406.

65. *Bulletin* (Honolulu), January 28, 1884.

66. *Bulletin* (Honolulu), February 15, 1884; *Pacific Commercial Advertiser,* February 16, 1884. The views of the chamber were substantially incorporated in the Gold Law of 1884.

67. *Bulletin* (Honolulu), April 30, May 3, 1884. The date when the coin was made legal tender to the same extent as U. S. silver was December 18, 1883.

68. *Bulletin* (Honolulu), May 8, 1884.

69. Because of a shortage of coin in outlying districts, many of the plantations had for years coined their own money which circulated in the plantation community and sometimes beyond.

70. *Bulletin* (Honolulu), May 8, 1884.

71. *Bulletin* (Honolulu), May 24, 1884.

72. *Hawaiian Gazette,* May 28, 1884.

73. *Pacific Commercial Advertiser,* May 24, 1884.

74. *Pacific Commercial Advertiser,* May 31, 1884.

75. *Hawaiian Gazette,* July 2, 1884.

76. *Pacific Commercial Advertiser,* July 1, 1884.

77. *Ibid.*

78. *Ibid.*

79. Journal of the Legislative Assembly, 1884, p. 248, AH.

80. *Hawaiian Gazette,* August 20, 1884, quoting *Gazette,* June 4, 1884; *Pacific Commercial Advertiser,* May 28, 1884; *Bulletin* (Honolulu), May 27, 1884.

81. *Pacific Commercial Advertiser,* August 19, 1884.

82. *Pacific Commercial Advertiser,* September 2, 1884; *Bulletin* (Honolulu), September 1, 1884. Gibson's estimate of three cents on the dollar would put the total profit on the coinage of $1,000,000 at $30,000. This is probably too low.

On the other hand, estimates of the profit at $150,000 to $250,000 are probably too high. The exact profit is of no great moment, but it was probably under $100,000.

83. *Bulletin* (Honolulu), June 19, 1884.

84. *Bulletin* (Honolulu), June 23, 1884.

85. *Hawaiian Gazette,* supplement, June 25, 1884. The entire report of the finance committee is printed in this supplement.

86. *Bulletin* (Honolulu), June 24, 1884.

87. *Hawaiian Gazette,* June 25, 1884.

88. *Bulletin* (Honolulu), June 28, 1884.

XIV: Fight over Gold Law

1. *Pacific Commercial Advertiser,* December 22, 1883.

2. *Bulletin* (Honolulu), May 20, 1884.

3. *Ibid.*

4. *Bulletin* (Honolulu), June 4, 1884.

5. *Bulletin* (Honolulu), June 13, 1884.

6. This 60-day period ended September 30, 1884.

7. For copy of Gold Law see *Session Laws,* 1884, pp. 20–23. Repeal of the Coinage Act of 1880 effectively prevented any further coinage of Hawaiian silver beyond the $1,000,000 already received. The important effect of the repeal of the Legal Tender Act of 1876 was to reduce from $50 to $10 the legal tender limit of silver. It was hoped thus to promote the circulation of gold.

8. *Hawaiian Gazette,* July 16, 1884.

9. *Ibid.*

10. *Ibid.* Just what Spreckels meant by this remark is not clear. He may have meant that C. Brewer & Co. would be in position to sell foreign exchange or gold at a premium. However, the Gold Law would hardly have been to the direct advantage of this company, because as a sugar factor it could obtain foreign exchange for exports of product. The company also had the possibility, without the Gold Law, of paying plantation labor, on plantations controlled by it, in silver. In fact, Z. S. Spalding, a prominent planter and lobbyist for continuation of the Reciprocity Treaty, later argued that the Gold Law was to the disadvantage of the planters. At the annual meeting of the planters' company in October, 1884, he said: "I have admired the action of the Opposition members in the Legislature, and their financial ability; but I think that they who carried through the Gold Bill have mistaken the situation. I have to pay out silver, I don't want to pay out gold. It seems to me that if I can pay off my labor in Kalakaua silver, and can purchase six silver dollars for one five dollar gold-piece, that it is better for me to have that silver instead of the gold. The question with me is not so much what the exchange on San Francisco is as it is whether I can get my labor cheap or not. If I have to pay that labor in gold it will not be cheap. The Japanese Consul, when here, told me that he had provided in the contracts that labor from Japan should be paid in silver of the United States standard of fineness; that is, in Kalakaua dollars. This I think is a wise provision. I think the Gold Bill is going to do exactly what Mr. Spreckels tried to explain to you that it would." (*Pacific Commercial Advertiser,* October 21, 1884.)

11. *Hawaiian Gazette,* July 16, 1884.

12. *Ibid.*

13. *Ibid.* Whether Spreckels was right or not was not really determined because the government seemed both unwilling and unable to enforce the Gold Law after it was passed. Spreckels was probably right in thinking that strict enforcement of the Gold Law, with contraction of the money supply, would not have been wise in the existing depression.

14. *Hawaiian Gazette,* July 16, 1884. For additional comment on Spreckels' speech, see *Bulletin* (Honolulu), July 12, 1884; *Pacific Commercial Advertiser,* July 15, 1884.

15. *Pacific Commercial Advertiser,* September 30, 1884.

16. *Report of Minister of Finance,* 1886, p. 4.

17. *Bulletin* (Honolulu), December 4, 1884.

18. *Bulletin* (Honolulu), December 6, 1884.

19. *Bulletin* (Honolulu), December 22, 1884.

20. *Hawaiian Gazette,* January 14, 1885.

21. *Bulletin* (Honolulu), December 4, 5, 1884.

22. *Bulletin* (Honolulu), November 29, 1884.

23. *Ibid.*

24. *Hawaiian Gazette,* February 18, 1885.

25. *Hawaiian Gazette,* June 10, 1885.

26. *Bulletin* (Honolulu), December 9, 1884; *Hawaiian Gazette,* December 17, 1884.

27. *Bulletin* (Honolulu), December 16, 1884.

28. *Bulletin* (Honolulu), January 22, 1886.

29. See Chapter 16.

30. *Hawaiian Gazette,* May 14, 1884.

31. *Thrum's Hawaiian Annual,* 1886, p. 61.

32. *Bulletin* (Honolulu), January 27, 1885.

33. *Bulletin* (Honolulu), January 28, 1885.

34. *Pacific Commercial Advertiser,* January 31, 1885.

35. *Ibid.*

36. "Report of Committee on Finance," in *Report of the Hawaiian Commission* (Washington: GPO, 1898), p. 92.

37. *Pacific Commercial Advertiser,* September 20, 1900.

38. *Hawaiian Gazette,* November 13, 1903.

39. *Report of the Governor of the Territory of Hawaii to the Secretary of the Interior,* 1907, p. 15.

40. *Pacific Commercial Advertiser,* December 31, 1903.

XV: Bank Bill Shenanigans

1. *Hawaiian Gazette,* May 28, 1879.

2. *Hawaiian Gazette,* July 23, 1879.

3. *Pacific Commercial Advertiser,* September 5, 1879.

4. *Hawaiian Gazette,* April 11, 1883; *Pacific Commercial Advertiser,* April 14, 1883; *Bulletin* (Honolulu), April 14, 1883.

5. *Thrum's Hawaiian Annual,* 1885, p. 56.

6. *Pacific Commercial Advertiser,* January 19, 1884.

7. *Bulletin* (Honolulu), January 16, 1884; *Pacific Commercial Advertiser,* January 19, 1884.

8. *Pacific Commercial Advertiser,* January 19, 1884; *Hawaiian Gazette,* January 16, 1884; Frederick Bagot, ed., *Hawaiian Directory* (San Francisco: 1884), p. 79.

9. *Hawaiian Gazette,* January 23, 1884.

10. *Bulletin* (Honolulu), May 24, 1884.

11. Alexander, *History of Later Years of the Hawaiian Monarchy,* p. 11.

12. *Pacific Commercial Advertiser,* September 2, 1884.

13. Parker and Campbell, both large landholders, were friends of Spreckels. Wilder and Foster were prominent businessmen with interests in Hawaiian railroads and interisland ships.

14. For full text of bill see *Hawaiian Gazette,* June 4, 1884. See also Journal of Legislative Assembly, 1884, p. 92, AH.

15. *Bulletin* (Honolulu), May 31, 1884.

16. *Ibid.*

17. *Hawaiian Gazette,* June 4, 1884.

18. *Pacific Commercial Advertiser,* June 7, 1884.

19. *Hawaiian Gazette,* June 4, 1884.

20. *Bulletin* (Honolulu), June 5, 1884.

21. *Ibid.*

22. *Ibid.*

23. *Bulletin* (Honolulu), June 9, 1884; *Hawaiian Gazette,* June 11, 1884.

24. *Bulletin* (Honolulu), June 2, 1884; *Pacific Commercial Advertiser,* June 7, 1884.

25. *Pacific Commercial Advertiser,* June 14, 1884.

26. *Ibid.*

27. *Bulletin* (Honolulu), June 9, 1884.

28. *Bulletin* (Honolulu), June 24, 1884.

29. *Ibid.*

30. *Bulletin* (Honolulu), June 25, 1884.

31. Under Hawaiian law ministers could vote in the legislature even on motions of no confidence.

32. *Bulletin* (Honolulu), June 26, 1884; *Pacific Commercial Advertiser,* July 1, 1884.

33. *Bulletin* (Honolulu), June 26, 1884; Journal of Legislative Assembly, 1884, p. 134, AH.

34. *Pacific Commercial Advertiser,* June 27, 1884.

35. *Hawaiian Gazette,* July 2, 1884.

36. On May 13, 1884, the *Bulletin* (Honolulu) reported: "Gov. Low takes a lively interest in the Legislature. He seems to have secured a season ticket."

37. *Hawaiian Gazette,* July 2, 1884; *Bulletin* (Honolulu), July 17, 1884.

38. *Bulletin* (Honolulu), June 13, 1884.

39. *Bulletin* (Honolulu), July 15, 17, 1884; full text of bill in *Bulletin* (Honolulu), July 16, 1884.

40. *Hawaiian Gazette,* July 16, 1884.

41. *Bulletin* (Honolulu), July 16, 1884.

42. *Bulletin* (Honolulu), July 12, 1884.

43. *Bulletin* (Honolulu), July 16, 1884.

44. *Hawaiian Gazette,* July 16, 1884.

45. *Ibid.*

46. *Ibid.*

47. *Bulletin* (Honolulu), July 21, 1884; *Pacific Commercial Advertiser,* July 22, 1884.

48. *Bulletin* (Honolulu), July 16, 1884.
49. *Ibid.* Davies was head of Theo. H. Davies & Co., a prominent sugar agency. Isenberg was head of Hackfeld & Co., also a prominent agency. Bishop was a partner in the Bank of Bishop and Company.
50. *Bulletin* (Honolulu), July 18, 1884.
51. *Bulletin* (Honolulu), July 17, 1884.
52. Journal of Legislative Assembly, 1884, pp. 199–203, AH.
53. *Ibid.*, p. 225.
54. For copy of bill, see *Session Laws*, 1884, pp. 26–38.
55. *Thrum's Hawaiian Annual*, 1920, p. 153. See also Petition of Bank of Honolulu, Ltd., for Dissolution, File 781, State Treasurer's Office, Honolulu, April 1, 1920.

XVI: *The Second Spreckels Bank*

1. *Hawaiian Gazette,* September 17, 1884.
2. *Bulletin* (Honolulu), October 1, 1884.
3. *Bulletin* (Honolulu), October 24, 1884.
4. *Pacific Commercial Advertiser,* November 4, 1884.
5. *Pacific Commercial Advertiser,* December 2, 1884.
6. *Pacific Commercial Advertiser,* January 1, 1885.
7. *Bulletin* (Honolulu), January 28, 1885.
8. *Hawaiian Gazette,* April 8, 1885.
9. *Pacific Commercial Advertiser,* April 28, 1885.
10. *Ibid.*
11. *Ibid.*
12. *Ibid.*
13. *Ibid.* The reason for this pledge of bonds as security is something of a mystery. There was no law requiring such action. The Bank of Bishop and Company, also a partnership, had not made any such pledge. Possibly Spreckels and Irwin thought the giving of bonds as security would make the bank more attractive to customers.
14. *Pacific Commercial Advertiser,* April 26, 1885.
15. *Pacific Commercial Advertiser,* May 5, 1885.
16. *Hawaiian Gazette,* May 6, 1885.
17. *Hawaiian Gazette,* May 13, 1885.
18. *Pacific Commercial Advertiser,* May 22, 1885.
19. *Hawaiian Gazette,* May 13, 1885.
20. *Thrum's Hawaiian Annual,* 1886, p. 61.
21. *Pacific Commercial Advertiser,* May 22, 1885.
22. *Pacific Commercial Advertiser,* January 18, 1886.
23. *Bulletin* (Honolulu), May 31, 1910.
24. Memorandum of Association of Bank of Honolulu, Ltd., File 781, State Treasurer's Office, Honolulu, May 31, 1910. Copy of the charter, dated June 1, 1910, is in the same file.
25. *Pacific Commercial Advertiser,* July 2, 1910.
26. *Thrum's Hawaiian Annual,* 1920, p. 153.
27. Petition of Bank of Honolulu, Ltd., for Dissolution, File 781, State Treasurer's Office, Honolulu, April 1, 1920. The Bank of Honolulu was

officially dissolved June 8, 1920. See also in File 781, In the Matter of Dissolution of Bank of Honolulu, Ltd.

XVII: London Loan: Original Loan Act

1. *Hawaiian Gazette,* December 29, 1885.
2. *Ibid.*
3. *Ibid.*
4. *Hawaiian Gazette,* January 19, 1886.
5. *Ibid.*
6. *Bulletin* (Honolulu), March 17, 1886. Celso Caesar Moreno was an Italian adventurer, well known in Washington, D. C., and Sacramento, California, as a lobbyist. He arrived in Honolulu in November, 1879, with dreams of a steamship line to China and a cable between Hawaii and the United States. He soon "gained unbounded influence over the King by servile flattery" and by encouraging him in such schemes as that of a $10,000,000 loan. On August 14, 1880, Moreno was appointed premier and minister of finance. As a result of outraged protests by Honolulu residents, he resigned five days later and left for Europe. Spreckels is said to have had a hand in his ouster. (Alexander, *History of Later Years of the Hawaiian Monarchy,* pp. 6, 7.)
7. *Bulletin* (Honolulu), March 17, 1886.
8. *Hawaiian Gazette,* March 23, 1886.
9. Draft letter, British Commissioner to British Foreign Office, March 27, 1886, British Consular Records, AH.
10. *Hawaiian Gazette,* August 3, 1886.
11. Alexander, *History of Later Years of the Hawaiian Monarchy,* p. 14.
12. *Pacific Commercial Advertiser,* May 3, 1886.
13. *Pacific Commercial Advertiser,* May 10, 1886.
14. *Bulletin* (Honolulu), May 17, 1886.
15. *Pacific Commercial Advertiser,* June 14, 1886.
16. *Bulletin* (Honolulu), June 1, 1886.
17. *Bulletin* (Honolulu), June 17, 1886.
18. *Pacific Commercial Advertiser,* June 28, 1886.
19. Draft letter, British Commissioner to British Foreign Office, July 31, 1886, British Consular Records, AH.
20. *Pacific Commercial Advertiser,* July 5, 1886.
21. *Bulletin* (Honolulu), July 2, 1886.
22. Draft letter, British Commissioner to British Foreign Office, July 3, 1866, British Consular Records, AH.
23. The official notice of the cabinet change (*Pacific Commercial Advertiser,* July 5, 1886) also included notice that Creighton had been granted "letters patent of denization" by King Kalakaua on June 29. In other words, Creighton had become a denizen (a kind of citizen) of Hawaii the day before he assumed the cabinet post. Dare had become a denizen less than two months before, on May 6 (*Bulletin,* June 26, 1886).

Section 433 of the Civil Code provided: "It shall be competent for His Majesty to confer upon any alien resident abroad, or temporarily resident in this Kingdom, letters patent of denization, conferring upon such alien, without abjuration of allegiance, all the rights, privileges and immunities of a native."

24. *Hawaiian Gazette,* July 6, 1886.

25. *Ibid.*

26. Draft letter, British Commissioner to British Foreign Office, July 3, 1886, British Consular Records, AH.

27. *Hawaiian Gazette,* July 6, 1886.

28. *Bulletin* (Honolulu), July 3, 1886.

29. *Ibid.*

30. *Hawaiian Gazette,* July 6, 1886.

31. *Pacific Commercial Advertiser,* July 26, 1886.

32. *Hawaiian Gazette,* August 3, 1886.

33. *Ibid.*

34. *Hawaiian Gazette,* July 13, 1886. The *Gazette* was mainly the organ of the Independents.

35. *Bulletin* (Honolulu), August 13, 1886.

36. *Ibid.*

37. *Bulletin* (Honolulu), July 31, 1886. It will be interesting to contrast this gay departure with the one in late October. That King Kalakaua frequently went to the wharf to see Spreckels off was a mark of royal favor and of his *aloha* for the sugar magnate.

38. Draft letter, British Commissioner to British Foreign Office, September 1, 1886, British Consular Records, AH.

39. Draft letter, British Commissioner to British Foreign Office, July 31, 1886, British Consular Records, AH.

40. *Ibid.*

41. Gibson to Hoffnung, March 13, 1886, Hawaiian Legation London, 1882–1893, AH. Some interesting but unanswerable questions may be raised about the last quoted sentence of this letter. Did it refer to new public improvements? To grandiose schemes of Kalakaua and Gibson for making Hawaii the prime power in the Pacific? Or did Gibson have in mind, as one "departure," action to loosen the grip of Spreckels on the government?

42. Hoffnung to Gibson, July 5, 1886, Chargé d'affaires, Consul General, Great Britain, London, 1886, AH. The humor of Hoffnung's statements about Armstrong can only be appreciated from later developments. It will be clear that Hoffnung and Armstrong regarded the Hawaiian kingdom as a lamb ready for the shearing.

43. *Hawaiian Hansard* (Honolulu: 1886), pp. 437–438.

44. *Hawaiian Gazette,* August 17, 1886.

45. Draft letter, British Commissioner to British Foreign Office, September 1, 1886, British Consular Records, AH.

46. *Hawaiian Gazette,* August 10, 1886.

47. *Pacific Commercial Advertiser,* August 11, 1886.

48. *Hawaiian Gazette,* August 24, 1886.

49. *Hawaiian Gazette,* August 31, 1886.

50. *Hawaiian Gazette,* August 11, 1886.

51. *Bulletin* (Honolulu), November 19, 1887.

52. Draft letter, British Commissioner to British Foreign Office, September 1, 1886, British Consular Records, AH.

53. *Bulletin* (Honolulu), November 19, 1887.

54. *Bulletin* (Honolulu), August 28, 1886.

55. *Pacific Commercial Advertiser,* August 30, 1886.

56. *Ibid.*

57. *Ibid.*

58. *Bulletin* (Honolulu), September 1, 1886.
59. *Ibid.*
60. See Section 4 of the original Loan Act, *Session Laws,* 1886, pp. 19–20.
61. *Bulletin* (Honolulu), September 1, 1886.

XVIII: Amended Loan Act: Downfall

1. *Hawaiian Gazette,* September 7, 1886.
2. *Bulletin* (Honolulu), September 1, 1886.
3. *Hawaiian Gazette,* September 7, 1886.
4. *Bulletin* (Honolulu), November 19, 1887.
5. The amendment, as finally passed, was not the same as that drawn up by Spreckels, Macfarlane, and Armstrong in San Francisco, but the schedule of uses for the funds was as they had recommended. For amended Loan Act, see *Session Laws,* 1886, pp. 57–59.
6. Gibson to Carter, October 22, 1886, Hawaiian Officials Abroad, 1886, AH.
7. Gibson to Carter, December 17, 1886, Hawaiian Officials Abroad, 1886, AH.
8. *Ibid.*
9. *Hawaiian Gazette,* October 5, 1886.
10. *Hawaiian Hansard,* p. 655.
11. *Ibid.,* p. 656.
12. *Ibid.,* p. 657.
13. Removal of this restriction was to Spreckels' advantage because he might be held to be a resident (he had a home in Honolulu), although he was not a citizen of the kingdom.
14. *Hawaiian Hansard,* p. 657.
15. *Pacific Commercial Advertiser,* October 8, 1886.
16. *Bulletin* (Honolulu), October 13, 1886.
17. *Ibid.*
18. *Ibid.*
19. See Section 2 of amended Loan Act, *Session Laws,* 1886, p. 57.
20. See pp. 211–212.
21. *Hawaiian Hansard,* pp. 698–699.
22. *Ibid.,* pp. 699–700.
23. *Ibid.,* p. 700.
24. *Ibid.,* p. 701.
25. *Ibid.,* p. 701.
26. Journal of Legislative Assembly, 1886, p. 380, AH.
27. *Hawaiian Hansard,* p. 702.
28. Gibson to Carter, October 22, 1886, Hawaiian Officials Abroad, 1886, AH. See also, in same file, letters of Gibson to Carter, December 17, 22, 1886.
29. Alexander, *History of Later Years of the Hawaiian Monarchy,* p. 15.
30. *Bulletin* (Honolulu), October 23, 1886; *Hawaiian Gazette,* October 26, 1886.
31. *Hawaiian Gazette,* October 26, 1886.
32. *Hawaiian Gazette,* December 7, 1886, citing San Francisco *Weekly Herald of Trade,* November 11, 1886; *Bulletin* (Honolulu), June 27, 1887.

33. *Bulletin* (Honolulu), November 19, 1887.
34. *Bulletin* (Honolulu), October 25, 1886.

XIX: *Aftermath of Loan*

1. *Hawaiian Gazette,* November 23, 1886.
2. *Bulletin* (Honolulu), November 18, 1886, citing *San Francisco Call,* October 31, 1886.
3. *Ibid.*
4. *Ibid.*
5. *Bulletin* (Honolulu), November 18, 1886, citing *San Francisco Examiner,* November 10, 1886.
6. *Ibid.*
7. *Bulletin* (Honolulu), November 19, 1887; *Report No. 100, Special Committee, Legislative Assembly, Extraordinary Session,* 1887, December 2, 1887.
8. *Bulletin* (Honolulu), January 12, 1887, citing *San Francisco Bulletin,* December 24, 1886.
9. *Ibid.*
10. *Ibid.*
11. *Bulletin* (Honolulu), November 19, 1887; *Report of Minister of Finance to Legislature of 1887,* November 8, 1887; *Report No. 100, Special Committee, Legislative Assembly, Extraordinary Session,* 1887, December 2, 1887; *Biennial Report of Minister of Finance,* 1888, pp. 28–29.
12. *Biennial Report of Minister of Finance,* 1890, p. 41.
13. *Report No. 100, Special Committee, Legislative Assembly, Extraordinary Session,* 1887.
14. There is some question about the amount of the open account. Gibson said in the legislature on June 30, 1886, that it was $170,000 and had been as high as $220,000 (*Bulletin* [Honolulu], July 1, 1886).

According to Spreckels, it was $220,000 in November, 1886 (*Hawaiian Gazette,* November 23, 1886).

In March, 1887, it was estimated that the amount at which it had been paid off was $200,000 (Draft letter, British Commissioner to British Foreign Office, March 16, 1887, British Consular Records, AH).

According to an official (but not completely reliable) report, it was $138,000 at the time it was paid (*Intermediate Report of Minister of Finance,* 1887, p. 27).
15. *Bulletin* (Honolulu), January 12, 1887, citing statement by George Macfarlane in *San Francisco Bulletin,* December 24, 1886.
16. Draft letter, British Commissioner to British Foreign Office, March 16, 1887, British Consular Records, AH.
17. *Bulletin* (Honolulu), November 19, 1887.
18. *Report of G. W. Macfarlane to Minister of Finance,* November 4, 1887.
19. Dr. R. S. Kuykendall has commented on this section as follows: He doubts that the London loan influenced the U. S. Senate and the administration on the Reciprocity Treaty. "Delay in renewal in 1887 was due to objections of the Hawaiian government [because of the Pearl Harbor amendment], not of the United States. The United States government was satisfied as soon as it learned

the facts about the loan bond." (Private note from Kuykendall, January 10, 1959.)

20. Draft letter, British Commissioner to British Foreign Office, July 14, 1886, British Consular Records, AH.

21. The following is a sample of statements appearing in San Francisco newspapers:

"It seems hardly possible that Hawaii can meet the interest on the bonds if they are negotiated. If the bonds are sold to Englishmen and default is made in the payment of the coupons, pressure will be brought to bear on the British Government to interfere on behalf of the creditors.... It is unfortunate that the Kingdom of Hawaii should, at this crisis, be on its last legs—financially, politically and morally." (*Bulletin* [Honolulu], December 18, 1886, citing *San Francisco Bulletin,* December 2, 1886.)

22. *Bulletin* (Honolulu), December 22, 1886. Later events bore out the accuracy of this appraisal. The treaty was renewed in 1887.

23. Copy of the prospectus, dated December 11, 1886, file Consul General at London, 1887, AH.

24. See Section 1 of amended Loan Act, *Session Laws,* 1886, p. 57.

25. Secretary of State Bayard wrote to the United States Minister in Hawaii, in early January, 1887:

"My attention was lately drawn to the proposed negotiation of a loan of $2,000,000 in England to the Hawaiian Government, by the terms of which the revenues of Hawaii were to be pledged as collateral security.

"The terms, so reported to me, were practically the creation of a right of inspection and possible control by foreign creditors over the financial measures and administration of the Hawaiian Government, and as such were not in accordance with the spirit, if not of the letter, of the existing treaty between the Hawaiian Islands and of the United States, which was intended to prevent any cession of territory or grant of a political nature by Hawaii to any other government than that of the United States.

"I ... suggest to you that it would be well for you discreetly to intimate to His Majesty King Kalakaua, the lively interest we feel in the autonomy and self-preserving force of his Government, and the satisfaction experienced by the President in learning that the late loan ... did not involve the pledge of the revenues ... and the possible embarrassments to which he might otherwise have been internationally subjected.

"The safety and welfare of the Hawaiian group is obviously more interesting and important to the United States than to any other nation." (*Report of the Committee on Foreign Relations,* II, p. 1973.)

26. Gibson to Carter, December 17, 1886, Hawaiian Officials Abroad, 1886, AH.

27. Carter to Gibson, January 7, 1887, H. A. P. Carter file, AH.

XX: *Fall of the Monarchy*

1. *Hawaiian Gazette,* October 26, 1886.

2. Aki stopped payment on a $4,000 check, so his net loss was $71,000. There is ample evidence that Kalakaua got the $71,000, though he claimed it was a gift. Surprisingly, much of the evidence concerning this "gift" was spread on the records of the Hawaiian Supreme Court in 1888. See 7 *Hawaiian Reports* 401.

3. Sylvester K. Stevens, *American Expansion in Hawaii, 1842–1898* (Harrisburg: Archives Publishing Co., 1945), p. 152.

4. Elisha H. Allen is not to be confused with his father of the same name who died in 1883. Elisha H. Allen, Sr., had been Hawaiian minister at Washington, and played an important part in negotiating the Reciprocity Treaty of 1876.

5. *Pacific Commercial Advertiser,* March 14, 1889.

6. *Bulletin* (Honolulu), August 7, 1890; *Hawaiian Gazette,* August 12, 1890.

7. *Hawaiian Gazette,* August 19, 1890.

8. Ethel M. Damon, *Sanford B. Dole and His Hawaii,* pp. 227–229.

9. In July, 1889, R. W. Wilcox, a part-Hawaiian, and about 150 followers tried to seize control of the government. His purpose seems to have been to overthrow the Constitution of 1887 and to oust the Reform administration. In brief, he wanted a return to the old order. It was rumored that he had the support of Kalakaua himself. Another rumor had it that he planned to replace Kalakaua with his sister, Liliuokalani. At any rate the rebellion was easily crushed.

10. Claus Spreckels, "Future of the Sandwich Islands," *North American Review,* vol. 152 (March, 1891), 287–291. So far as I know, this is the only journal article that ever appeared under Spreckels' name.

11. Thurston to Blaine, May 27, 1892. Misc. letters, USDS, NA. This memo, though well known, is treated extensively by the present writer because it throws much light on subsequent bitter controversy between Spreckels and Thurston over the Hawaiian Revolution of 1893.

12. *Ibid.*

13. *Ibid.*

14. *Ibid.*

15. *Ibid.*

16. Stevens, *American Expansion in Hawaii,* p. 207.

17. *Ibid.,* p. 209.

18. *Ibid.,* p. 187.

19. William A. Russ, Jr., *The Hawaiian Revolution, 1893–1894* (Selinsgrove, Pa.: Susquehanna University Press, 1959), p. 98.

20. Thurston, *Memoirs,* p. 283.

21. *San Francisco Chronicle,* July 27, 1893.

22. *San Francisco Chronicle,* January 27, 1893.

23. *Ibid.* Of the meeting in the Palace Hotel, Commissioner Castle wrote in his diary: "Claus takes the floor, talking in a general sort of way of the vital importance of himself and the trust; of how annexation will fail without it and of his great power and influence. The others look on and listen but Dimond takes the floor and purrs softly of the mighty Spreckels and his influence. It wins! The mighty Claus is won! He says he will cause annexation to become an accomplished fact." (*Reminiscences of William Richards Castle* [Honolulu: Advertiser Publishing Co., 1960], p. 81.)

Thurston wrote to Dole that the meeting resulted in "unanimous approval of the action taken at Honolulu and the proposition for annexation. . . . Mr. Spreckels has gone into the matter with both feet." (Thurston to Dole, January 29, 1893, Local Officials, 1893, AH.)

24. *San Francisco Chronicle,* July 27, 1893.

25. *Hawaiian Star,* May 22, 1893, citing *San Francisco Examiner,* January 29, 1893.

26. *San Francisco Chronicle,* January 29, 1893. W. G. Irwin, then in New

York, said: "As far as the United States is concerned, it was not, of course, to the interest of this country to annex the Sandwich Islands as long as affairs were running smoothly. It would be an expensive place to protect. . . . Now that trouble has broken out, however, I see no other course for this country to pursue than to annex. United States would not allow any other country to annex." (*San Francisco Examiner,* January 29, 1893, New York date line, January 28.)

27. For S. B. Dole's instructions to the commissioners, see Hawaiian Officials Abroad—Washington Minister and Commissioner, January 18, 1893, AH.

28. In the fall of 1892 the Hawaiian planters had signed a contract with the Western Sugar Refinery, controlled jointly by Spreckels and the sugar trust. The contract provided that upon annexation the bounty of two cents a pound under the McKinley Act would be divided between the planters and the trust. Thurston (rightly) claimed "that if it were made a condition precedent to annexation that the Hawaiian planters should waive the benefits of the bounty . . . they would do so." (*San Francisco Chronicle,* March 8, 1893. See also *Brooklyn Citizen,* March 17, 1893.)

Castle, reporting on a conversation in Washington, D. C., with B. F. Dillingham, Honolulu entrepreneur, wrote: "He thinks the action of the Planters in Hawaii, acceding to demands of the Sugar Trust to *divide* benefits of U. S. bounty on sugars is very bad! He is right! It is suicidal! (*Castle Reminiscences,* p. 94.)

Secretary of State Foster had been inclined to recommend a bounty of one-half cent a pound for Hawaii. But then he found out about the agreement between the planters and the trust to share any bounty. In these circumstances Foster felt that approval of a bounty to Hawaiian planters, together with continuance of contract labor, "would have the same effect upon the opposition that a red flag would have upon a bull." (Julius W. Pratt, *Expansionists of 1898* [Baltimore: Johns Hopkins University Press, 1936], pp. 118–119.)

29. *Bulletin* (Honolulu), March 4, 1893.

30. *Ibid.*

31. *San Francisco Chronicle,* July 27, 1893.

32. *Castle Reminiscences,* p. 85.

33. Stevens, *American Expansion in Hawaii,* pp. 232–235.

34. *Ibid.,* pp. 245–247.

35. *Hawaiian Star,* April 7, 1893, New York date line, March 23, 1893.

36. *Ibid.*

XXI: *The Sugar King Returns*

1. On the "Australia's" trip, see *Bulletin* (Honolulu), April 18, 1893; *San Francisco Chronicle,* May 4, 1893.

2. Commissioner Blount reported Spreckels' version of his talk with Stevens in a letter of April 26, 1893, to Secretary of State Gresham (*Report of the Committee on Foreign Relations,* II, p. 1289). For a statement by Spreckels on this interview, see *San Francisco Chronicle,* July 27, 1893.

According to Nordhoff, Stevens added that he wanted to leave the islands by May 24 and he wanted to get the annexation business settled before he left (*New York Herald,* June 27, 1893).

3. *Hawaiian Star,* April 21, 1893. But according to Liliuokalani's diary for 1893, when she saw Spreckels at noon, April 20, and asked him for help, he said he would help by not making any loans to the Provisional Government "and they would naturally collapse."

4. *Hawaiian Star,* April 20, 1893. The queen complained of "much maneuvering and wire pulling with Mr. Spreckels." She wrote that the Provisional Government had been trying to turn him against her. (Diary, April 25, 1893, AH.)

5. *Hawaiian Star,* April 21, 1893.

On April 19, S. E. Bishop wrote that Spreckels was in favor of an independent republic under a United States protectorate. On April 24, Bishop wrote: "Claus Spreckels is vapouring a good deal. Is making up his mind & going to act vigorously when decision is reached between Annexation and an Independent Republic. In the latter, he evidently intends to run it himself! Good Lord deliver us!" He also wrote that Spreckels appeared likely to cause trouble. (S. E. Bishop to G. D. Gilman, April 15, 1893 [Letter evidently begun on that date], HMCS.)

Thurston wrote Dole from Chicago on April 23 that he heard Spreckels had gone to the islands to fight annexation and work for an oligarchy. He did not think Spreckels would find much support in Honolulu, and said an oligarchy could be permanently maintained only by force. Further, it would ruin the public and private credit of Hawaii. "I believe in securing S's assistance if possible," wrote Thurston, "but it may come too dear." (Local Officials President with Hawaiian Commissioners to Washington, 1893, AH.)

6. There is some evidence that Spreckels favored putting Samuel Parker at the head of the government. See Liliuokalani Diary, April, 1893, AH.

7. The term *kanaka* ("person") is now generally considered derogatory.

8. See p. 249.

9. *San Francisco Chronicle,* May 4, 1893, Honolulu date line, April 25.

10. *Hawaiian Star,* April 25, 1893.

11. *Hawaiian Star,* April 27, 1893. Liliuokalani told of a meeting (of the Chamber of Commerce?) where two-thirds of those present voted against some proposal that Spreckels made. He then told them he would have nothing more to do with them. Sam Parker offered Spreckels the queen's "power of attorney," to run the government. "Spreckels said he did not want it. I admonished Sam. It was not for him to offer." (Diary, 1893, AH.)

12. *Bulletin* (Honolulu), June 6, 1893.

13. *Ibid.*

The *New York Tribune* published on May 13, 1893, a letter which it described as giving "a suggestive insight of political affairs in the Hawaiian Islands." Purportedly the letter, dated Honolulu, April 26, was from a member of the Hawaiian Annexation Commission to a friend in New York. (There can be little doubt that the letter was written by someone having intimate knowledge of the facts.)

When Spreckels reached Honolulu, so went the letter, he called on Blount and made known to him his opposition to annexation unless the contract labor system were kept. He said he wanted a republic under a United States protectorate. Blount was noncommittal but asked Spreckels to make a written statement to be sent to Washington. With the help of "two planters" (presumably Irwin and Baldwin) Spreckels drafted the statement. He met next day with the most prominent planters and businessmen to demand that they sign it. They quietly demurred. They explained that "safe and responsible government was far more important than contract labor."

Spreckels retorted: "You shan't get annexation. I'll block it! You will never get into the United States!" He boasted that he would use his money in Washington to get what he wanted.

The writer of the letter concluded: "In view of the statement that Mr. Cleveland entered the White House with an ugly suspicion that the whole annexation movement was a move on the part of the [Sugar] Trust to get in, I think these facts are very significant. We are feeling rather depressed, for he may be able to accomplish his purpose, and if we are delivered over to the tender mercies of a Spreckels oligarchy protected by the United States, we shall soon have the floodgates opened to the ignorant hordes of Asia."

14. *Hawaiian Gazette,* May 23, 1893, quoting *New York Herald,* May 2, 1893.

15. *Hawaiian Gazette,* May 30, 1893.

16. *Ibid.*

17. *Ibid.* The attitude of the planters is well summed up in interview of H. P. Baldwin with Blount on April 26, 1893. Blount asked: "Suppose you were cut off from the power to make contracts to bring labor into this country, what would be the effect on your plantations?"

"Some of the planters consider it absolutely essential for us to have contracts," said Baldwin, "but I think that in order to bring about annexation most of them would be ready to yield that point." (*Report of Committee on Foreign Relations,* II, p. 1492.) See also letter, Baldwin to Blount, June 23, 1893, *ibid.,* p. 1875.

18. "I had quite an interview with Claus Spreckels, who was trying to persuade me & S. M. Damon to fall in with his Independent Republic scheme" (S. E. Bishop to G. D. Gilman, May 17, 1893, HMCS).

19. *Report of the Committee on Foreign Relations,* II, p. 1784.

From Honolulu on April 25, Dole wrote Commissioner Carter: "The Provisional Government has the greatest confidence that the Government of the United States when fully aware of the necessity of a system of labor for the maintenance of our agricultural industries will make such arrangements as will aid in their continued progress and development." (Hawaiian Officials Abroad, Minister and Commissioner to Washington, April, 1893, AH.)

20. *Report of the Committee on Foreign Relations,* II, p. 1784.

21. *Report of the Committee on Foreign Relations,* II, pp. 1787–1788.

22. The notes were as follows: $30,000, September 16, 1892, at 7½ per cent; $25,000, September 16, 1892, at 7½ per cent; $25,000, September 29, 1892, at 7½ per cent; and $15,000, November 11, 1892, at 8 per cent (*Hawaiian Star,* June 1, 1893).

23. Blount to Gresham, April 26, 1893, *Report of the Committee on Foreign Relations,* II, p. 1296. See also Liliuokalani Diary, May 29, 1893.

24. *Hawaiian Star,* May 29, 30, 1893.

25. *Hawaiian Star,* May 30, 1893; *Hawaiian Gazette,* June 6, 1893. One report had it that Spreckels demanded repayment of the loan because his plans for a republic had not got proper attention (*New York Times,* June 7, 1893). S. E. Bishop wrote to G. D. Gilman on June 3: "Claus Spreckels has been raging about because of his failure to enlist support for an 'independent republic' for himself to boss. He has been talking loudly about putting the queen back, from which her adherents have derived great rally to their waning hopes, & are full of plots and conspiracies."

26. *San Francisco Interocean,* June 19, 1893.

27. *Pacific Commercial Advertiser,* June 2, 1893. A. B. Spreckels later claimed that the money to pay the $95,000 came mostly from S. M. Damon (*New York Advertiser,* June 30, 1893).

28. *Pacific Commercial Advertiser,* June 2, 1893; *Hawaiian Star,* June 3, 1893.

29. *Hawaiian Gazette,* June 6, 1893.

30. *Hawaiian Gazette,* October 3, 1893.

31. *Hawaiian Star,* June 9, 1893.

32. *Ibid.*

33. *Ibid.*

34. *Hawaiian Star,* June 13, 1893. The *Star* and other forces favorable to the Provisional Government forces made a great show of not being afraid of Spreckels. But some of this may have been just whistling in the dark. Bishop wrote to Gilman on June 19: "Claus Spreckels is a bad element and is doing his utmost to force the Gov't to feel themselves in his hands or be broken up by his royalist plots. I do not know whether there are elements in the P. G. sufficiently prompt and resolute to meet him. He thinks he can overcome everything."

When former Minister Stevens heard of Spreckels' continued pressures on the Provisional Government, he wrote from Augusta, Maine: "What at this distance from you I now most fear is the disorganizing & damaging influence of Claus Spreckels in the Islands. The exposure of his cause & his motives in the United States helps the cause of Annexation & the Pro. Government. Can you hold your ground securely against him in the Islands? I hope you can & will, & I so pray." (Stevens to Dole, July 16, 1893. Local Officials President, 1893, AH.)

35. *Hawaiian Star,* December 13, 1893.

36. *Bulletin* (Honolulu), June 22, 1893. A photograph of the sign is in the Victor S. K. Houston collection, AH.

Spreckels' wife and daughter urged him to return to San Francisco. "There is no question," said the *New York Tribune* correspondent, "that his family are thoroughly alarmed over this placard and believe that his life is in danger. They know that Honolulu is full of reckless fellows who would assassinate Spreckels for a few hundred dollars." (*New York Tribune,* July 5, 1893.)

37. Blount succeeded Stevens as U. S. Minister to Hawaii.

38. Blount to Dole, June 23, 1893. FO & Ex, U. S. Ministers and Consuls, 1893, AH.

39. *Hawaiian Gazette,* June 27, 1893.

40. *Hawaiian Star,* June 23, 1893.

41. *Hawaiian Gazette,* June 27, 1893.

42. *Ibid.*

43. *Hawaiian Star,* June 23, 1893.

44. *Pacific Commercial Advertiser,* June 23, 1893.

45. *Bulletin* (Honolulu), June 22, 1893.

46. *Hawaiian Gazette,* July 25, 1893.

47. Affidavit of Harry A. Juen, December 12, 1893. Document 941 in Attorney General file, AH.

48. Thurston, *Memoirs,* pp. 89–90.

49. *Hawaiian Star,* July 19, 1893.

50. *Ibid.*

51. Liliuokalani Diary, July 15, 1893.

52. *Bulletin* (Honolulu), July 18, 1893. Most members of the Royal Hawaiian Band had been discharged for refusal to take the oath of allegiance

to the Provisional Government. They then formed their own band in support of the royalist cause.

53. *Hawaiian Star*, July 19, 1893.

54. *Ibid.* In its July 25 issue the *Star* commented: "That this boozy lot of flunkeys . . . should compare their new found political lord and master to the brutal Caesar of The Roman empire was more appropriate than the parties themselves probably realized. Irresponsible power, exercised with contemptuous and ostentatious disregard of other people's rights, . . . for purposes selfish and sordid, appears to be his ideal and aim. Great is Claus Imperator!"

S. E. Bishop wrote of the cane incident as resulting from the "insane foolishness of some leading Royalists." He said the names on the cane were not those of the donors but of persons marked for death according to an Associated Press report printed on the Coast. These persons were to be killed in case the royalists carried out a dynamite plot against the Provisional Government. Bishop wrote, further: "I cannot learn that any such plan existed, beyond some such wild talk as always arises at such times." (Bishop to Gilman, July 24, 1893, HMCS.)

55. *Bulletin* (Honolulu), July 19, 1893.

56. *Hawaiian Gazette*, July 25, 1893. The *Hawaiian Star* said: "In his address at the steamer, John E. Bush could not have voiced Mr. Spreckels' idea of his own personal glory in phrases more like those which the Sugar King is accustomed to use on the street, if he had taken dictation from the admiring potentate himself. Perhaps, indeed, he did so. There is much more of Spreckels than of Bush in those labored sentences of esteem for His Saccharinity. In fact, Bush, when left to himself, is much more sententious, as witness his brief but comprehensive toast to the Kaiser at Samoa: 'D––n the German Emperor,' said the chief of the Hawaiian Embassy to the assembled Germans at a royal katzenjammer." (*Hawaiian Star*, July 20, 1893, referring to the time in 1887 when Bush was envoy to Samoa in connection with Kalakaua's dream of "Primacy of the Pacific," which the Germans opposed.)

57. *Hawaiian Star*, July 19, 1893.

58. *Bulletin* (Honolulu), July 19; *Hawaiian Star*, July 19, 1893. Liliuokalani wrote in her diary (AH): "Mr. Spreckles [*sic*] will go right on to Washington. . . . While making a speech on the wharf . . . to the people who flocked down to see them [the Spreckels] off Mr. A. F. Judds two sons who are on their way to Harvard College hooted and stamped and made all the noise they could helped by Mr. C. M. Cooke and Mr. Hosmer & another teacher. . . . How little and how small."

59. *Hawaiian Star*, July 19, 1893.

XXII: *The Struggle for Restoration*

1. *Hawaiian Star*, July 19, 1893.

2. Blount to Dole, U. S. Ministers and Consuls, July–December, 1893, AH.

3. Minutes of Executive Council of Provisional Government, January 6, 1893, to March 26, 1894, AH.

4. *Bulletin* (Honolulu), July 20, 1893. The *Hawaiian Star* denied that Johnstone of the *Pacific Commercial Advertiser* was author of the list published in the San Francisco newspapers on July 6, 1893.

5. Dole to Creighton, July 24, 1893, Local Officials, Minister of Foreign Affairs to Local Officials, AH.

6. Creighton to Dole, July 26, 1893, AH.

7. Dole to Creighton, July 26, 1893, AH.

8. Dole later sent the correspondence to Minister Albert S. Willis, Blount's successor. Willis wrote Secretary of State Gresham on November 19, 1893: "I will file these letters in the Department and presume that the matter will end here" (Willis to Gresham, No. 6, U. S. Legation, Honolulu. November 19, 1893, *Report of the Committee on Foreign Relations,* II, p. 2090).

When Blount arrived in San Francisco on August 15 he said: "The story of a murder society recently formed at Honolulu is nonsense. It is a most peaceful community. Everyone sleeps with his doors and windows open. At my house the doors were not closed night or day while I was there." (*Hawaiian Gazette,* September 12, 1893, citing *New York Advertiser,* August 16, 1893.)

9. *San Francisco Chronicle,* July 27, 1893.

10. *Hawaiian Star,* August 25, 1893, citing interview in *San Francisco Bulletin,* n.d.

11. *San Francisco Chronicle,* July 27, 1893. The *New York Commercial Advertiser* (July 29) jibed at Spreckels' opinion that the masses would restore the queen even if blood had to flow. "Still, he ought not to give expression to these views unless he is willing to remain in Honolulu and witness the ensanguined restoration, and the fact that he has arrived in this country impresses us with the belief that he will be satisfied with mail accounts of it."

12. *San Francisco Chronicle,* July 27, 1893.

13. *Hawaiian Gazette,* September 26, 1893, citing *San Francisco Bulletin,* n.d. C. T. Wilder, Hawaiian consul general at San Francisco, wrote on July 28 to Thurston at Washington: "Claus Spreckels arrived on the S.S. 'Australia' and I have heard that he intends going to Washington to buck annexation, so be prepared to down any assertions that he may make which no doubt will be an easy matter" (Hawaiian Officials Abroad, Minister and Commissioner Washington, 1893, AH).

14. *Hawaiian Star,* September 19, 1893.

15. *Hawaiian Star,* September 29, 1893. The *Hawaiian Gazette* (October 24, 1893) reported that Senator Perkins was "said to owe his political advancement entirely to Spreckels," and that Perkins was a stockholder and director of Spreckels' Oceanic Steamship Company. F. P. Hastings, Thurston's aide and secretary to the Hawaiian legation in Washington, called on Spreckels on September 19 and found him surrounded by friends, including Senator Perkins. "The Colonel [Spreckels] told me I was on the wrong side," wrote Hastings, "that he was going to beat us, that we could not get annexation, etc., etc., etc." (Hastings to Dole, September 22, 1893, President with Hawaiian Commissioners to Washington, 1893, AH.)

16. As cited in *Hawaiian Star,* October 19, 1893.

Spreckels' opposition to annexation had many aspects, emotional, political, and economic. A letter to the editor of the *New York Sun* (August 10, 1893) signed "One who knows," throws light on one aspect. In effect, the letter said: Spreckels opposes annexation because it would loosen his grip over the Hawaiian planters in the refining of sugar. In his San Francisco refining operation he is in league with the sugar trust. He is a planter too, and therefore has more than one string to his bow. He buys island sugar below the New York price, refines it, and sells it on the Pacific Coast at a price to the consumer that is higher than elsewhere in the United States. The Hawaiian planters have no satisfactory market for their raw sugar except San Francisco. Freight rates to New York are too high. Under the Reciprocity Treaty unrefined sugar was admitted to the United States free of duty. With annexation, refined sugar would also be admitted free of duty. Therefore Hawaiian planters (other than Spreckels) would have the incentive to start refineries in Hawaii in opposition to Spreckels and the sugar trust. Therefore he does not want annexation. Even if he suffered losses as a planter (without annexation) he would more than make up such losses on refining in San Francisco.

So in substance wrote "One who knows." Plausible the argument sounds, but the present writer does not put much stock in it. No one in the islands had a knowledge of refining even remotely approaching that of Spreckels.

17. *Hawaiian Star,* September 30, 1893; October 19, 1893, citing *Washington Post,* September 19; *Hawaiian Gazette,* October 3, 1893.

18. *Hawaiian Gazette,* October 10, 1893, citing *Washington Post,* September 19, 21.

19. *Ibid.*

20. *Hawaiian Star,* September 29, 1893.

21. *Hawaiian Star,* October 7, 1893.

22. *Hawaiian Star,* October 9, 1893. W. D. Alexander, special commissioner to Washington, wrote Dole: "Mr. Spreckels visit did good as he stated his reasons for opposing annexation so bluntly, and made the alleged necessity of semi-slave Asiatic labor his main argument." (Alexander to Dole, October 4, 1893, Local Officials President with Hawaiian Commissioners to Washington, 1893, AH.) And later Alexander wrote to Thurston: "If Claus Spreckels becomes convinced that the restoration of monarchy is impossible, and will agree to join with other property owners of the islands in sustaining a decent government, I would welcome him, but I would take care not to let him get hold of the helm.

"It is likely that he will disagree with us on at least two points, viz. on the importation of Chinese, and on the policy of working for future annexation, to say nothing of Crown land matters. . . .

"If anybody can reason with Spreckels it will be Baldwin and my brother Sam. Baldwin is probably right in saying that Claus has been influenced much more by his interests as a sugar refiner than as a plantation owner, in opposing annexation. But that is not the issue at present. As a large property owner, his true interests are certainly on the side of good government, and it would be a great point gained to break his 'unholy alliance' with Wodehouse and Mrs. Dominis [Liliuokalani]." (Alexander to Thurston, October 31, 1893, Minister and Commissioner to Washington, AH.)

23. Armstrong to Thurston, November 1, 1893. Hawaiian Officials Abroad, Minister and Commissioner, AH.

24. "Knowing the unwillingness of Congress to sanction any resort to armed force for the restoration of the Queen, Mr. Thurston can confidently press on the Hawaiian Government a policy of resistance which will make the return of Liliuokalani to the throne impossible except through actual bloodshed" (*New York Tribune,* December 9, 1893).

Even earlier, the *New York World* (November 16, Washington date line, November 15) was saying: "Minister Willis has been instructed not to use force in accomplishing the restoration of the Queen of Hawaii, without communicating with the Secretary of State." The paper said that semiofficial sources amply confirmed this.

25. Liliuokalani Diary, AH.

26. *Hawaiian Star,* November 24, 1893, San Francisco date line, November 11, 1893.

27. *Hawaiian Star,* December 26, 1893.

28. *San Francisco Examiner,* April 25, 1897.

29. *Chicago Record,* April 10, 1897.

30. Statement by F. M. Hatch, Sugar Trust and Annexation, December 22, 1897, U. S. Minister to Washington, 1897, AH; *San Francisco Chronicle,* August 22, November 7, 1897; *San Francisco Examiner,* June 9, 1898; *New York Journal,* May 28, 1898.

31. *Washington Star,* June 11, 15, 1898.

INDEX